About This Book

D1537569

Why is this topic important

Creativity is an increasingly critical topic for contemporary organizations. One of the most crucial reasons for organizations to promote creativity has been global competition. In today's competitive business environment where innovation and "speed to market" are crucial, teaming also plays a vital business role in bringing key contributors together to focus on joint work objectives, common problems, and how to develop innovative solutions. Advances in information technology have enabled the foremost minds to work together on dispersed, virtual teams without relocating these individuals. Virtual teams with an eye for *creativity* are helping businesses of all kinds meet these new market conditions. Those who manage and are part of virtual teams must be aware of how to *create the appropriate conditions to foster and support creativity in their virtual teams.*

What can you achieve with this book?

This book provides virtual team designers, leaders, and managers with a theoretical understanding of what components are necessary for high levels of creativity in virtual teams. The book also describes the necessary tools to assess and develop these needed components in their virtual teams. The book includes a variety of assessment tools for you (and your team members) to use, including diagnostic instruments, reflection questions, checklists, and exercises. You may choose to either read through the book in a linear fashion from beginning to end, or use the initial diagnostic tool in the *Introduction* to focus on components most in need of development. In addition, you will gain insight from a series of practical lessons learned from conversations with nine highly creative virtual teams. Furthermore, although the theoretical model and tools outlined in this book are specifically developed from research on virtual teams, you may transfer the principles to all types of teams (not just virtual ones) that are striving to be more creative in achieving their goals and objectives.

How is this book organized?

This book is divided into five parts that cover the key components for creativity in virtual teams. In **Part I**, the component of *Design* is reviewed. Within the design component, you will learn how to map out an effective creative process and work design approach for your virtual team. You will also learn how to choose an appropriate leadership structure to guide your virtual team toward higher levels of creativity. **Part II** deals with the essential component of *Climate*, the attitudes, feelings, and behaviors that characterize life within a team and organization. Climate includes both building and maintaining a sense of task and interpersonal connection between team members, and developing and practicing appropriate management and team member skills to support creativity. **Part III** focuses on *Resources* virtual team members may draw on to produce creative work. Resources include available communication tools to support a virtual team's creative process, linear and intuitive creativity techniques used to foster higher levels of creativity and idea generation, and various software tools that enhance individual and team creativity. In **Part IV**, appropriate communication and project—task management *Norms and Protocols* for virtual teams are outlined. The book culminates in **Part V** with a discussion of the fifth key component, *Continual Assessment and Learning*. A series of practical lessons learned are shared. However, opportunities for assessment and learning may also be found in each chapter within the book.

About Pfeiffer

Pfeiffer serves the professional development and hands-on resource needs of training and human resource practitioners and gives them products to do their jobs better. We deliver proven ideas and solutions from experts in HR development and HR management, and we offer effective and customizable tools to improve workplace performance. From novice to seasoned professional, Pfeiffer is the source you can trust to make yourself and your organization more successful.

Essential Knowledge Pfeiffer produces insightful, practical, and comprehensive materials on topics that matter the most to training and HR professionals. Our Essential Knowledge resources translate the expertise of seasoned professionals into practical, how-to guidance on critical workplace issues and problems. These resources are supported by case studies, worksheets, and job aids and are frequently supplemented with CD-ROMs, websites, and other means of making the content easier to read, understand, and use.

Essential Tools Pfeiffer's Essential Tools resources save time and expense by offering proven, ready-to-use materials—including exercises, activities, games, instruments, and assessments—for use during a training or team-learning event. These resources are frequently offered in looseleaf or CD-ROM format to facilitate copying and customization of the material.

Pfeiffer also recognizes the remarkable power of new technologies in expanding the reach and effectiveness of training. While e-hype has often created whizbang solutions in search of a problem, we are dedicated to bringing convenience and enhancements to proven training solutions. All our e-tools comply with rigorous functionality standards. The most appropriate technology wrapped around essential content yields the perfect solution for today's on-the-go trainers and human resource professionals.

Essential resources for training and HR professionals

www.pfeiffer.com

THE **COLLABORATIVE WORK SYSTEMS** SERIES

Building collaborative capacity in the world of work

Other Collaborative Work Systems Series Titles:

Integrating Lean Six Sigma and High-Performance Organizations:
Leading the Charge Toward Dramatic, Rapid, and Sustainable Improvement
Tom Devane

Guiding the Journey to Collaborative Work Systems: A Strategic Design Workbook
Michael M. Beyerlein and Cheryl L. Harris

The Collaborative Work Systems Fieldbook: Strategies, Tools, and Techniques
Michael M. Beyerlein, Craig McGee, Gerald D. Klein, Jill E. Nemiro,
and Laurie Broedling

Beyond Teams: Building the Collaborative Organization
Michael M. Beyerlein, Sue Freedman, Craig McGee, and Linda Moran

THE **COLLABORATIVE WORK SYSTEMS** SERIES

CENTER FOR THE STUDY OF WORK TEAMS

Creativity in Virtual Teams

KEY COMPONENTS FOR SUCCESS

Jill E. Nemiro

Pfeiffer

A Wiley Imprint

www.pfeiffer.com

Copyright © 2004 by John Wiley & Sons, Inc.

Published by Pfeiffer
An Imprint of Wiley
989 Market Street, San Francisco, CA 94103-1741   www.pfeiffer.com

No part of this publication may be reproduced, stored in a retrieval system, or transmitted in any form or by any means, electronic, mechanical, photocopying, recording, scanning, or otherwise, except as permitted under Section 107 or 108 of the 1976 United States Copyright Act, without either the prior written permission of the Publisher, or authorization through payment of the appropriate per-copy fee to the Copyright Clearance Center, Inc., 222 Rosewood Drive, Danvers, MA 01923, 978-750-8400, fax 978-646-8700, or on the web at www.copyright.com. Requests to the Publisher for permission should be addressed to the Permissions Department, John Wiley & Sons, Inc., 111 River Street, Hoboken, NJ 07030, 201-748-6011, fax 201-748-6008, e-mail: permcoordinator@wiley.com.

For additional copies/bulk purchases of this book in the U.S. please contact 800-274-4434.

Pfeiffer books and products are available through most bookstores. To contact Pfeiffer directly call our Customer Care Department within the U.S. at 800-274-4434, outside the U.S. at 317-572-3985 or fax 317-572-4002 or www.pfeiffer.com.

Pfeiffer also publishes its books in a variety of electronic formats. Some content that appears in print may not be available in electronic books.

ISBN: 0-7879-7114-6

Library of Congress Catalog Card Number 2003024912

Library of Congress Cataloging-in-Publication Data
Nemiro, Jill E., 1954-
   Creativity in virtual teams : key components for success / Jill E. Nemiro.
       p. cm.
Includes bibliographical references and index.
   ISBN 0-7879-7114-6 (alk. paper)
   1. Virtual work teams. 2 Teams in the workplace. 3. Creative ability in business. I. Title.
   HD66.N45 2004
   658.3'14--dc22

                                                                                    2003024912

Acquiring Editor: Matthew C. Davis   Senior Production Editor: Justin Frahm
Director of Development: Kathleen Dolan Davies   Manufacturing Supervisor: Bill Matherly
Developmental Editor: Susan Rachmeler   Cover Design: Bruce Lundquist
Editor: Elyse Lord

Printed in the United States of America
Printing   10   9   8   7   6   5   4   3   2   1

CONTENTS

LIST OF TABLES AND FIGURES

Chapter 7

Chapter 8

DEDICATION

To Sara, Rachel, and Mikey, who have taught me about creative passion and love.

PREFACE FOR THE COLLABORATIVE WORK SYSTEMS SERIES

I N LAUNCHING THIS SERIES, it is the editors' intention to create an ongoing, dynamic forum for sharing cutting-edge ideas and practices among researchers and those practitioners involved on a day-to-day basis with organizations that depend on collaborative work systems (CWS) for their success.

Proposed publications in the CWS series include books devoted to specific topics, workbooks to guide planning and competency development, fieldbooks that capture lessons learned in organizations experimenting with collaborative work systems, software for facilitating learning, training materials, and assessment instruments. The goal of the series is to produce four new products per year that will build a foundation for a perspective on collaboration as an essential means of achieving high levels of performance in and across organizations. Our vision for the series is to provide a means for leveraging collaborative work practices around the world in for-profit, government, and not-for-profit entities.

Collaborative work systems are those in which conscious efforts have been made to create strategies, policies, and structures as well as to institutionalize values, behaviors, and practices that promote cooperation among different parties in the organization in order to achieve desired business outcomes. While many organizations vocalize support for teamwork and collaboration, collaborative work systems are distinguished by intentional efforts to embed the organization with work processes and cultural mechanisms that enable and reinforce collaboration. New forms of organization continue to emerge with CWS as an essential facet. Team-based organizations and self-managing organizations represent types of collaborative systems. The computer revolution has made possible network, cellular, and spherical forms of organizing, which represent more transorganizational forms of collaboration.

Why the urgency? The challenges organizations face seem to be escalating rapidly. The number of global issues that impact an organization proliferate, including the terrorist threat, continued deforestation of ancient lands by debtor nations, wars, famine, disease, the accelerating splitting of nations' consciousness into the haves and the have-nots around the globe, which fuels hatreds—all aspects of interrelated political, social, economic, environmental challenges that will ultimately reduce quality of life on a worldwide scale if not addressed. These are the systemic, wicked problems that depend on many minds lodged in a common value set committed to improving human welfare in all settings. The business community must work with city, county, and state governments, with nation states, and with transnational organizations, such as the United Nations and the World Bank, to bring enough intellectual and financial capital to bear on the problems to do something about them—demanding collaborative initiatives at all levels.

Individuals working well together—this seems like a relatively simple proposition. Yet barriers abound in organizations that tend to inhibit collaboration at every turn. Social barriers are erected for a variety of reasons, including turf wars and mindsets that lead to hoarding of specialized knowledge rather than sharing. Fear of loss seems to be amplified during economic downturns as operating budgets are trimmed, fueling a multiplicity of negative personal scenarios, including loss of jobs, promotional opportunities, titles, and perks, which in turn can threaten self-esteem and professional identity. Barriers to establishing effective collaborative work systems can also reflect lack of cross-training, cultural norms and reward systems that reinforce individual performance, organizational political realities that reinforce competition for scarce resources among units, and differing technical languages that make communication challenging. However, despite these difficulties, some companies appear to overcome the significant barriers and benefit from the positive consequences of effective collaboration.

People in and around organizations have been experimenting with and learning about designing effective work processes for millennia. Researchers and practitioners have been capturing the lessons learned since the early part of the 20th Century. That process continues as we embark on the 21st Century. There will be much to document as changes in global business practices and new generation technologies enable more effective ways of organizing, operating, competing, innovating, and collaborating. Technical developments during the next quarter century will create unheralded challenges and opportunities in an increasingly interdependent world.

The move from muscle-based work to knowledge-based work has been so profound that some writers have called it the age of the knowledge economy. It demands new levels of collaborative expertise and a shift in focus to intangible forms of capital.

Knowledge grows through the development of organizational routines. Knowledge includes knowing what, but also knowing how and why. Each employee carries a somewhat different library of knowledge and a unique perspective on how to apply it—termed intellectual capital. The network of interaction among knowledge workers creates a rich environment where ideas can grow and blossom in stair-step fashion—termed social capital—and where there is widespread competency around teamwork at all levels of the organization in various forms—termed collaborative capital. This form of capital provides the foundation for leveraging what the other forms contribute, but it demands radically different ways of organizing work and involving employees in its design and practice.

In summary, collaborative work systems provide one of the key competency areas that organizations can focus on for building vitality and excellence, including competitive and collaborative advantage. On a daily basis, people come together to make decisions, solve problems, invent new products and services, build key relationships, and plan futures. The effectiveness of those gatherings and the effectiveness of the systems that emerge from them will depend greatly on the collaborative capacity that has been built in their organizations.

A high level of collaborative capacity will enable more effective work at the local and daily levels and at the global and long-term levels. We can solve our immediate problems more effectively, and we can cooperate more effectively to take on the emerging global issues that threaten us in the 21st Century, when we have the skills, values, and processes for effective collaboration. This series of publications is intended as a catalyst in building that collaborative capacity at both local and global levels.

Michael M. Beyerlein, Ph.D.
Susan T. Beyerlein, Ph.D.
Center for the Study of Work Teams
University of North Texas

James Barker, Ph.D.
United States Air Force Academy

APPRECIATIONS

My sincere appreciation goes to the following people:

- Susan Rachmeler, my editor at Pfeiffer, whose remarkable insight, expertise, and creativity greatly enhanced this book.

- The Collaborative Work Systems series editorial team—Michael Beyerlein, Susan Beyerlein, and James Barker—for their wisdom and sound suggestions. A genuine and special thanks goes to Michael Beyerlein, whose is my mentor and friend. Mike has taught me the true meaning of collaboration, and without him, this book would still be a dream yet unrealized.

- JD Eveland, my mentor and friend for many years. I am greatly indebted to JD for his initial and continual support, expertise, and guidance of my work.

- Dale Berger, Mark Runco, and John Regan, who each provided unique contributions to this project.

- Kathleen Dolan Davies, Matthew Davis, Justin Frahm, Gabriela Bayardo, Laura Reizman, Elyse Lord, Bruce Lundquist, Chris Wallace, Bill Matherly, and all the others at Jossey-Bass/Pfeiffer who contributed to this book.

- Caleb Anderson and Camarin Santos, my research assistants at Cal Poly Pomona, who were helpful in compiling information for this book. I am also greatly appreciative of the meetings we shared during the development of this book, which afforded me a safe and supportive environment where initial ideas could grow into full-length chapters.

- The students in my creativity seminar at Cal Poly Pomona, for allowing me the opportunity to test and refine some of the creativity exercises.

- The anonymous reviewers who constructively challenged me to move in directions I had not thought of.

- Teresa Amabile and William C. Miller, whose own work in creativity has fascinated and inspired me.

- The virtual team members who shared their creative experiences with me. It was an honor to "virtually" meet each one of them and to have the opportunity to share their stories in this book.

- My close friends. David, who supported and put up with me during the creation of this book and who served as a loving uncle to my girls while I was writing; Beverly, whose encouragement and wisdom helped me stay on the path; and Nancy, who believed in me even when I was not quite sure where I was going.

- My family: Sara, Rachel, and Mikey, for being the creative, precious gems in my life.

- You, the reader, for allowing me to share my thoughts with you!

Getting the Most from This Resource

We did the whole thing fast and in three different weekends. And we did it totally by computer and telephone conferencing with each other, until we got face-to-face in front of the client. What really was kind of exciting about that was we started communicating with e-mail and conferencing calls to get the creativity [going] about how to even think about approaching the project and working on an overall strategy. Then we were able to go off, and each one of us [was able to] take responsibility for building different parts of the project. And then come back together through e-mail and make adjustments. Then somebody could take the clean-up chore each time. One of the advantages was not everybody was on the same schedule. So the burden of develop-ment over that period of time would shift from one person to the other based on what else was going on in their lives, what the deadline was, what else had to still be done.

Pam, ACI

CREATIVITY IS INCREASINGLY BECOMING a critical topic for contemporary organizations. One of the most crucial reasons for organizations to promote creativity has been global competition. Global competition has not only created a dire need for organizational creative efforts, it has forced companies to get products out faster. In today's competitive business environment where innovation and "speed to market" are crucial, teaming also plays a vital business role in bringing key contributors together to focus on joint work objectives, common problems, and how to develop innovative solutions. Advances in information technology have enabled the foremost minds to come together wherever they reside. Teaming opportunities today exist not only with co-workers in your office, but with people everywhere. As Pam's quote reveals, more and more teams are having to communicate with colleagues in modes besides typical face-to-face interactions in order to develop and implement creative results. Thus, a new type of team called a *virtual team* is developing. Virtual teams allow companies to tap into the best talent to create the highest quality and fastest response to customer needs. As competition has grown, the need for expertise and information has expanded. Dispersed or virtual teams can leverage their expertise by putting people together on projects without relocating them. Meanwhile, the traditional notion that an office is a collection of cubicles in a high-rise is shrinking as individuals are finding themselves working in an "anywhere-anytime" mode, connected to co-workers through information technology (O'Hara-Devereaux and Johansen, 1994).

Virtual team structures may actually lead to *higher* levels of team creativity as a result of more openness, flexibility, diversity, and access to information than exists in traditional group structures. However, it also may be extremely difficult to develop and maintain a social context that is conducive to high levels of creativity. In designing virtual teams, we cannot ignore the context of such arrangements. Technology allows for the electronic connection of geographically spread-out individuals, but it does not necessarily lead to effective personal connection, communication, and creativity. Virtual teams cannot function without information technology. But technology alone is not the answer to the problems of working across geographical and cultural boundaries. The ultimate answers to these problems lie in the realm of human and organizational relations and in creating work environments that bring out the best in people involved in these virtual structures.

ity are helping businesses of all kinds
who manage and are part of virtual
levels of creativity in these new vir-
team designers, team leaders, and
heir creativity? The answer to that
opriate dimensions to foster and sup-
. provide you with an understand-
high levels of creativity in virtual
y tools to assess and develop these
ιs.

Enjoy!
K.

growing as a vehicle to pull together key human
resou... ...ιe globe to respond to and overcome the pressures and
demands of our competitive global marketplace. And those virtual teams with
a creative edge are even better equipped to successfully meet these pressures
and demands. This book is for everyone who is, will be, or potentially could be
a part of virtual teams. The overall goals of this book are to provide those who
design, manage, lead, or are members of virtual teams with the knowledge and
tools they need to lead their virtual teams to high levels of creativity. Virtual
teams of all shapes and sizes can benefit from this book. Small consulting firms
will gain just as much as virtual teams that are embedded in larger organizational structures. Readers from across the globe will also be able to gain insight
into how to foster creativity in their virtual teams. And even those readers who
are not part of virtual teams will still find the content of this book transferable
to all types of teams (not just virtual ones) that are striving to be more creative
in achieving their goals and objectives.

Purpose

Although several good books have already been written on designing effective virtual teams, what makes this book unique is its focus on how to design,
establish, and maintain the proper dimensions to foster and support *creativity*
in virtual teams. As you read this book, you will develop both a theoretical

understanding of what key components are necessary for high levels of creativity in virtual teams, and the ability to assess and strengthen these components in your own virtual teams. Along the way, you will find assessment tools, discussion questions, checklists, and exercises. Case stories and lessons learned from real virtual teams doing creative work will also be shared.

This book reflects several years of my in-depth research with virtual teams and even more years of my exploration into what conditions are necessary for creativity to soar within individuals, teams, and organizations—virtual or not. For much of my professional life, I worked in the entertainment field as a film editor. When I began the research for this book, based on my own experiences of working in the film industry, I was puzzled as to how creativity and idea generation could take place without face-to-face contact. I questioned and quite honestly doubted how a process I felt was dependent on real time, physically close human contact could be accomplished electronically. My motivating questions for this book were—Can creativity be accomplished in virtual teams? If so, what needs to be in place to guarantee success? This book provides answers to those questions. I hope this book leads you and your virtual team to many wonderfully creative and successful experiences.

The Key Components and How This Book Is Organized

This book is divided into five parts that cover the key components for creativity in virtual teams. (See Figure I.1 for a graphical representation of the model of key components.) These components emerged from extensive qualitative data analysis of interviews with virtual team members. In Part I, the component of *Design* is reviewed. In Chapter One you will learn how to map out an effective creative process and work design approach for your virtual team. In Chapter Two you will learn how to choose an appropriate leadership structure to guide your virtual team toward higher levels of creativity.

Part II discusses the essential component of *Climate,* the attitudes, feelings, and behaviors that characterize life within a team and organization. Chapter Three details how to build and maintain a sense of connection within a virtual team, a necessary element for creativity in virtual teams. Connection involves the elements that need to be in place for a team to develop and maintain identity and a sense of community. Connection involves both task and interpersonal

Figure I.1. Key Components for Creativity in Virtual Teams

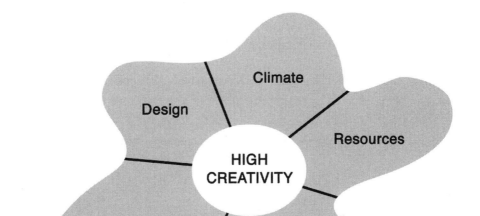

connection. As the creative work is under way, a series of team member and management conditions and competencies must be in place to stimulate creativity. These conditions and competencies will be covered in Chapter Four.

Part III focuses on *Resources* that virtual team members may draw on to produce creative work. Once a connection between team members is established, team members need to be supplied with sufficient resources to accomplish their creative work. Chapter Five describes a series of communication tools available to support a virtual team's creative process. The first portion of Chapter Six describes both linear and intuitive creativity techniques that may foster higher levels of creativity and idea generation. The second portion of the chapter reviews a variety of software tools that have been developed to enhance the creativity of individuals and teams. In this chapter, you will be able to pull resources together into your team's own creativity toolbox.

In Part IV, the appropriate *Norms and Protocols* that virtual teams need to consider, agree on, and respect and adhere to while working virtually are outlined. Chapter Seven reviews a series of norms and protocols to assist virtual teams to communicate and manage tasks and projects.

The book culminates in Part V, Chapter Eight, with a discussion of the fifth key component, *Continual Assessment and Learning.* This component is discussed throughout the book as well. Opportunities for assessment and learning exist in each chapter within the book, including in this introduction. (See the section on initial assessment.)

Creativity is highest, then, at the intersection of these five components, where the design is appropriate, the climate is supportive of creativity, the resources are sufficient, the proper norms and protocols are agreed on and adhered to, and the team takes the time to continually assess and to learn from its assessments.

A Study of Virtual Teams

This book is about creativity and about how creativity can best be accomplished in virtual teams. To ensure common understanding, let's clarify what we mean by a virtual team and by creativity.

Virtual Teams

Virtual teams are being touted as the optimal way to work in the 21st century to assist organizations in meeting the challenges of global market competition and turbulence. But what are virtual teams? What are the defining characteristics of these teams? In this section, I put forth a definition of virtual teams that emerged from discussions with thirty-six virtual team members from nine different virtual teams. (See the following sections on "Methodology" and "Description of the Virtual Teams" for further detail on the nine teams interviewed.)

To begin with, some team members had not thought about their teams as being "virtual." They simply saw themselves *as a team.* They had not set out to become virtual, but rather to work with people they enjoyed, who had the necessary competencies to get the job done, and to live in the communities they wanted. And even when team members did acknowledge their team was virtual, they still saw it as a *team first,* with team characteristics such as interdependence, shared values, and common goals. Members felt united by "having common tasks, common goals, and basically a common calling to do the work." [Rob, ACI]

Although team members defined virtual teams as a team first, most of them were aware that how they were working was different from teams in the traditional workforce. Factors that made their teams different from face-to-face, co-located teams include the following:

Geographic, Temporal, and Organizational Separation

One of the distinguishing characteristics of a virtual team is that members are separated from one another physically. As one team member shared, "we are a virtual team because namely we're in so many different locations, yet it's as if we are in one building but in different offices." [Melissa, VTG]

Geographic separation is amplified by temporal separation. One team member elaborated, "we are trying to master the art of being physically and temporally separated but not lose any of the flow of work among ourselves and our clients. So it's different time, different places that defines us as virtual." [Chad, Jacobs/Taylor] Virtual teams are also frequently composed of members from different departmental affiliations within a particular organization or even of members from entirely different organizations.

Alternative Methods of Communication

Because virtual teams are geographically separated, they most frequently use electronic communication tools to help them transcend the barriers of geographic separation. Team members stressed that the majority of their communication was through electronic means, rather than face-to-face interactions. One team member suggested her team was "linked by technology instead of geography." [Cheryl, ACI] Interestingly, people have been using alternative methods to communicate across distances—and have even been working in virtual teams for years. However, the evolution of sophisticated communication methods has made working in virtual teams seem like something new. One team member's definition of a virtual team reflects this thinking.

> A virtual team is a group of people who use technology, some of which has been available for fifty years, and some of which is relatively new, to stay hooked [up] and [to] do their tasks. I'm not sure I see the difference between what people call a virtual team and people collaborating over distances when they can't get together face-to-face. Before, when we could not get together, we would do our collaborative work via the telephone. Now we've thrown in the use of available information technology through emails and Faxes and whatever else people may want to choose

from. But to me it's just working together with somebody who you're not in the same office with. And that's something that has been going on for a long time. So, in one sense you're looking at a new phenomenon, but in another sense, you're looking at a very old phenomenon. [Jason, ACI]

Loose Boundaries

Although membership may be relatively clear in a co-located team, in a virtual team, membership can become fuzzy. Virtual teams have been characterized as having permeable boundaries. For example, team members spoke of belonging to teams with core and peripheral members (who offer assistance when needed), of belonging to smaller virtual teams that are a part of larger virtual teams, and of belonging to teams with members from differing departments or functions.

And Now, a Definition

So for the virtual team members interviewed, three crucial factors characterized their teams—common goals, geographic separation of team members, and the majority of their team's communication taking place through methods other than face-to-face. Additionally, team members characterized boundaries as loose and often unclear, with membership made up of core and peripheral members, members from multiple departments, and smaller virtual teams being a part of larger virtual teams. Here is a formal definition of a virtual team, which encompasses what the members shared.

> A virtual team is first of all a team, characterized by interdependence, shared values, and common goals. Additionally, it is characterized by members who are geographically separated from one another, who communicate mostly through electronic means, and whose boundaries may be stretched by the inclusion of core and peripheral members, members from multiple departments, and smaller teams subsumed by larger teams.

Creativity

Creativity has been typically defined as the process through which individuals or teams produce something that is both *new or novel* and potentially *useful or appropriate.* Novelty implies that what has been created is different from what has been done by the individual or team before. However, genuine creativity within a business setting requires something more than just novelty. A creative outcome must be relevant, effective, appropriate, and offer a genuine solution to a particular problem or presented task. Creative responses that are novel but not of any particular use are therefore not creative. The tangible results of creativity are often referred to as either incremental innovation (improvements to existing processes) or radical innovation (creation of entirely new activities).

Methodology

The findings in this book are grounded in a two-year inquiry I conducted with members of virtual teams. Thirty-six members from nine different virtual teams (described in the next section) were asked a series of questions about their virtual teams, how they created, and what determined high and low creative experiences in their teams. Each team member was interviewed over the telephone. Interviews were audiotaped with the individual team member's consent and verbatim transcripts were generated; these transcripts were then subjected to qualitative data analysis. In the interviews, team members were asked to: (1) provide background on the organization in which the team resides, (2) discuss their specific role in the team and describe a typical work day, (3) describe the characteristics, behaviors, and norms of their virtual team, (4) describe what they liked and did not like about working in a virtual team, (5) address the strengths and limitations of virtual teams, (6) describe how the creative process evolves in their virtual team, and (7) share two stories of projects completed by their team—one story that they felt exemplified high creativity and one story that exemplified low creativity. The members candidly shared stories of how creativity occurred (or did not occur) within their teams.

Throughout this book, the virtual team members' words are frequently shared. These quotes offer an absorbing, coherent, and candid account of what is involved in creativity in virtual teams.

After the interview, team members completed a background survey (either electronically or through regular mail). The survey was a mixture of both closed-ended and open-ended questions asking about the individual virtual team member, the virtual team (size, duration, mission, specific tasks, frequency of communication, and types of information technology used), and the organization in which the virtual team resided. (See the Appendix for information about how the trustworthiness—validity, reliability, and generalizability—of the inquiry was achieved.)

Description of the Virtual Teams

This section profiles the nine participating virtual teams to help readers gain a sense of the teams' characteristics such as: (1) the nature of the team's work, (2) the size of the team, and (3) the amount of time (tenure) the team had been in existence. (*Please note that throughout this book, names of teams and individual team members—and other company-specific information—have been disguised to ensure the anonymity of those individuals who were kind enough to share their thoughts with me.*)

The nine teams varied with respect to the nature of their work. Three teams were organizational consulting firms: Alpha Consultants Incorporated (ACI), specializing in assisting clients with organizational change; Vital Training Group (VTG), specializing in personal productivity and time management training and in helping clients streamline their workflow; and Jacobs/Taylor (J/T), who assisted clients in technological diffusion.

Two teams were in the education field. The Job Search Consortium (JSC) team was composed of a group of career development professionals from universities with small, but high-quality MBA programs that had come together to put on an annual recruiting event for their students. The Electronic Learning Consortium (ELC) team was composed of four developers responsible for developing and maintaining a text-based, educational virtual community for primary, secondary, and university students.

Three teams were on-line service providers. Two of these teams resided in the same organization, Worldwide Network Software Development (WNSD), a large software development company. The WN–Current Events team was responsible for producing an on-line publication that featured a calendar of events and directory of content of what was happening on the on-line service network. The WN–Religion Forum team managed an on-line chat on religion. The third on-line service provider team resided in OfficeTech, a large, multinational organization that manufactures business machines and computers. The major work of the OfficeTech team was to develop and sustain a company virtual community to foster knowledge sharing among globally dispersed workers in the corporation.

The final team was made up of product design engineers who worked for AutoMax, a large auto manufacturing company. The engineers were responsible for designing circuit boards for car radios, clusters, odometers, anti-lock brakes, and electric windows.

Members of the nine teams were mostly located within the United States (although there were some internationally dispersed team members), but were widely dispersed across the country. The size of the teams varied from three to twelve individuals. Team tenure (defined as the time from when the team was initially formed to the time of the interviews) also varied, ranging from one team who had been in existence for only six months to one team who had been in existence for fifteen years. Table I.1 briefly profiles each of the virtual teams. In some cases, I was not able to interview the entire team. The number of team members that were interviewed per team is indicated in parentheses in the following table.

Table I.1 Profile of the Virtual Teams

Team	Nature of Work	Size/(# int.)	Tenure
Organizational Consultants			
Alpha Consulting Incorporated (ACI)	Consulting firm that assists clients with organizational change	6 (6)	15 years
Jacobs/Taylor (J/T)	Consulting firm that assists clients with technological diffusion and implementation	8 (2)	6 years
Vital Training Group (VTG)	Consulting firm that specializes in personal productivity, time management training, and helping clients streamline workflow	6 (5)	3 years
Education Teams			
Electronic Learning Consortium (ELC)	Team of designers responsible for developing and maintaining an educational virtual community for primary, secondary, and college students	4 (3)	1 year
Job Search Consortium (JSC)	Team of MBA career development professionals that put on an annual job recruiting event for students	12 (6)	5½ years

Table I.1 Profile of the Virtual Teams, Cont'd

Team	Nature of Work	Size/(# int.)	Tenure
On-line Service Providers			
OfficeTech	Team that develops and sustains a company virtual community to promote internal knowledge sharing	3 (3)	1 year
Worldwide Network-Current Events (WN–CE)	Team that produces an on-line publication	5 (4)	6 months
Worldwide Network-Religion Forum (WN–R)	Team that manages an on-line forum on religion	4 (3)	1½ years
Design Engineers			
AutoMax	Team of product design engineers who design circuit boards for the electronics in cars	5 (4)	6 months

Guidelines for How to Use This Book

The most obvious way to use this book is to simply read through from beginning to end. This will allow you to gain a thorough understanding of the key components presented and to try the tools that are designed to help you develop each of these components in your virtual team. I'll also offer an alternative way to make your way through this book. Following this section is a brief diagnostic tool on each of the key components for virtual teams. If you chose to direct your attention first to only those components your team is most in need of developing, you should complete the initial assessment tool and then read the appropriate chapters first.

If you do not have the time to work through all the tools provided in this book, you may also read the entire text first to gain an overall awareness of what is needed for creativity in virtual teams. Then take the initial assessment and re-visit and complete only the assessment tools in the chapters on topics for which your team needs further development. Pick the option that works best for your team.

To assist virtual team designers, managers, and team members in assessing the functioning of their virtual team, a series of assessment activities are provided throughout this book. Take the time to work through the assessments thoroughly. Merely reading without doing the appropriate work will not produce the same amount of learning as actively completing the assessments will. There are two major types of assessment activities for you to partake in. Some chapters have assessment questions provided for the team to reflect on. Other chapters have assessment tools with checklists and specific exercises to work through. In completing the assessment activities in this book, it is best if all team members and key stakeholders are involved in the assessment process. Furthermore, it is important to remember that the process of assessment takes time. Don't rush the process by attempting to answer all the questions or complete all exercises in one team meeting. You may find it beneficial to circulate the assessment questions or tools to individual team members and stakeholders for personal review before beginning collaborative dialogue.

Once individual members have reviewed the questions or tools, bring team members together for focus group sessions to address and discuss the questions presented in the assessment activities. If at all possible, record the sessions (through note-taking, electronic exchanges, audio taping, or video taping). Otherwise your team's discoveries and subsequent learning may be lost. However, it is imperative that team members be comfortable with recording methods; if they are not comfortable, honest dialogue and discussion could be inhibited. After answers and responses have been shared and captured, the responses need to be summarized in some fashion. This may involve pulling together the responses into major themes or categories that emerged. This list of themes or categories should then be presented back to team members and stakeholders for clarification, review, and further discussion. This same process should be engaged in at periodically agreed-upon intervals. That means the team may come back to specific assessment activities at these agreed-upon intervals. This re-assessment is crucial for continual learning and development.

Because the very nature of virtual teams means that members are not co-located, you might wonder how this assessment would take place. Is it best done face-to-face or can electronic methods of exchange achieve the same results? Just as virtual teams can generate ideas in a variety of ways (discussed in Chapter 1)—by meeting face-to-face, by listing ideas electronically and then meeting face-to-face to sort through ideas, by relying on tools and technology, and so on—there are also many approaches teams can take with assessment. While assessment is probably best begun with members coming together face-to-face, this may not be practical, especially if the assessment is to be ongoing. Virtual teams need to consider which methods of communication are feasible and likely to lead to a productive and honest assessment procedure. The type of methods used should be tailored to the specific virtual team and to the members of that team. All members should be comfortable sharing responses in the methods chosen for assessment.

By engaging in the assessment process, your virtual team is really beginning the creative process as well. Assessment helps a team to sense current problems, challenges, and opportunities for growth in the functioning of the team. From the mess, data, and facts gathered through the team members' sharing and discussion, areas of improvement in the themes that emerged are identified. Ideas then are generated for solving these identified problems, and these solutions are evaluated. Development then begins producing action plans to achieve workable solutions. Implementation of the action plan takes place and the action is then evaluated (ongoing assessment). As a result, the assessment process begins again. In actuality, the assessment process mirrors the creative process itself (which will be discussed in Chapter One). So you are on your way, embarking on the process of becoming a more creative virtual team. Enjoy your journey.

Initial Virtual Team Assessment

Answer each of the following questions with regard to your virtual team. You may find it helpful to have all team members complete this assessment. After you have completed the initial assessment, look at the questions you circled or rated with a 1 or 2. These are areas in which you might strive for improvement. Questions that you circled or rated with a 3 indicate that you also might want to strive for further improvement. Even for the questions that you circled or rated with a 4 or 5, you still might want to search out ways in which the team can move to even higher levels of functioning within that component.

Component 1: Design

Creative Process and Work Design Approach (refer to Chapter One)

1. How effective do you think your team's current overall creative process is in leading to promising creative results?

    Very Ineffective   1   2   3   4   5   Very Effective

2. How effective do you think your team's current method of generating ideas is in leading to promising creative results?

Very Ineffective   1   2   3   4   5   Very Effective

3. How effective do you think your team's current method of developing ideas into workable products is in leading to promising creative results?

Very Ineffective   1   2   3   4   5   Very Effective

4. How effective do you think your team's current procedure for finalizing and bringing a project to a close is in leading to promising creative results?

Very Ineffective   1   2   3   4   5   Very Effective

5. How effective do you think your team's current method for evaluating the strengths and weaknesses of a completed project are in leading to future promising creative results?

Very Ineffective   1   2   3   4   5   Very Effective

6. How effective do you think your team's method of assigning portions of the work to team members is in leading to promising creative results?

Very Ineffective   1   2   3   4   5   Very Effective

Leadership Structures (refer to Chapter Two)

7. How appropriate do you think the current leadership structure is for guiding the creative efforts of your team?

Inappropriate for   1   2   3   4   5   Appropriate for
creative work   creative work

Component Two: Climate

Connection (refer to Chapter Three)

8. Overall, how dedicated are team members to the team's work?

Not dedicated   1   2   3   4   5   Extremely
at all   dedicated

9. How effective do you think your team is in establishing clear goals?

Very Ineffective   1   2   3   4   5   Very Effective

10. How effective do you think team members are in sharing information with one another?

    Very Ineffective   1   2   3   4   5   Very Effective

11. How strong is the personal bond between members of your team?

    Very weak   1   2   3   4   5   Very strong

12. The level of trust between the members of our team is:

    Very weak   1   2   3   4   5   Very strong

Team Member and Management Conditions and Competencies (refer to Chapter Four)

13. How accepting are team members of the ideas offered by other team members?

    Not accepting   1   2   3   4   5   Extremely
    at all   accepting

14. How constructively is tension utilized within the team to stimulate creativity?

    Not constructive   1   2   3   4   5   Very
    at all   constructive

15. How challenged are team members by the team's work?

    Not challenged   1   2   3   4   5   Extremely
    at all   challenged

16. Overall, the level of collaboration among the members of our team is:

    Very weak   1   2   3   4   5   Very strong

17. Overall, the degree of freedom given to team members in pursuing their work is:

    Very low   1   2   3   4   5   Very high

18. How encouraging are team managers and leaders of creative behavior within the team?

    Not encouraging   1   2   3   4   5   Extremely
    at all   encouraging

19. In general, how much time is allotted to complete projects?

    Leaves no time   1   2   3   4   5   Is the ideal
    to be creative   amount to
                                                      think creatively

20. Rate how much you agree or disagree with each of the following statements concerning members of your team. Use the following scale:

    Strongly disagree   1   2   3   4   5   Strongly agree

    The members of our team . . .

    _____ possess a high degree of self-awareness.
    _____ have a high degree of interpersonal awareness.
    _____ communicate supportively with one another.
    _____ resolve conflict effectively.
    _____ are adept at problem solving and making decisions.
    _____ are able to communicate well with individuals from various cultures.
    _____ can manage stress effectively.
    _____ can manage time effectively.
    _____ are adept at using positive political skills to improve interpersonal relationships.
    _____ can manage and access needed knowledge, data, and information.
    _____ take an active part in advancing their own careers.

21. Rate how much you agree or disagree with each of the statements below concerning the leader or manager of your virtual team. Use the following scale:

    Strongly disagree   1   2   3   4   5   Strongly agree

    Our team leader (or manager) . . .

    _____ possesses a high degree of self-awareness.
    _____ has a high degree of interpersonal awareness.
    _____ communicates supportively with team members.
    _____ resolves conflict effectively.
    _____ is adept at problem-solving and making decisions.
    _____ is able to communicate well with team members from various cultures.

_____ can manage stress effectively.

_____ can manage time effectively.

_____ is an effective coach.

_____ empowers the members of our team through delegating tasks appropriately.

_____ rewards and recognizes the members of our team for effective performance, significant achievements, or important contributions.

_____ is adept at using positive political skills to improve interpersonal relationships.

_____ can manage and access needed knowledge, data, and information.

_____ takes an active part in advancing his or her career.

Component Three: Resources

Communication Tools (refer to Chapter Five)

22. How adequate do you feel the technological resources (tools used to communicate with one another) allocated to your team are?

Sorely lacking   1   2   3   4   5   Ideal

23. How effective do you think your team's integration of information technology and face-to-face contact is in leading to promising creative results?

Very Ineffective   1   2   3   4   5   Very Effective

Creativity Techniques and Software Tools (refer to Chapter Six)

24. In the pursuit of creative work, how often does the team utilize specific techniques (some examples might be brainstorming, analogical thinking) for stimulating creativity?

Not often at all   1   2   3   4   5   Regularly
                                                                when needed

25. How useful do you consider the techniques your team uses to stimulate creativity?

Not very useful   1   2   3   4   5   Extremely
                                                               useful

26. How adequate are the creativity software tools (software programs developed to assist in generating, trying out, recording, and finally implementing ideas) that have been allocated to your team?

    Sorely lacking   1   2   3   4   5   Ideal

Component Four: Norms and Protocols
(refer to Chapter Seven)

27. Overall, team members know how and when they can get in touch with one another.

    Not at all   1   2   3   4   5   Most of
    the time

28. Typically, how effective are the tools selected by your team to communicate and convey intended messages to one another?

    Very ineffective   1   2   3   4   5   Very effective

29. Your team's plan to guide communication between subsets of the team is:

    Not at all useful   1   2   3   4   5   Very useful

30. How balanced are opportunities for formal and informal communication between team members?

    Way off   1   2   3   4   5   Just right

31. Overall, most of the projects accomplished by our team flow through lifecycles that are:

    Not clearly   1   2   3   4   5   Logical
    defined and   and well
    understood   understood

32. Overall, how effective is the process of assigning roles and responsibilities to team members?

    Very ineffective   1   2   3   4   5   Very effective

33. Overall, how accountable are team members for completing assignments and delivering quality results on time?

    Not at all   1   2   3   4   5   Extremely
    accountable   accountable

34. How effective is the team's plan for ensuring individual team member accountability?

    Very ineffective   1   2   3   4   5   Very effective

35. Overall, how effective are existing protocols in helping team members work with shared database systems and files?

    Very ineffective   1   2   3   4   5   Very effective

36. Overall, how useful is feedback given to the team on its work?

    Not at all useful   1   2   3   4   5   Very useful

37. Overall, how consistently is feedback given to the team on its work?

    Not consistent at all   1   2   3   4   5   Very consistent

Component Five: Continual Assessment and Learning
(refer to Chapter Eight and assessment tools throughout the book)

38. Our team takes the time to properly assess the work it has performed.

    Strongly disagree   1   2   3   4   5   Strongly agree

39. Our team takes the time to properly assess the functioning of the team.

    Strongly disagree   1   2   3   4   5   Strongly agree

40. Our team takes the time to learn from its past experiences.

    Strongly disagree   1   2   3   4   5   Strongly agree

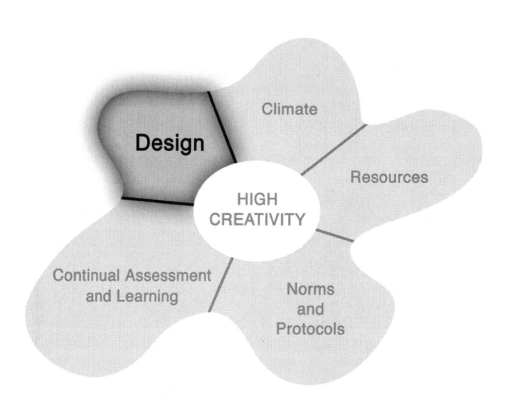

PART I

Design

IN DEFINING THE NATURE OF A VIRTUAL TEAM, the technology that supports virtual teams often gets most of the attention. However, the process through which a team creates, the approaches a team uses to organize its creative work, and the leadership structures that guide and manage the team's creative efforts—all elements of team *design*—must also be understood. Chapter One outlines the stages involved in the creative process of virtual teams and the work design approaches commonly used by virtual teams to accomplish their creative outcomes. Chapter Two describes the types of leadership structures that typically occur in virtual teams to move creative behavior forward.

CHAPTER 1

Mapping Out the Creative Process and Work Design Approach

There is a kind of iteration or reiteration cycle that keeps happening, individual work and then back out to the group. Some people will tear the project apart, others will say it looks great, and still others will offer a couple of ideas. And over a period of a month or so, it comes together into a final product, which gets together in a reasonable form and then [is] sent back out again. So there seems to be this kind of cycling of individual work, send it out, get comments, and bring it back.

Matt, ACI

IT IS NOT SURPRISING that contemporary organizations, faced with global competition and external environmental turbulence, require highly creative teams to survive. The need for creativity is particularly critical for virtual teams, teams that join individuals from across the globe to meet the demands of this fierce competitive global marketplace. The literature on virtual teams is expanding. Many (including myself) have argued that virtual teams are no different from more traditional face-to-face teams and that the skills and processes needed for effective virtual teams are the same as those for co-located teams. However, it has also been suggested that for virtual teams these same skills and processes may be more difficult to establish and take more time and effort to develop than in face-to-face teams.

In this chapter, one of the key processes of virtual teams is examined—the process through which members of these teams create. What is involved in a virtual team's creative process? How is a virtual team's creative process similar to or different from that of traditional, co-located teams? The purpose of this chapter is to address these questions.

This chapter contains several different threads of discussion. The chapter begins with an overview of the major approaches in the study of the creative process—linear, intuitive, and componential approaches. Then it presents a model of the unique stages of the creative process for virtual teams. This model is then compared and contrasted with the more traditional creative process models. Following that, three work design approaches commonly used by virtual teams to accomplish their creative efforts are described—the wheel, modular, and iterative approaches. Finally, an assessment tool is offered to assist virtual teams in appraising the current functioning of their creative process.

Major Approaches in the Study of the Creative Process

The creative process refers to the activities that occur while a person is creating. For years, a myriad of researchers and practitioners have examined the creative process. Theoretical models that attempt to conceptualize the creative process typically fall into one of three major approaches: (1) A linear approach, in which the creative process is viewed as a logical problem-solving process, (2) An intuitive approach, in which the creative process involves the use of insight, intuition, imagery, and a sudden change in perception, and (3) A componential approach, in which the creative process is only one element among the entire set of abilities, skills, traits, and processes that are involved in creative behavior.

These major approaches are described in more detail next.

The Linear Approach: A Logical Path of Problem Solving

Here the creative process is viewed as a logical, patterned sequence of steps or stages through which an individual or team moves to define, clarify, and work on a problem and then produce a solution to that problem. Individuals or teams make a conscious attempt to sit down and attack a problem or task using several linear creative problem-solving techniques.

Many theoretical models of the creative process further clarify and elaborate on the exact steps included in the process leading to a workable solution to a problem. One example is the "Complete Creative Problem Solving Process" developed by Min Basadur (1994). In this model, creative behavior is defined as a three-stage process that includes problem finding, problem solving, and solution implementation. Within each of these stages are two thinking processes, ideation (idea generation without evaluation) and evaluation (judging how useful a generated idea is). Eight steps then occur across these three stages.

Three steps are involved in the first stage of problem finding: problem finding, fact finding, and problem defining. In the *problem-finding* step, problems are initially sensed and anticipated, as the environment is scanned for present and future problems. Information related to these newly sensed problems is then actively gathered in the *fact-finding* step. The facts are subsequently evaluated, and the most useful are utilized to develop a workable problem definition in the *problem-defining* step. Then, the problem definitions that appear to be most advantageous to solve are selected.

The process then evolves into the problem-solving stage, which contains two steps: idea finding (solution-finding), and evaluation and selection. In *idea finding*, a large number of potential solutions for the problem definitions are generated. Following that, a smaller number of the most useful solutions are selected in the *evaluation and selection* step. During evaluation and selection, criteria are established to determine which solutions are most appropriate for moving forward into the third stage, solution-implementation. A key characteristic of the solution-implementation stage is recognizing that problem solving does not end with having developed a good solution. Three steps comprise the work of solution-implementation: (1) *action-planning*, where specific action steps are created for successful implementation of the solution; (2) *gaining-acceptance*, where alternative ways are generated to create ownership among those affected by the suggested action; and (3) *taking-action,* which involves the actual doing of the action. The model takes a circular form, where the ninth step is in actuality the first step of the next rotation or cycle to the creative process. Each action taken to implement a new solution automatically results in new problems, changes, and opportunities as it interacts with new elements in the environment.

Some of the models within the linear approach take on a more flexible view of the creative process. Stages or steps are not viewed as a fixed number to be applied in a predetermined order, but are viewed as tools that are available when and as needed, for individuals or teams working on problems or open-ended tasks. One such example is the Creative Problem Solving (CPS) model. The model was initially developed by Alex Osborn (1963), the creator of the popular brainstorming technique used for idea generation. Osborn's model was further refined by creativity experts Sidney Parnes (1981) and Treffinger, Isaksen, and Dorval (1994). In the current form, the CPS model has six stages, which have been clustered into three general components: (1) Understanding the problem (mess finding, data finding, problem finding); (2) Generating ideas (idea finding); and (3) Planning for action (solution finding, acceptance finding).

The Intuitive Approach: Intuition and Insight

For those who view creativity from a more intuitive perspective, the creative process is viewed as involuntary. It involves a relatively rapid change in one's current way of thinking or perceiving. What occurs is a mental transformation that allows new ideas, meaning, or solutions to be suddenly discovered. There is little or no experience of a particular path one follows to a solution (as in the linear approach). The creative individual is often left to wonder "Where did the thought come from?" Intuitive techniques (discussed in detail in Chapter Six) emphasize developing in an individual or team a state of inner calmness (through the use of imagery, meditation, or visualization) to prepare individuals to access the intuitive solution when it arises.

In this approach, the use of intuition and insight are necessary to achieve promising creative results. Intuition has been characterized as an unconscious process that is created out of one's past experiences. It involves relying on one's gut feeling about what is the right decision or direction to follow. Insight has been formally defined as a process where an individual or team suddenly moves from not knowing how to solve a problem to just simply knowing how to solve that problem (Mayer, 1999). Although the phenomena of intuition and insight may overlap, they can be distinguished from one another. According to Emma Policastro, "Intuition entails vague and tacit knowledge, whereas insight involves sudden, and usually clear, awareness. In the context of creativity, *intuition may precede insight*" (italics added) (1999, p. 90).

Intuitions are frequently used early in the creative process to guide decision-making. Experts often use intuition to size up situations quickly and accurately to decide on a specific and effective course of action. Evidence from several sources supports the importance of intuition in the creative process of both artists and scientists. In addition, top executives frequently rely on intuition to assist in making important decisions. These same executives have indicated that in most circumstances their initial intuitive hunches proved to be right. The creative process then continues after this initial use of intuition, as the individual or team moves through a sequence in which a vague and implicit sense of what is right transforms into an explicit and integrated knowledge of how to produce the needed creative results (Policastro, 1999, p. 91).

Intuition is often regarded as most useful in situations characterized by high stakes and uncertainty, by limited facts to assist in decision-making, by several plausible alternatives to choose from, and by pressure to make the right decision in a limited amount of time. In situations that require urgent action, there simply may not be the time to go through the logical stages and steps outlined in the linear creative process models. In urgent and pressing situations, one may choose intuition out of necessity—there isn't always time to analyze each existing alternative.

Although intuition may be the initial spark in a long path toward a creative outcome, insight is often characterized as a sudden revelation, transformation, change in perception, or "ah-ha" experience. In reality, insight is rarely as sudden as it may appear. Creative insights are generally the result of much prior reflection, knowledge, and action.

Insight is sometimes seen as one stage of several that occur in the course of the creative process. The most traditional analysis of stages in the creative process was originated by Graham Wallas in 1926 in *The Art of Thought*. Wallas proposed a four-step model of the creative process: preparation, incubation, illumination, and verification. *Preparation* involves exploring and clarifying the situation, looking for what the real problem is, thinking about what may be needed to work toward a solution, and gathering and reviewing relevant data. In the *incubation* stage, conscious work on the problem is suspended. The creative individual does not consciously work on the problem presented, but rather engages in things totally unrelated to the creative activity. Even though conscious work is suspended, a series of unconscious and involuntary mental events are stirring about, ready to spring forth into a revelation of sudden insight in the *illumination* stage. An "ah-ha" or "Eureka" feeling is experienced. There is a sudden change in perception, a new idea combination, or a transformation that produces an acceptable solution to the problem at hand. This period is usually accompanied by a feeling of excitement and renewed interest in the creative activity. Insight, then, plays a key role in the illumination stage. *Verification* involves the use of logical and rational thought to translate this sudden insight into an appropriate solution. Evaluation of proposed solutions is made against objective criteria.

The Interplay of Linear and Intuitive Approaches

In real life situations, both linear and intuitive thinking are needed to produce highly creative results. A typical pattern in the creative process may involve logic preceding and following intuition and insight. The key difference between the two ways of thinking is that in more linear views the creative process is sequential. In intuitive approaches to creative activity, the process is holistic. Thus the creative process is a combination of hard work, logic, and intuitive insight.

The Componential Approach: Capturing the Complexity of Creativity

The creative process is only one element in componential models of creativity, which specify abilities, skills, personality traits, and processes involved in creative behavior (Lubart, 1999, p. 295). Although the exact components necessary for creativity vary from model to model, what they have in common is their capacity to capture the complexity of creativity with one framework. Componential models add further value by providing components on which highly creative individuals and teams may be assessed and identified, and by providing areas in which training may be developed for creativity enhancement. One of the first componential models of creativity was proposed by Teresa Amabile (1983, 1996) in her work on the social psychology of creativity.

Amabile described a set of three components as necessary and sufficient for creative production: (1) Domain-relevant skills such as factual knowledge, technical skills, and special talents; (2) Creativity-relevant skills such as appropriate cognitive style, knowledge of heuristics, and conducive work style; and (3) Task motivation such as the individual's attitude toward the task and self-perception of motivation for undertaking the task.

The process with the highest creativity contains high levels of all three components. In addition, each of the three components contributes in varying degrees to five stages of the creative process. In the first stage of the creative process, a *task or problem is presented*. The component of task motivation is crucial, for it determines whether the individual will engage in the task at all. In the second stage of the creative process, individuals *prepare to generate solutions* by building up or reactivating a store of information relevant to the task or problem. Domain-relevant skills are of particular importance in this stage. In the third stage of the creative process, the individual *generates possible responses and solutions*. Both creativity-relevant skills and task motivation are important and can affect both the quality and quantity of ideas generated. In the fourth stage of the creative process, the *responses or solutions generated are evaluated and validated* for their appropriateness or correctness to the task at hand and *communicated* to relevant stakeholders. Domain-relevant skills provide the knowledge and assessment criteria to be used in this stage. In the fifth stage of the creative process, *an outcome is achieved* that is based on the results of stage four. If an idea is accepted, indicating success, or rejected, indicating failure, the creative process ends. If the idea is not wholly appropriate but does contribute significantly to solving the problem, the process returns to stage one. (For more information on other componential models of creativity, see Finke, Ward, and Smith, 1992; Mumford and others, 1991; and Runco and Chand, 1995 [cognitive-components approach]; Woodman and Schoenfeldt, 1990 [interactionist approach]; Sternberg and Lubart, 1991 [investment approach]; and Feldman, Csikszentmihalyi, and Gardner, 1994; Gruber, 1989 [systems approach]).

Stages of the Virtual Team Creative Process Model

Until recently, knowledge about the creative process had been limited to the study of individuals and organizations and, in some cases, groups or teams. However, the groups investigated have been traditional, face-to-face problem-solving groups. In this section, a new model of the creative process is presented, one that has emerged from my discussions with virtual team members about how the creative process evolves in their teams. As will be seen, the virtual team creative process model has much in common with the more traditional creative process models discussed in the previous section. However, there are intriguing differences as well.

Virtual teams follow a path of four stages in their quest toward the production of creative results—idea generation, development, finalization and closure, and evaluation. The *idea generation* stage is ignited when someone on the team recognizes an unmet need, asks a question, or simply feels that exploring a specific endeavor would be intriguing. As Rick, a member of the ELC team, explains, "Well, when I instigate something, it's usually because I see the need. But sometimes it's just creativity, you know, this would be cool." An individual team member (or a group of individuals within the team) then becomes the kicker and suggests an idea to the entire team. If the rest of the team agrees that the idea is worth pursuing and committing some initial time and resources to, the kicker then champions and begins to further define and mold the idea.

After the kicker's efforts are drafted, presented, and disseminated to the rest of the team, an iterative stage of *development* follows. Here, the team (or subset of the team) works to develop a product, project, or service that meets the initially-proposed need, answers the initially-proposed question, or brings into action the specific endeavor that was found to be intriguing. Team members exchange drafts, designs, or prototypes back and forth, offer feedback to one another, and, as a result, continue to make revisions. Matt (of the ACI team) describes this period as a cycling of individual and group work. (More about this iterative process will be described in the section on work design approaches.)

> A creative experience typically would start with two people saying, "What if we did X," or "We need to do X." And typically one person would say, "I'll take a lead on this. Let me scratch out some possibilities we ought to consider." Initiators will usually share possibilities on-line. People will respond electronically: "I like that, let me take A, you take D, and she'll take X." And they will do a little work around that and then put that up for a reaction. So the process begins with one initiator deciding "It's about time and I'll take the lead." Then, a template is developed that allows team members to grab pieces that interest them and do some creative individual work. Then, members will bounce their efforts off of one another. Such are the stages. An individual initiates, a couple of oth-

ers kick ideas around, come back to a starting nucleus of possibilities, divvy up those possibilities, respond to possibilities, and then bring their initial work back to the team to consider and assess. And there is usually one person who takes responsibility for kind of guiding the development work through all that iteration.

Once ideas are developed into workable outcomes, the creative products are *finalized* and implemented. Here the team makes one last review and pulls together any last-minute loose ends. *Closure* occurs just before implementation of the product, project, or service. It's almost like the last push in the birth of bringing the creative result into the world. After implementation, an *evaluation* period follows, in which team members get together and assess the strengths and weaknesses of the completed project.

Although four stages to the creative process for virtual teams have been proposed, it is crucial to realize that these stages may not be mutually exclusive. Activities in one stage may overlap and recur in another. For example, idea generation can also occur in the development stage; ideas need to be developed while they are being generated, and ideas are often evaluated before being fully developed. The trouble with viewing the creative process from a stage perspective is it attempts to linearize a process which in reality may be non-linear. Nevertheless, stage models are useful for organizing the decisions and activities involved in the creative process. Perhaps a better way to think about the stages of the creative process is, as Eveland (1990) suggests, to not "think of the sets of behaviors defined in most stage/phase models as steps on a stairway, but rather as rooms connected by a finite number of doors. Each room has core behaviors that take place within it; movement between rooms is divided by marker events that tell us when we are making significant behavioral transitions from one kind of activity to another" (pp. 30–31).

Comparing Traditional and Virtual Team Creative Process Models

As I began to undertake a comparison of the creative process models discussed thus far, a series of overall steps in the process leading toward a creative result began to emerge. The process begins with an initial scan of the environment for pressing problems, challenges, or opportunities. Facts are then gathered to further clarify the problems identified in the initial scan. After the facts have been sorted through, the problem or problems are more formally defined. What follows is a progression of steps leading to taking action, which include: (1) Generating and then evaluating solutions to the defined problem(s), (2) Creating an action plan for implementing solutions, (3) Gaining acceptance from those who will be affected by the proposed action, and (4) Taking the action. After implementing an action, an evaluation period may occur to clarify needed modifications and revisions. In Table 1.1, the columns list each of the overall steps in the creative process (across the top). The corresponding steps and/or stages in each of the specific models discussed are listed in the rows. Arrows indicate that a step or stage of a particular model includes more than one of the overall steps of the creative process. An empty box indicates that a particular model does not have a corresponding step or stage for that particular overall step of the creative process.

What is evident is that not all of the overall steps are included in each individual creative process model. In addition, in some creative process models, several of the overall steps are subsumed in a particular step or stage of an individual model. Interestingly, only three out of the five models (Amabile, 1983, 1996; Basadur, 1994; and the virtual team creative process model proposed in this chapter) address creating an action plan and taking action.

At first glance, the virtual team creative process appears simplistic compared to the other linear creative process models (Basadur, Creative Problem Solving). This may be partly because virtual teams have been created around the need to develop cost-effective, instantaneous responses to customer and market demands. This electrifying pace with which business can and does take place electronically may leave little room for all the steps outlined in a more traditional linear approach to creativity. Intuition and insight may play a role in helping team members gain initial agreement on what intriguing ideas should be taken into the development phase. Additionally, in virtual teams, clients or managers often present team members with problems and challenges, which eliminates the need for protracted work on finding and defining problems. It does appear that in the creative process of virtual teams there is more of a push to get to development quickly. There is less emphasis on sorting through an abundance of problem definitions, and more of a focus on assessing whether presented or sensed problems are worthy to pursue. In addition, as previously stated, the iterative stage of development in the creative process of virtual teams implies a more flexible view of the creative process, where activities occurring in one stage may overlap or recur in another stage. The boundaries between the four stages of a virtual team's creative process can often become blurred.

Table 1.1 Comparison of the Stages and Steps Across the Creative Process Models

Model	Initial Scan	Gather Facts	Define Problem	Generate Solutions	Evaluate Solutions	Action Plan	Gain Acceptance	Take Action	Evaluate Action Taken
Basadur	Problem finding	Fact finding	Problem defining	Idea finding	Evaluation and selection	Action planning	Gaining acceptance	Taking action	
Creative Problem Solving	Mess finding	Data finding	Problem finding	Idea finding	Solution finding	Acceptance finding	→		
Wallas	Preparation →	→	→	Incubation (unconscious), Illumination (conscious)	Verification				
Amabile	Preparation →	→	Problem and Task Identification	Response generated	Responses validated	→	Communication	Outcome	→
Virtual teams—Nemiro	Idea generation →	→	→	Development →	→	→	→	Finalization and closure	Evaluation

The virtual team creative process model contains many similarities to the other creative process models. The idea generation stage of the virtual team creative process includes a kicker actively scanning or searching for an intriguing problem or sensed need. The kicker finds additional data and facts, further molds the problem, and then presents initial problem definitions to the team. The period of development can begin with illumination, solution finding, and response generation, where the team, now committed to the initial challenge and to some initial ideas for solving that challenge, begins further work on generating and evaluating appropriate solutions. Verification, acceptance finding, and response validation and communication also occur during the development period.

The stages of finalization and closure and evaluation are similar to Amabile's outcome stage where a solution is reached and implemented and some kind of outcome occurs as a result. However, the virtual team creative process model that emerged in this investigation is probably most similar to the model suggested by Basadur (1994), with the three stages of problem finding, problem solving, and solution implementation. The last stage, which emphasizes implementation, action planning, and gaining acceptance, is not included in most of the other creative process models, which typically end once the appropriate idea has been selected.

Traditionally, creativity has been viewed as the generation and selection of new ideas, and innovation as the implementation of those new, creative ideas. Creativity and innovation, for the most part, have been characterized as two separate processes. Creativity involves only "thinking up new things" and innovation only "doing new things" (Peters and Waterman, 1982, p. 206). This is a simplistic view, as it implies that creativity is largely cognitive and innovation largely behavioral. In a conceptual paper on group creativity, Nemiro and Runco (1995) pointed out the difficulty with viewing creativity and innovation as two separate processes.

> Surely innovation requires some thought, and creative insights
> may follow from actual activity. Just as surely there can be some
> interplay; a creative idea may suggest an innovation, which in
> turn suggests new and creative possibilities. Part of the problem
> is the either–or assumption, the dichotomy that artificially sepa-
> rates creativity and innovation.

In the virtual team creative process model, there is no dichotomy between creativity and innovation. They are intertwined, as ideas are generated, developed, finalized, and then evaluated. Teams may, however, proceed through each of these stages using different methods to accomplish the work. The work design approaches that were used by the teams I interviewed are discussed in the next section.

Work Design Approaches Used During the Creative Process

Three work design approaches—the wheel, the modular, and the iterative approach—emerged from the virtual team members' stories of how they moved from initial idea generation, through development, to finalization and closure of a creative effort. These approaches were not mutually exclusive, as most of the teams used more than one.

The Wheel Approach

The wheel is a classic type of communication network (Katz and Kahn, 1978), in which there is one key person who communicates to all team members. Members on two different status levels make up the network—a high-status member (the leader or supervisor) and lower-level members or assistants. The higher-status member is usually referred to as the hub or center of the network, through which all communication must pass. In a classic wheel communication network, there are no direct communication links between any of the lower-level members.

One team investigated, the WN–Religion Forum team, used the wheel approach to communicate and exchange information while creating. Although all team members did potentially have access to one another (through e-mail and phone), rarely did any of the assistants actually communicate with one another. The creative process began with either the team leader parceling out assignments to each team member, or individual team members proposing their ideas directly to the leader. Development of a creative idea occurred between the team leader and an individual team member.

The Modular Approach

One of the most common work design approaches used during the creative process of these virtual teams was the modular approach. In this approach, team members met initially to decide on the need, task, or project to be pursued. Then, as a group, the work was parceled out or distributed among team members, usually based on each individual team member's expertise or interest. Team members then went off to work on their "pieces of the pie," sometimes by themselves, sometimes with one or two other members of the team. After the work was completed, the efforts were presented to the group for feedback before finalization and implementation. Revisions were done as needed. The entire team, then, assessed the creative outcome, which in reality was a compilation of all the individual pieces put together. One team member succinctly describes the modular approach: "Oh, when everybody had a job and they were able to do it, and everyone did these tiny little pieces, then the final project is something impressive" [Alan, ELC].

Melissa, a VTG team member, points out a major drawback to the modular work design approach—the loss of feedback from others not working on a particular project.

> I think before we became so virtual we had more traditional meetings where everybody would just sit around and shoot the breeze about different projects and offer different ideas. Now, it's like a Catch-22 because the roles are so defined only certain people usually are involved in certain projects, so sometimes we lose other peoples' creativity who might not have anything to do with a project, but would see different things outside the dotted line.

To avoid this drawback, many teams used the iterative approach in conjunction with the modular approach.

The Iterative Approach

In the iterative approach, team members engaged in back-and-forth development cycles. Members worked a little, presented those results to the team, got feedback, worked a little more, presented those results, got more feedback, and so on until the project was finalized. E-mail technology allowed team members to throw out their ideas in a more or less random fashion. Ideas could bounce back and forth and build on one another with ease. Although several teams used the iterative approach, mostly in conjunction with the modular approach, two teams, ELC and OfficeTech, used the iterative approach frequently. For example, Richard, an OfficeTech team member, characterizes the team's creative process as a series of steps, alternating between thought and action.

Ours is more a very iterative close contact. [We] talk about it either via e-mail or via voice as you go along, and brainstorm ideas. One of the keys to our success is, as far as creativity is concerned, this frequent contact between team members. We're trying to do what, in software terms, is sometimes referred to as rapid prototyping, where you think a little, you do a little, you think a little, you do a little, you think a little, you do a little, rather than thinking a whole lot and then trying to come out with something that everybody agrees with the first time.

When To Use Each Work Design Approach

Typically, the most common work design approach used for virtual work is the modular approach. As seen in Table 1.2, seven out of the nine teams I spoke with used this particular approach in completing their work. However, the three work design approaches are not mutually exclusive. Table 1.2 outlines the work design approaches used by the virtual teams I interviewed. Most of the teams used more than one work design approach in accomplishing their work.

Table 1.2 Work Design Approaches Used by Teams When Creating

Team	Work Design Approach
Organizational Consultants:	
Alpha Consulting Incorporated (ACI)	Modular, Iterative
Jacobs/Taylor	Modular, Iterative
Vital Training Group (VTG)	Modular, Iterative
Education Teams:	
Electronic Learning Consortium (ELC)	Modular, Iterative
Job Search Consortium (JSC)	Modular, Iterative
On-line Service Providers:	
OfficeTech	Iterative
WN-Current Events	Modular
WN-Religion Forum	Wheel, Iterative (between team leader and individual members only)
Design Engineers:	
AutoMax	Modular, Iterative

Not every creative effort (or for that matter, less creative effort too) may be easily divided into sections. In those cases, a modular approach may be a poor choice for accomplishing that particular task. Virtual team designers need to consider seriously whether the creative task at hand can be effectively accomplished within the specific work design approach the team is using. Some teams may find it better to adapt a more flexible design, using one work design approach for one situation, and switching to another when the circumstances call for it. You may find Table 1.3 helpful in deciding what work design approach might work best for your team and when.

Table 1.3 Work Design Approaches

Work Design Approach	Works Well When
Wheel: Leader communicates to all team members; individual team members have little interaction with one another.	• Decision-making is centralized. • Leadership is permanent. • Work completed by individual team members does not require a lot of input and feedback from other team members. • Work completed by individual team members does not substantially overlap. • Team leader integrates individual work elements from all team members. • Individual team members have necessary expertise to accomplish their work. • Team members trust their fellow team members' expertise and are willing to let each handle their own work.
Modular: Work is parceled out to qualified team members; elements are integrated together later on.	• Task can be parceled out or divided among team members. Especially useful for creative tasks that can be easily broken down (such as writing a technical document, preparing a client proposal). • Team member roles and responsibilities are clearly defined. • Development work does not require extensive feedback or joint effort among members of the entire team. • Team has access to technology that can allow and support the exchange of shared work. • A democratic decision-making system is in place to support the team's assessment of the creative outcome. • Clearly-defined methods for ensuring accountability are in place and followed to guarantee team members will deliver their work on time. • One team member or support person is responsible for assembling all pieces of the project at the end.

Table 1.3 Work Design Approaches, Cont'd

Work Design Approach	Works Well When
Iterative: Work may be parceled out to qualified team members but members work together in back-and-forth development cycles.	• The nature of the work necessitates more frequent interactive input from and among all members or subsets of the team. • There is sufficient time to go through several back-and-forth development cycles. • Team members are willing to share their work in early stages of development. • Team members give one another honest, constructive, and open feedback. • Team members are accepting of and comfortable with divergent points of view (feedback from other members). • There is a well-designed system for communicating during the creative process. • Team norms support regular and open communication. • Technology is available to support the exchange of shared work.

Assessment Tool: Appraising the Creative Process and Work Design Approach

Now it's time to take a look at the creative process as it unfolds in your own virtual team. Use the questions presented in this section to reflect on and assess the functioning of the creative process within your virtual team and the specific work design approaches your team is using (or should be using). And remember this. By engaging in assessment, your virtual team is really mirroring the creative process as well. (Revisit the guidelines for using chapter assessment tools described in the Introduction if you need to.)

Assessment Questions

Overall Creative Process

1. How would you explain to a new member joining your team how creative results (products, projects, services, other outcomes) are achieved? In other words, how does the creative process evolve in your team? (Having team members share stories about the creative process underlying specific creative results provides insight into commonalties and variations in the creative process across different types of creative efforts.)

2. How do team members currently use linear (structured) approaches in their creative process?

3. What role do insight and intuition play in the team's creative process?

Idea generation

4. Is there a disciplined procedure in place that team members use to scan the environment for possible unmet needs or problems?

5. Is there a forum team members may use to share ideas they find intriguing? In this forum, are ideas initially shared without judgment and evaluation by others?

6. To what degree are team members open to hearing ideas offered by other team members?

7. Is there a disciplined procedure for using specific criteria to evaluate alternative solutions once generated?

Development

8. Is there a system in place for organizing development work (organizing the exchange of working drafts, designs, or prototypes)? How effective is this system? What would you change? What would you not change?

9. Do team members take the time to offer valuable and constructive feedback to one another?

Finalization and closure

10. Is there adequate time set aside to make last minute adjustments and revisions before implementation?

11. Is there a forum where team members can gather consensus on the proposed action before taking action? If so, how effective is the decision-making system that is in place to gain agreement?

12. Is there a system in place for gaining agreement from individuals outside of the team who may be affected by the proposed action?

13. To what degree can team members reach closure within the appropriate timeframe on a particular creative effort?

Evaluation

14. Is there a formal, disciplined process for evaluating action taken?

15. To what degree are multiple criteria used when evaluating action taken?

16. To what degree is feedback from evaluation used to further refine the action taken?

Work design approaches

17. What are the most frequently used work design approaches (wheel, modular, iterative, or others your team may use)?

18. To what degree are projects parceled out to individual team members? How effective is this process (in terms of divvying up the work fairly, assigning sections to those who have appropriate expertise, assigning sections that individuals are motivated to work on, holding team members accountable for delivering results of their individual efforts on time)?

19. To what degree is there a sense of iterative exchange in the development of a creative result? Are forums established for this? If so, how effective are they?

Final Thoughts

There needs to be *an appropriate balance of togetherness and apartness on the path of the creative process.* Although many of the virtual teams I interviewed relied heavily on the modular work design approach, each had their own unique creative cycle in which members oscillated between periods where they would come together (whether electronically or face-to-face) and periods where they would work apart and by themselves. The appropriate balance of togetherness and apartness varied for each team, with some teams (Jacobs/Taylor, JSC) needing more time together to create and other teams preferring time apart (VTG, WN–Religion Forum). Lipnack and Stamps (1997) referred to this oscillation between togetherness and apartness as the "rhythm of aggregation and dispersion," a rhythm they suggested has been around since ancient times. Lipnack and Stamps likened the pulse of virtual teams to foraging societies that survive even today, such as the !Kung of the Kalahari Desert in Botswana.

There was a pulse to the ancient life of nomads: groups of families came together and then went apart. Foragers had to follow the rhythm of the seasons dictated by their sources of food. Even today, !Kung households move to the same beat which literally 'goes with the flow.' Access to water moves the !Kung through seasonal cycles that cause groups of families to diverge and converge. The !Kung beat holds for the way most people work—coming together and going apart. People work alone and then join up in a group. We do what we do best independently and then work with others to expand our capabilities. The basic social rhythm of human beings has not really changed in two million years. [1997, p. 110]

Thus, these virtual teams worked and created in the same manner as humans have done for ages. However, the technology through which these teams did so has evolved quite considerably. In addition, the leadership structures used to guide virtual teams have also changed from the more traditional autocratic models. Chapter Two outlines the typical leadership structures used by virtual teams and offers some suggestions on how to choose an appropriate leadership structure for your virtual team.

Points to Remember

- Virtual teams follow a path of four stages in their quest toward the production of creative results: idea generation, development, finalization and closure, and evaluation. However, the boundaries between the four stages can become blurred.

- In the creative process of virtual teams, it appears there is more of a push to get to development quickly. Less of an emphasis is placed on sorting through a variety of problem definitions, and more focus is put on assessing whether presented problems are worthy to pursue.

- Three work design approaches guide the work of virtual teams as they proceed from initial idea generation, through development, to finalization and closure, and to evaluation of a creative effort. These approaches are the wheel, modular, and iterative approaches.

- The most common work design approach used by virtual teams during the creative process is the modular approach, in which the work is parceled out or distributed among team members based on their expertise or interest.

- The loss of feedback from others is a disadvantage of the modular approach. To avoid this drawback, many virtual teams use the iterative approach—in which team members engage in back-and-forth development cycles—in conjunction with the modular approach.

- Team members need an appropriate balance of togetherness and apartness as they work toward achieving creative results.

CHAPTER 2

Choosing an Appropriate Leadership Structure

We don't have a hierarchy. There are people that have been in the company longer, but it's more of an even playing field. So, on a four-month basis we rotate leadership. The position became dubbed as the Rotating Intergalactic Overlord of the Universe, the RIOU. We have someone that's the RIOU, and they hold that role for four months, and then it goes to the next person. And that is the cycle that works. And it's worked out pretty well.

Barbara, ACI

We don't differentiate the roles of leadership that much. I mean, everybody knows, in the business, ultimately who has responsibility to make final decisions. That's the people who own the business, the partners. But after that, it gets pretty muddy

Chad, Jacobs/Taylor

L EADING A VIRTUAL TEAM is not the same as leading a more traditional, co-located team. For one thing, as a manager or leader of a virtual team you will most likely spend 70 to 80 percent of your time with team members who are *not* co-located with you. Much of what has been written on virtual team leadership includes a series of suggestions for new competencies and skills needed by leaders or managers of virtual teams. Some of these new competencies include technological proficiency and appropriate use of technology; cross-cultural management skills; ability to coach distant team members; ability to build trust among dispersed team members; networking with others outside the team, such as customers or other stakeholders; and remote project management skills. (For more information on competencies and skills needed by virtual team managers or leaders, see Chapter 4 and Duarte and Snyder, 1999; Fisher and Fisher, 2001; and Haywood, 1998).

Not only are the competencies and skills needed by virtual team leaders potentially different from those necessary for leaders of traditional co-located teams, but the leadership structures in which they will lead may differ as well. Wilson, George, and Wellins (1994), in their book, *Leadership Trapeze: Strategies for Leadership in Team-Based Organizations,* suggest that leadership success in virtual organizations will require a new set of leadership tolerances. These include a tolerance for horizontal moves in the organization, organizational ambiguity, and for playing both a member role and a leader role within a team. They write, "In a virtual environment, power comes from what an individual accomplishes for the customer—not from position within the hierarchy" (p. 264). This last tolerance for simultaneously playing team leader and member roles was one that became especially evident in the leadership structures I witnessed in the virtual teams I interviewed.

Virtual Team Leadership Structures

This chapter details the different categories of leadership structures that guided the nine virtual teams I shared conversations with. The leadership structures that will be described include the following:

1. Permanent team leadership (the same individual or partners)

2. A rotating team leader (every member of the team is at one time the team leader)

3. Managing partners who govern the overall business and rotating project leaders who supervise individual projects and tasks

4. A facilitator or coordinator (rather than a full-fledged leader)

5. Leaderless (or led by all the team members)

Another issue that emerges side-by-side with leadership structure as important for the success of virtual teams is role clarity. Although role clarity is important for virtual team members, the roles they play are often multiple and flexible due to the dynamic nature of virtual teams. The different types of roles that members held in their teams will also be shared.

Permanent Team Leadership

In my conversations with virtual teams, oddly enough the most common leadership structure that emerged is the traditional style of having one team member (or partners who own the firm) function as the primary permanent team leader(s). Out of the nine teams I interviewed, five were led by permanent team leader(s). Each case is described in more detail.

For the *Electronic Learning Consortium (ELC)* team (in the field of education), one team member is the guiding force behind the team and also the entire ELC educational virtual community. This individual is responsible for developing the vision, for developing and setting new policy, and for handling public relations. His philosophy on leading the team is simple and engaging: "I've always considered myself a jack-of-all-trades looking for masters. The Internet just gets all these masters. And all I have to do is keep them happy and they'll keep working with me. I guess that's the real meaning of power. Being able to get something done." [Alan, ELC]

The other team members work both in conjunction with the leader and each other to develop new areas and interact with visitors to the community. Individual team members take on responsibilities based on their expertise, personality, and interest. One team member primarily interacts and counsels students on-line, another handles the maintenance of the computer system, and the other assists the rest of the team with procedural tasks.

One team member clearly leads the *WN–Current Events* team (an on-line service provider). As a team member shares, "Lianna is the leader and if Lianna says, 'I like it this way,' that's the way it's going to go" [Lisa, WN–Current Events]. However, Lianna may serve as the permanent leader but she also gives her team members operational autonomy to follow through on the tasks she assigns. As Lianna of WN-Current Events explains, "I have a spreadsheet that has a list of all the events that we've been promoting, and I asked Lisa to verify that they were actually occurring. I wanted Lisa to feel like she could address this task however she wanted to. I didn't want it to sound like, here's a spreadsheet, go through and check these off. I wanted to leave it up to her how she handled it."

The WN–Current Events team consists of five core team members. Lianna, as discussed, is the team leader. Three other team members do similar work, scheduling electronic chats and other events that will occur on the on-line service, and then putting together materials to publicize and promote these events in the on-line publication. A final team member functions as the builder who assembles all the information from the other team members and puts them all together into the final on-line publication. Peripheral team members, artists, and copywriters are used as needed.

One team member is also in charge of the *WN–Religion Forum* team (another on-line service provider team). The three other members of this team are assistants employed by the team leader who then subcontracts out to the larger organization, Worldwide Network Software Development (WNSD), for which this team supplies work. Team members are responsible for hosting chats and responding to bulletin board/message boards in their specific content area. (Each team member is responsible for a particular religion.) Team members interact mostly with the team leader and very little with one another. The leader decides what work is to be done and delegates tasks to her assistants. Scott, a WN-Religion Forum team member, describes the importance of the relationship with the team leader, Eryn. "Eryn is the ringleader and she is the core of the group, and I think the relationship between Eryn and the other assistants determines the success and the comfort range and the warmth of the entire community. I think it's very important for each assistant to identify and relate personally with Eryn."

The *OfficeTech* team (the third on-line service provider team) is the smallest of the teams I interviewed, with only three members (two core members and one peripheral member joining in as needed). The two core members work together to build an electronic virtual community for their organization. The two members characterize their relationship as "a strong synergy, almost a symbiotic relationship" [Richard, OfficeTech]. The peripheral team member is brought in when needed for additional programming and graphic support.

Although OfficeTech is a small team, there is clearly a team leader, who is based in the company's corporate office. The other two team members are dispersed from the corporate office. Having the team leader based out of the corporate office has a definite advantage. According to the team leader, being based out of the corporate office "allows me to stay politically better connected, and I can therefore champion our team and, where necessary, defend our team with the powers that be." [Richard, OfficeTech]

The *Vital Training Group (VTG)*, an organizational consulting firm, is headed up by two permanent leaders—partners who own the firm—one primarily focusing on sales and the other on consulting and training. The rest of the team members have well-defined areas of responsibility. Because the firm is small (six individuals), many of the members have three or four different roles they fulfill. For example, one team member said she was a consultant, manager of the coaching department, software program manager, account manager, and kitchen person. Another team member said his responsibilities included information technology coordinator, office manager, sales office administrator, and receptionist.

Why It Works

Why did these five virtual teams choose a relatively traditional leadership structure to manage and lead their teams? One common element in these teams (with the exception of OfficeTech) is the high degree of role differentiation between team members. Each team member has a distinct area of knowledge and expertise and is assigned to and responsible for a specific portion of the overall outcome or product. (For example, the WN–Religion Forum team members are each responsible for a different chat room; WN–Current Events team members are responsible for different elements of the on-line publication.) The different work products produced by individual team members are then integrated into a whole by the team leader (who also is the one who began the process by dividing up the work and assigning out appropriate tasks). A high level of interaction is necessary between the team leader and each individual team member, but not between individual team members.

Rotating Team Leader

The *Alpha Consulting Incorporated (ACI)* team (organizational consultants) began its life (when the team was larger in size) led by a president of the organization and one team leader that functioned as a general manager. The general manager had the role of overseeing all the organizational consultants, being aware of what each was doing, where they were, and relaying that information back to the office staff. As the number of consultants making up the team diminished, the need for a general manager role also diminished. Along with that, so did the available financial resources to pay for such a position. It was at that point the team decided to change its leadership structure to a system in which the team leadership position is rotated every four months among the four consultant members. The team members fondly call their leader "the Rotating Intergalactic Overlord of the Universe." Barbara of ACI explains,

> We do have a unique role in this company called the Rotating Intergalactic Overlord of the Universe. We call it the RIOU. We started rotating that because we really are all on pretty much of an equal plane. We don't have a hierarchy. There are people who have been in the company longer, but it's more of an even playing field. In order to make it fair, we do it on a four-month basis. We have someone who's the RIOU; he or she holds that role for four months, and then it goes to the next person. That is the cycle that works, and it's worked out pretty well.

The ACI team has six members, four consultants and two staff members. The two staff members (one who serves as the firm's business manager and accountant, the other who functions as a support person for the consultants in editing and formatting their work products) do not serve as rotating team leaders. The four consultants all perform similar tasks, including client consulting work, marketing, sales, and development of client prospects.

Why It Works

The rotating leadership structure works well for this particular virtual team because the roles that consultant team members play are not that different. The four consultant team members all perform the same type of work. The consulting projects are divided based on either customer or client preference (or who recruits which client), or the type of project the consultants enjoy and favor. However, in reality, any of the consultants could do any of the projects brought into the company. In addition, all team members have equal ability to effectively lead the team. They all understand the ins and outs of the business and know what it takes to lead it. The team has put in place several formal meetings throughout the year where all team members get together (through teleconferencing or in person) to discuss the business. These meetings keep all team members equally informed and help to foster high levels of interpersonal connection and trust among the members. Trust is essential in a rotating team leadership structure because all team members have to trust that each member (when it is his or her turn) will lead the team effectively. This leadership structure requires that all team members have a tolerance for filling both the role of a team member and team leader. When consultants take on the role of RIOU, they still have their consulting work to perform as well. Further, within the rotating team structure, there are consistent stable elements built in. The team's two staff members do not rotate and are there to assist whichever team member is "up to bat" as the current rotating team leader. The team also has attempted to standardize procedures and create templates to minimize variability of operations from one rotating leader to the next.

Managing Partners and Rotating Project Leaders

Combining permanent team leadership and rotating team leadership structures yields a structure in which the overall business is led by the same managing partners, but a particular project is led by whoever has the expertise needed for a particular assignment. One of the teams I interviewed (the Jacobs/Taylor team, an organizational consultant team) used this leadership structure.

Two partners own and lead the *Jacobs/Taylor* firm and have ultimate responsibility for making final decisions concerning the business. However, for specific projects, leadership is rotated. Typically, knowledge, expertise, and individual interest determine who becomes the leader of a particular project. Then, the rest of the team members function as support to the project leader. Since several projects often exist at the same time, team members play multiple roles (can be a leader on one project and a support person on another). Chad, one of the senior partners in the Jacobs/Taylor team, explains, "When we take on an engagement, one of the people is assigned as the lead person on that. Then we assign people in coordinating and support roles behind it. We try to even that out so everybody gets the lead, everybody gets the support, everybody gets to consult. We all play multiple roles at the same time."

Why It Works

This particular leadership style works well for virtual teams that offer multiple products or services for different customers. The nature of the team's business must be diverse enough to support the need for members with a variety of expertise areas. In turn, the team must be composed of team members who can support each needed area of expertise. Trust is also essential in the use of this leadership structure. Team members must trust the level of expertise each team member offers and trust their leadership abilities as well. This means that all team members, if they are to fill the role of project team leader at one time or another, must possess different levels of expertise and be trained in project and task management. This leadership structure requires that all team members have a tolerance for filling both the role of team member and team leader. With a multiplicity of projects, team members may fill the role of team leader on one particular project and concurrently fill the role of a support team member on another project. Virtual teams that use this type of structure tend to be larger in size.

A Facilitator or Coordinator

For virtual teams coming together to work on a particular project, formal team leaders may not always be needed. Knowledge workers from different functional units are often brought together to produce a product or service. Typically, these kinds of teams are self-managing. One of the teams I interviewed fell into this particular category—the *AutoMax* team, a product design engineering team. Rather than relying on a formal team leader, the AutoMax team has one team member who functions as a facilitator or coordinator. This individual assists in coordinating the sharing of dialogue and information among team members, but does not have any formal authority over the team and its work. Dana, an AutoMax team member, describes the role of their team's facilitator: "Bryan runs the Connection Plus system [a shared remote communications program] we use to communicate during our design process. When we need to talk to the plant, he showed us how to use Connection Plus so that we don't have to fax information or have it mailed there. We and they can see information as it's happening. So, Bryan is part of the virtual team but he really doesn't have anything to do with the design part as much as facilitating the sharing of information."

The other members of the team are product design engineers, working collaboratively together to design circuit boards to be used in an anti-lock brake module of a car.

Why It Works

The use of a facilitator or coordinator to guide a virtual team works well for teams that are self-managing but need additional support (for example, in terms of how to use technology or in facilitating team meetings and decision-making sessions). These virtual teams often are project teams whose members are part of a larger organizational structure as well. Team members need to be in constant communication with one another and to communicate their needs for information exchange and communication to the facilitator. Those who facilitate or coordinate the activities of these teams need to be trained in several areas, such as technical proficiency in electronic forms of communication, interpersonal skills (such as decision-making, conflict resolution), and project and task management.

Leaderless

The final leadership structure I encountered is one with no team leader at all, in which leadership is truly shared by all team members. For the Job Search Consortium (JSC), a team in the field of education, one team member, David, described their leadership structure as "kind of leaderless, leadership is equally shared." All team members have the same status and no one individual functions as a team leader. Responsibilities are divided equitably and along the lines of what individual team members have expertise in and do well. David of JSC further describes how this occurs: "We divide the responsibilities in the team fairly equitably and it's along the lines of what do you do well. We don't object to rotating assignments and will take different assignments if need be. But we found there are some schools that have an expertise, and it's great to just continue to tap that expertise."

The clarity of roles is evident when examining what task each team member is responsible for. All twelve team members work in their own university sites, and in those settings each has the responsibility of preparing their students for the Job Search Consortium. The team's main task is to put on a yearly job recruiting event for the students from the twelve participating schools. Each team member is also required to recruit organizations to participate in the Consortium event. Aside from those overall responsibilities, each team member is accountable for a separate task leading to the final Consortium event. For example, one team member is in charge of overseeing the registration database; another team member produces the resume book (with participating students' resumes) that is sent out to all participating companies. Still another team member manages the finances and collects registration payments. A fourth team member interfaces with the hotel where the event will take place. Another team member creates the brochures to market the event, and still another is in charge of creating and maintaining a Web site for the Consortium.

When decisions need to be made within the team, members bow to an individual team member's area of expertise.

As Raymond, a JSC team member, shares, "If we have a responsibility and someone has the skill or the drive to do it, we say, 'It's your task, take care of it. Assign us the way you'd like.' I'll use the resume book as an example. We ask that the resume book elements come in a certain format, and some schools have been uncomfortable with that format. But because it's our responsibility and our system that is producing it, we set the rules there. And they respect that."

Decisions are also made democratically with input from the entire group. Democratic decision-making is made simpler because of the ease of being able to get the information out to all members of the group through the e-mail forum. As Elaine, a JSC team member, describes,

> I prefer to do everything through the e-mail forum if someone's asking me to do something that impacts the whole group. That way, if someone wants to comment on it, they are informed as to what's happening and, once again, I'm not taking the full credit. I'm not taking the action and making the decision on behalf of the whole team. Everyone knows what I'm doing and when I'm doing it, and if someone has a problem with the request, then he or she can share those concerns in the forum. If someone doesn't respond, we just infer that they consider it a good idea. If you don't voice your objections, then we go with it.

When leaders in the team do emerge, they do so naturally. Says Raymond of JSC, "When leadership is needed, there's someone who takes it. It just happens and it literally is not defined."

Why It Works

This leadership structure worked for this virtual team because all twelve members were in positions of similar status or rank in their primary organizational settings. (All were directors of career development centers for MBA programs.)

Additionally, all team members chose to be part of the virtual team because it benefited the student population they served. Leaderless structures work well for teams whose members have equal status and rank, who have similar background and expertise levels, and who are all equally invested in and will benefit from the team's outcome or results. Trust also comes into play. With no team leader, each team member needs to trust that the other members will produce their section of the work at a high level of quality and on time.

Assessment Tool: Choosing an Appropriate Leadership Structure

What I learned from talking with these virtual teams about their leadership structures is that there appears to be *many different ways to lead virtual teams*. All team members indicated in their interviews that they felt their teams were highly productive, yet they followed a variety of leadership structures. Some teams had clearly defined team leaders, while others had rotating team leaders or project team leaders. Some teams functioned either without a leader or only with the assistance of a facilitator or coordinator.

Even though there is no one best way to lead, the stories shared in this chapter can be of assistance in pulling out some characteristics of situations in which each type of leadership style might work best. Your team may find Table 2.1 helpful in assessing what leadership structure may work best for leading the members of your team in achieving their creative work.

Table 2.1 Leadership Structure

Leadership Structure	Works Well When
Permanent leadership	• Centralized decision making and assignment of work tasks; sections of the team's work can be individually assigned to team members and later integrated into a final product or service by the team leader. • Individual team members with high levels of expertise in their unique areas. • Knowledge generated by one team member is not necessary for another member to complete his or her task. • Team members with clearly distinct roles. • Individual team members who interact mostly with the leader rather than other team members in completing their work.

Table 2.1 Leadership Structure, Cont'd

Leadership Structure	Works Well When
Rotating team leader	• Team members have less differentiated roles; all team members could potentially do the same task. • Projects are primarily assigned based on customer or client preference, or team member preference, not necessarily on level of expertise in particular area. • All team members have equal ability to effectively lead the team (are trained to do this). • Standards and templates have been created and are practiced and utilized so that the chain of command can be easily passed from one person to another without disrupting the team's operation. • All team members understand the business and know what it takes to lead it. • A consistent administrative staff supports rotating leaders. • There is a high level of trust among team members. • Team members are comfortable and able to fill both the role of a team member and team leader. • Teams of small size (no more than 6 team members). Recall the ACI team had 6 team members, 4 of who served as rotating project leaders.
Permanent leadership with rotating project leaders	• The nature of the team's business is diverse enough to support the need for members with different types of expertise. • There is a high level of trust among team members (trust in the expertise of fellow members). • Team members are not only trained in their level of expertise, but also in project and task management. • Team members are comfortable and able to fill both the role of a team member and team leader. Sometimes, multiple projects require team members to be team members on one assignment and leaders on another. • Teams fairly large in size (8 or more team members). The Jacobs/Taylor team that used this leadership structure had eight members.
Facilitators or coordinators	• Self-managed teams requiring additional support in a particular domain (for example technological assistance, team meeting assistance). • Teams composed of members from various functions. • Team members all of equal status or rank. • Teams brought together for the purposes of developing a particular project. • Adjunct teams composed of members who also are part of another larger organizational context (have internal supervision in that setting).

Table 2.1 Leadership Structure, Cont'd

Leadership Structure	Works Well When
Leaderless (leadership is shared)	• Self-managed teams. • Team members all of equal status or rank. • Team members who are equally invested in and will benefit from the team's outcome. • There is a high level of trust among team members that each will be accountable for the work he or she has been assigned (without prodding by a formal leader). • Strong accountability systems in place and followed.

It may be beneficial to further narrow down the leadership structures that emerged from the interviews with virtual teams into three major categories—permanent leadership, rotating leadership, and self-managing leadership (leaderless). Table 2.2 offers a checklist of these types of leadership structures. Use this checklist to assess whether the current leadership structure in your virtual team is appropriate or to select a leadership structure for a virtual team that may just be starting out. Check off the items that are (or will be) characteristic of your team. Then, examine which of the leadership structures has the most "checks." Is this the current leadership structure for your team? If not, why? Consider whether your team might benefit from moving more in that direction.

Table 2.2 Leadership Structure Characteristics Checklist

Permanent Leadership

_____ Decision making is centralized, made by one person or a few.

_____ The work can be divided and parceled out to team members based on their different areas of expertise.

_____ Individual team members possess distinct roles and different areas of expertise.

_____ Team members do not require high levels of interaction with other team members (other than the leader) to accomplish the tasks parceled out to them.

Table 2.2 Leadership Structure Characteristics Checklist, Cont'd

Rotating Leadership

_____ Team members' roles are less differentiated; all team members could potentially do the same tasks.

_____ Project assignments are based on either client/customer preference or team member's level of interest.

_____ All team members have the necessary knowledge of the business to effectively lead the team.

_____ All team members have equal ability to effectively lead the team.

_____ Standard operating procedures are established to assist in maintaining stability.

_____ Support staff do not rotate.

_____ There is a high level of trust among team members.

Self-Managed Leadership (Leaderless)

_____ Team members come from various functions.

_____ Team members are of equal status or rank within their various functions.

_____ Team members are equally invested in and will benefit from the team's outcome.

_____ There is a high level of trust among team members.

_____ Members are accountable for their work (deliver quality results on time).

Appropriate leadership structures do not emerge by chance. They are matched appropriately with the values and skills of team members and the vision, objectives, and tasks that guide the team's work. Whatever leadership structure a virtual team uses, members will most likely be required to make one critical shift. Members in these types of teams will need to develop the tolerance for and comfort level with performing the dual roles of team member and team leader and the ability to shift back and forth between these roles as the need arises.

In choosing an appropriate leadership structure, you may also want to consider the stage of development of the virtual team. In the initial stages of a virtual team (its birth), leaders are needed to communicate vision to external stakeholders, acquire technology, recruit key personnel, and inspire commitment of team members. When the team is in its growth period, team leaders are often responding to internal demands. As the team matures, leaders turn to the task of structuring work to increase efficiency and maintain employee morale. And finally, in possible decline and hopefully revitalization, leaders strive to help the team adapt and survive (Yukl, 2002).

Another issue to consider in developing a leadership structure is the type of leadership behavior it will support. Leadership behavior is frequently categorized according to three categories: (a) Task-oriented behaviors such as planning and scheduling work, clarifying roles and objectives, and monitoring operations; (b) Relations-oriented behaviors such as supporting team members (showing trust and confidence, being considerate, listening to problems, soliciting input), coaching and developing team members in advancing skill acquisition and career development, and recognizing team members' contributions; (c) Change-oriented behaviors such as strategic decisions, adapting to change, and increasing flexibility and innovation.

Not every leadership structure may be able to effectively accomplish all these behaviors, or may require the same amount of skill from a leader in each behavior. For example, permanent leadership structures may require leaders to exert stronger task-oriented behaviors, whereas with rotating and self-managed leadership structures, the need for relations-oriented leadership behaviors may increase. In addition, if virtual team members are to take on the role of team member and team leader interchangeably, they will need to be trained in how to effectively manage team tasks, support and encourage team relations, and strategically plan for change and innovation. This seems like a lot to ask for. In some cases it may be possible. However, in other cases, leadership structures may need to be adapted and be flexible, allowing for rotation of leaders based not only on their expertise related to different project assignments, but their abilities to manage different types of leadership behaviors as well.

Whether you are considering starting up a virtual team or are part of a virtual team already in existence, it will benefit your team to assess what leadership structure best fits your team with respect to the following:

- The team's stage of development
- The team's philosophy and vision
- The nature of the team's work
- The skills and abilities of the potential team members

Final Thoughts

Perhaps it is more effective to view leadership in virtual teams (or in any team for that matter) as a relationship, and management as a position (Crawford, Brungardt, and Maughan, 2000; Gardner, 1990). With the emphasis on virtual team members needing to develop a new tolerance for filling both a team member and leadership role, the relevance of viewing leadership as a process rather than as a position seems particularly important. Positions come and go, and the people in those positions may also come and go. Effective leaders are those individuals who can create relationships with others and can inspire them. True leadership then is based on relationships and context and occurs independent of position. One element of context, the climate in which a team is embedded, most certainly can impact a team's level of creativity. Part II includes two chapters that reveal necessary elements for creating a climate for creativity in virtual teams.

Points to Remember

- Several types of leadership structures are used by virtual teams, ranging from permanent leadership structures, to rotating leadership structures, to either a leaderless structure or a structure in which teams are assisted by a facilitator or coordinator.

- Although there are many different ways to lead a virtual team, selecting a structure that best suits the values and skills of the team's members and the vision, objectives, and tasks that guide the team's work will enhance the team's overall effectiveness. The more democratic forms of leadership structures (rotating, self-managed) used by virtual teams also enhance a team's level of creativity by allowing team members higher levels of autonomy and input into the decision-making process.

- Leadership structures may not remain constant throughout the team's lifecycle. Different leadership structures may be appropriate for various stages of the team's lifecycle.

- Different leaders and leadership structures may be needed to successfully perform various leadership behaviors, such as task-oriented, relations-oriented, and change-oriented behaviors.

- Leadership is best viewed as a relationship rather than a position.

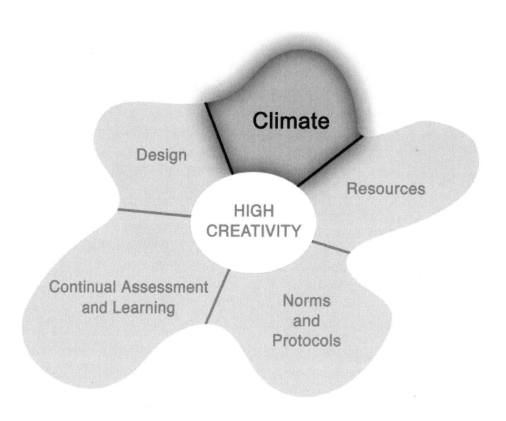

Climate

Design

Resources

HIGH
CREATIVITY

Continual Assessment
and Learning

Norms
and
Protocols

PART II

Climate

COLLABORATIVE TECHNOLOGY MAKES IT EASIER to coordinate virtual teams of all sizes by enabling team members to post questions, work jointly on documents, schedule meetings, and track progress toward goals. However, collaborative technological tools simply will not work if the *climate* within an organization and within the teams that make up an organization does not foster and encourage people to work together. The same requirements hold for creativity. Virtual team members will only use collaborative tools to design creative work if the climate supports and fosters creativity. A creative climate for virtual teams includes solid connections (at the task and interpersonal level) among team members and appropriate team member and management conditions and competencies that support creativity. Chapter Three discusses the dimensions that build a strong sense of connection. Chapter Four addresses the appropriate team member and management conditions and related competencies necessary to foster high levels of creativity.

CHAPTER 3

Building Task and Interpersonal Connection

Trust is a definite challenge in a virtual team environment when you have never met anybody. We know each other through the computer keyboard, and that is it. We're a bunch of computer screens, but not really, you know what I mean? We see people on the other side, that's essentially how we communicate. But it is a bigger challenge to build the trust through a computer terminal than it is face-to-face. I don't think there's a lack of personal connection. It's just part of the technology. Unless you take it one step further and meet each other face-to-face, it's always going to have a slight limitation. Trust can be built. It can be built reliably. But it has to be through a diligent effort and over a period of time, and through a series of good experiences with each other.

Scott, WN–Religion Forum

AS THE QUOTE ABOVE SUGGESTS, it may be extremely difficult to build a sense of interpersonal connection and trust in virtual teams. But interpersonal connection and trust are crucial to high levels of team creativity (Isaksen, 1985, 1988; Stein, 1975; West, 1990). Thus, in designing virtual teams to accomplish creative tasks, we cannot ignore the social context of such arrangements. Technology links messages between geographically dispersed individuals, but it does not necessarily lead to effective interpersonal connection, joint commitment to goals and tasks, and high levels of creative behavior.

One of the key tasks that virtual team designers, team leaders, and managers need to undertake to help virtual teams realize high levels of creativity is relatively simple, and yet difficult to implement—*create a connection between team members*. In my investigation of virtual teams, connection emerged as one of the key elements necessary for creativity in virtual teams. Connection involves both *task* connection (made up of dedication/commitment and goal clarity) and *interpersonal* connection (made up of information sharing, personal bond, and trust). In the first section of this chapter, the concept of connection and each of the accompanying dimensions are illustrated. In my discussions with the members of the nine virtual teams, they shared stories of both high and low creativity within their teams. To better describe and explain the dimensions within connection, the virtual team members' own words are frequently shared. In the second section of the chapter, an assessment tool consisting of a series of questions is included for virtual teams to assess their current level of task and interpersonal connection and to assist in establishing action plans to work on areas of needed improvement.

The Pitfalls in Building Connection

One of the problems with virtual work structures is that electronic interaction eliminates much of the work context, stripping off everything but the message and leaving the rest for inference. Two major considerations for virtual teams are (1) How much contextual information do individuals need to feel connected on an interpersonal level and to have a joint commitment to team tasks and goals?, and (2) How much of this contextual information can actually be communicated across the boundaries of time and distance?

More specifically, one of the key contextual factors often stripped away in virtual interactions is nonverbal communication. Nonverbal behavior can be used to control, regulate, and modify exchanges. Although certain etiquettes have been established to communicate some form of nonverbal behavior through text, it cannot be ignored that many virtual teams who communicate through media in which the message is shared in text or audio format (Faxes, e-mail, phones) lose valuable visual cues. Technology such as videoconferencing and computer conferencing with video links allow for the transmission of an image of the speaker as well, but, in most cases, the absence of visual nonverbal feedback is a characteristic of day-to-day virtual team interactions. Virtual teams then face unique challenges as they attempt to interact, share meaning, and reach consensus in the absence of rich face-to-face interaction. It is simply difficult to transmit the entirety of a message through electronic communication methods that are limited in information richness and are often used by virtual teams.

Another condition of electronic communication is the level of dehumanization and social isolation that may develop in this type of communication. Some research has suggested that communication through electronic means is dehumanizing, creating a sense of social anonymity (Kiesler, Siegel, and McGuire, 1991). As a result, messages in electronic mail tend to be stronger and more uninhibited and assertive.

Finally, another contextual factor that can lead to miscommunication in virtual teams is cultural differences or diversity. Virtual teams may be dispersed all over the globe, indicating that these teams may be made up of members from varying cultural backgrounds. For one thing, creativity itself is defined differently in different cultures (Lubart, 1990). Cultural diversity may be a boon for creativity, as individuals from varying backgrounds may offer differing perspectives and insights. However, since the virtual work environment usually offers little social context, cultural differences, if not properly addressed, may lead to problematic miscommunication between team members, hampering connection and, as a result, creativity.

Connection and Virtual Team Effectiveness

The study of virtual teams has exploded in the last few years. Much recent evidence suggests dimensions of connection, such as goal clarity and trust, are crucial to the effectiveness of virtual teams. Lipnack and Stamps (1997) view purpose and goal clarity as the essence of a virtual team and the best predictor of virtual team success. Shared purpose and goal clarity are necessary to build loyalty and trust among geographically dispersed and culturally diverse virtual team members. O'Hara-Devereaux and Johansen (1994) see shared goals as crucial to the effectiveness of virtual teams. "Distributed team members stay oriented to each other and their tasks through high-level shared vision, goals, and roles rather than through detailed implementation plans. This level of understanding is a critical substitute for the informal, face-to-face meetings that play such an important role in keeping on-site teams in tune with one another" (p. 125).

Trust, in actuality, may be the most crucial element necessary for virtual team effectiveness. Davidow and Malone (1992) emphasize trust as a defining feature for virtual corporations. "The road to world-class supply chain management meanders through a series of cultural changes—to a new plateau of trust. To achieve true partnership, customers and suppliers must share information—on new products, designs, internal business plans, and long-term strategy—that once was closely guarded" (p. 145).

O'Hara-Devereaux and Johansen (1994) also suggest that building trust in the early stages of team development is perhaps the most effective measure in guaranteeing the success of virtual teams. The key rule in building trust is to take the time to build relationships, to create "the human glue of teams" (p. 171).

Trust may develop more slowly among virtual team members than among face-to-face team members. With less visual contact, it simply may take longer to identify and adjust to the habits, quirks, and skills of team members. Unfortunately, mistrust is likely, as employees from different locations, cultures, and technical backgrounds are apt to question how the information they offer will be used, whether their contribution will be recognized outside the team, and whether other team members will make an equal contribution to the work.

Connection and Virtual Team Creativity

In my study of virtual teams, *connection* emerged as a key element of an environment that encourages the realization of creativity in virtual teams. Table 3.1 summarizes each of the dimensions of connection, which are further illustrated in this section.

Table 3.1 Dimensions of Connection in Virtual Teams

Task Connection

> *Dedication and Commitment*—a sense of dedication, intense involvement, and commitment to the work; the ability to work hard on difficult tasks and problems and to persevere.

> *Goal Clarity*—clearly defined, developed goals (through constant clarification and feedback) shared by all members.

Interpersonal Connection

> *Information Sharing*—regular communication; sharing the results of one's efforts; providing needed information; updating information quickly.

> *Personal Bond*—a personal connection among team members; a "family-like" feeling; a sense of connectedness that goes beyond common goals and commitment to the work, to a bond in which team members are also committed to and care for one another.

> *Trust*—a sense of trust that team members will do their designated tasks within the designated time frame; trust in the accurateness of the information provided by other team members; trust that team members will give honest and constructive feedback on ideas, thoughts, and creative efforts shared electronically; trust in one another's expertise and ability to do the work effectively; and trust that team members will hold ideas shared in confidence if requested.

Task Connection

For virtual teams to have a solid task connection, two dimensions are essential—*dedication/commitment,* and *goal clarity.*

Dedication/Commitment

In their high creativity experiences, virtual team members spoke of having a strong sense of dedication, intense involvement, and commitment to a project or task. They worked hard on difficult tasks and problems and persevered. Melanie of JSC describes the importance of dedication on her team. "The bottom line is we've had people who are committed, who really want the thing to succeed, even if the personalities have some kind of conflict. People are able to sort of disconnect the personality from the fact that the job is being done, how it's being done, and that it's getting done properly."

On the other hand, when team members differ in the degree of commitment to a particular project or goal, creativity suffers. Oftentimes differing levels of commitment not only hamper creativity, but cause the mere existence of a project to be in jeopardy as well. Richard (of the OfficeTech team) candidly shares how he and his partner differed in terms of their levels of commitment to a project. As a result, a potentially creative outcome was dropped.

> Keith was keen to develop a model of knowledge sharing and learning in a professional services practice, and got the software and did some preliminary work in developing a simulation. He sent me a copy of his model electronically, and I was going to analyze his work and we were going to collaborate on it. The long and the short of it is it didn't work. The reason for failure is pretty darn simple. It wasn't as high a priority for me as it was for him. It's one of those things that I professed to be extremely interested in, but when push comes to shove, other things take precedence. This experience was clearly an example of a low level of creativity within our team. I really needed to be able to walk away from the office for a week or more and say, "I'm unreachable, I'm doing something else." For better or for worse, I didn't choose to do that.

Goal Clarity

Goals that lead to the realization of purpose need to be clear for members of virtual teams to maintain a team identity and stay connected. When the virtual team members I interviewed were asked how they maintained a sense of connectedness, sharing common goals was the most frequent response. Rob (of the ACI team) shares, "I would say that common goals is probably close to the root of our cohesiveness as a team." Eric (of the AutoMax team), in his sharing of a highly creative project within his team, echoes this focus on common goals. "I think the end goal, what you're trying to achieve, to me is very key. This project is a big project and everyone in the team has really considered it their own little baby. That really brought people together." Thus, a team's goals, and the clarity of those goals, was a prevalent characteristic of the high creativity stories shared by the members across the nine virtual teams.

Although goals were crucial for success in creative work, some virtual team members felt it took more effort in a virtual team to make sure those goals were clear. Constant checking, feedback, and asking questions were needed to ensure clarification. Matt, of the ACI team, explains, "Goals need to be more clear and checked more frequently, because of the distance, the separation, the lack of personal contact, to keep people on board. So that you're not expecting a horse and you get a camel by the time you're finished."

Interestingly, although goal clarity was seen as necessary for high creativity, a few virtual team members reported high periods of creativity during the discovery and creation of goals. Laura, a member of the ELC team, describes one such experience. "We had a highly creative period this past year where we as a team began to really consolidate and feel out just exactly what we wanted to do. It was kind of a consensus or sort of a melding that happened where through talking together and so forth we began realizing that this was the real vision, that this was what we wanted to create."

In low creativity stories, virtual team members described situations in which goals were fuzzy or unclear. As a result, misunderstandings and faulty assumptions occurred, and valuable time was wasted. The rapid pace at which business often takes place electronically sometimes creates the context for confusion when the proper amount of time is not taken to make sure goals are clearly outlined and communicated. Ironically, then, the speed at which the work moves can actually slow the creative process down through unclear goals. Patricia (of the WN–Religion Forum) describes how her team's leader frequently moves so fast that goals are not clearly communicated or updated in a timely manner. "The clarity of the goals can get fuzzy sometimes. Sometimes Eryn's [the team leader's] goals will change or things will change so fast that what was communicated to me is not necessary anymore. And if you have someone who communicates fast, and sometimes Eryn does have to do that because she's in such a hurry to get things done, you are left wondering. I'll have to sit kind of going, 'hmm, what's trying to be said?'"

Melissa, a member of the VTG team, further reveals how a lack of clarity around the team's goals and roles led to frustration, misunderstandings, and faulty assumptions.

> A marketing project that we did with a sister company of ours digitally was the least creative project. It also was the least fun, the most aggravating, and it was where everybody was just pulling their hair out. There was a tremendous lack of clarity, and there were a lot of assumptions made about which party would do what, who would pay for what, what the end result would be, and basically what people's roles would be. I think sometimes that

is a problem with a virtual environment. Assumptions are made
by one party sitting in their office, [behind a] closed door, typing
away, and they fire off an e-mail. We interpret it in a completely
different way. We don't have the luxury of a dialogue back and
forth. Instead we have the aggravation of one-shot e-mails back
and forth.

Creativity also suffers due to indecision that results from unclear goals. Consequently, some projects become unwieldy. Cheryl, a member of the ACI team, relates a low creativity story about her team's "Manual from Hell" project. Her story illustrates how lack of goal clarity turned one of their virtual team's projects into a frustrating, massive undertaking.

We have had a few little mishaps in my career here. The major one
was what now we affectionately refer to as the "Manual from
Hell." It was a project where three consultants were writing this
manual and they each had a different section that they were supposed to write. I was to edit it and put it together and it was going
to go to the client. It was actually pretty simple but it turned into
this massive undertaking. It was like opening Pandora's box. Once
they started writing, it was like, "Oh, we've got to talk about this
and we've got to go out here" and then "Oh let's talk about this." It
just grew and grew and grew. It got to the point where there was
no way it was going to be finished when it was supposed to be.

Even when goals were communicated clearly in initial face-to-face meetings, sometimes when virtual team members dispersed, goals were sometimes forgotten or dropped, and creativity was low. Jeff, a member of the JSC team, reports how his team talks about goals: "In January, we plan some things, then we have the agenda, and we're like, 'Oh yeah, that's great, let's do this, this, and this.' Then each day that goes by, the more likely people are to forget."

Interpersonal Connection

Virtual teams that have a strong interpersonal connection have high levels of information sharing and trust, and are personally bonded with one another above and beyond the nature of the team's work.

Information Sharing

Information is the fuel that feeds the fire of creativity in virtual teams. Information sharing is closely tied to the degree of trust between team members, and both trust and information sharing were perceived by the virtual team members as crucial for creative work. Highly creative experiences involved team members who communicated regularly with one another, shared the results of their efforts, offered open and honest feedback, and updated information regularly. Dana (of the AutoMax team) stresses the critical role of information sharing in alleviating problems in the creative process early on. "We had one creative situation that really worked out well because we started sharing design information of the anti-lock brake electronically right from the beginning. We were talking to the plant and to the specialists. Engineers were together and we were saying, 'Okay, what do we do to make this work?' Every week we had these electronic sessions in which information was shared, so we always knew what the plant wanted. We didn't wait till the last minute, and then give them the drawings. That made the design work out really good."

Sharing of information not only alleviates problems in the creative process, but helps to spur new outlooks on potential problems as well, as Larry, another member of the AutoMax design engineering team, reveals in his high creativity story.

> When we had a portion of our design that we felt was important, and they wanted to change it for some reason, we needed to explain all of the information necessary for them to understand what was driving our concerns as far as keeping with the design that we had. Basically we had to explain the history and fundamentals of what was driving our design ideas. That gave them an understanding of what we were looking at. And then they would suggest things that we might not have thought of, because they had either a novel view of the situation or were coming from a different background, which sometimes drove our thoughts into other directions.

A prevalent characteristic then of the high creativity stories was the need for regular communication to stay connected and to exchange information. When people meet in a face-to-face meeting, individuals can be directly asked for information, feedback, or input. In virtual teams, individuals can also be directly asked electronically, but it is easier for individuals to disappear or drop out of the discussion. To avoid this, norms for communicating and exchanging information were created in many of the teams. (See Chapter Seven for more information on establishing norms and protocols to guide communication behavior.) For example, the ACI team established a series of norms to guarantee regular communication, including the following:

- Members agreed to respond to e-mail at least three to four times weekly, whether working at home or on the road at client sites.

- A conference call was scheduled every six weeks to review client marketing and business development, to assess ongoing client work, and for a personal check in.

- Members agreed to respond to all telephone calls within 24 hours, whether at home or traveling and working at client sites.

- Face-to-face meetings were scheduled quarterly (referred to by members as "the quarterly gathering of the clan"). These meetings took place in the homes of the team members and lasted for two to three days.

- The corporate office served as the hub and all consultants were required to update the hub daily as to their whereabouts.

However, in many of the low creativity experiences shared by the virtual team members, norms for communication were either not established or were unclear or ignored. As a result, communication became irregular, inconsistent, or nonexistent. And even when norms were in place for communication and information sharing (as in the ACI team), they were not always consistently adhered to. The ACI team itself had periods of tremendous information sharing and other periods in which information sharing was limited. Pam, an ACI team member, describes this as "kind of a yin and yang. At some point there is a lot of information sharing and at other points, you don't know that something might be relevant to somebody else. It has the impact of working and creating something in a vacuum."

Information sharing was also hampered by individual team members with a "self-serving attitude," who withheld information to protect their own interests. Todd, of JSC, discloses this in his low creativity story. "The biggest roadblock to working in this environment would be that somebody was being parochial and was only sharing part of what they knew to protect their own interests. It has to be a total, open communication, sharing, trusting environment because as soon as one person or two people start withholding information, then the team breaks down."

Although too little information can hamper creativity, so too can an overload of information. In several of the low creativity stories, team members shared experiences in which they were attempting to deal with the constant flow of information between themselves and their geographically dispersed team members. They felt at times overwhelmed with more information than they could effectively comprehend. Another problem that arose in low creativity stories was the distortion of information as it was filtered electronically from company headquarters to the team leader, and then out to team members. Scott, a member of the WN–Religion Forum team, describes how filtered information has been problematic for his team.

> Eryn (the team leader) is the mediator between us and WNSD who provides the great vision. She gets a lot of information that she has to filter down to us. So she will get a whole bunch of information that is relevant to a project I'm working on. It might be in the form of some new CDs, new manuals, or new technology. And the only way she can translate it to me is via e-mail or mailing the stuff to me. There is a degree of degradation and communication in the process as it filters down because WNSD refuses to deal directly with the assistants. Because it has to be filtered through Eryn, there is lack of clarity and clarification.

Personal Bond

One of the more intriguing themes that emerged from my discussions with members of the virtual teams was the ability of these teams to establish a personal bond. Team members, even though separated by distance and sometimes time, in many instances suggested they felt like a family. Developing and maintaining this kind of personal bond is critical for creativity to occur in virtual teams. A personal sense of connection can lessen the problematic misunderstandings and faulty assumptions that hamper creativity and help to develop the trust, respect, understanding, acceptance, and compassion that team members need to feel comfortable sharing ideas and taking risks across distances. This kind of connection goes beyond common goals and commitment to the work. Team members are also committed to one another and care for one another.

Personal bond was built through a variety of techniques, including the following:

- Scheduling face-to-face get-togethers
- Electronically sharing humorous stories or incidents
- Creating playful games to build and maintain team identity
- Taking the time to show personal interest in one another (by electronically passing along information they thought other team members might be interested in)
- Sharing personal issues and crises with other team members
- Functioning as a support network for one another

Each technique is touched on in more depth in the next section.

Although one of the teams had never met face-to-face, for the majority of teams, *face-to-face contact* was beneficial in beginning to develop a personal bond among team members. Several team members shared how their relationships with other team members changed after they had met one another face-to-face. For example, Eric, a member of the AutoMax team, shares that he went to the United States last October, which was "the first time anyone had gone over there from our area. I spent three weeks with them. Since I came back, we've had an excellent relationship because up until then it was just a big name. It really has made a big impact and a big improvement."

Sharing humor was another way virtual team members established a personal bond. Even for one of the teams that had never met face-to-face, humor helped to build a sense of community. Scott, a member of the WN–Religion Forum, describes how his team shares humor. "We don't feel impersonal because we translate our humor through the written word. We are using little bits of humor, and we're real loose and personal, we're not rigid. We're very comfortable with each other."

Sometimes, *playful games* were used to develop the team's identity. Chad, a senior consultant of the Jacobs/Taylor team, reveals: "We do crazy, silly little game things that build identity, little competitions, or silly things that we share. And those become the inside jokes that people outside don't know, but it forms identity and helps build community."

In any relationship, taking the time to show *personal interest* in another person helps to create a bond. The same holds true for virtual teams. Team members took the time to pass along information they thought other team members might be interested in. At times, taking a personal interest in one another went beyond simply forwarding interesting information or sharing jokes. It involved sharing *personal issues and crises* with one another, and supporting one another through these crises. This kind of sharing was instrumental in creating a family-like feeling between team members. Jason, of the ACI team, says about his virtual team family, "This group of six people is up there close to my family in terms of folks I feel connected with. It's not just because we're all in this one lifeboat called economic survival, but we have been through each other's personal crises. These people are just supportive. There's just no other way to say that. This is family."

Finally, functioning as a *support network* for one another, both personally and professionally, solidified the connection between virtual team members. Elaine, a member of the twelve-person JSC team, characterizes this level of support. "I feel that I have a built-in support system. I think having people that you know are always going through the same thing that you are, and being able to call and bounce ideas off of each other, that is a very supportive environment, and something that I really enjoy."

So, it is possible to establish a real personal bond in a virtual team, even in those teams where no face-to-face contact occurs. Scott, a WN–Religion Forum team member who has never met face-to-face his fellow team members, discusses how his team has bonded.

> There is a very personal connectedness between us. A very human one. I think a lot of people who are not familiar with virtual teams would definitely expect that we're all a bunch of robots, you know what I mean? You just automatically assume that if you're just communicating through a computer, how could there be any connection, how could there be anything personal, how could there be anything warm about it, and there is.

Trust

Team members felt it took a great deal of trust to share ideas and accomplish creative work electronically. Melissa, a VTG team member, discloses, "There's a level of trust with putting everything that you're doing on the computer and knowing everybody's seeing everything you're doing." In a virtual environment, without the nonverbal indicators available in face-to-face encounters, trust was viewed as essential. Trust was seen by the virtual team members as crucial not only for the team to be creative, but for the team to even exist. Eryn, the WN–Religion Forum team leader, reveals, "Well, if you don't have trust, it's not a team. The person you can't trust isn't a member of the team. Period. That's it. They either get fired or they leave. Trust is the foundation of the team."

Trust was composed of the following elements:

- A sense that individuals would do what they said within the designated time frame

- Trust in the accurateness of the information provided by other team members

- Trust that team members would give honest and constructive feedback on ideas, thoughts, and creative efforts shared electronically

- Trust in one another's expertise and ability to do the work effectively

- Trust that other team members would hold ideas shared in confidence if requested

Trust in these virtual teams developed from positive ongoing experiences among members of the team. Trust also emerged from team members believing in the individual expertise of one another. Finally, and perhaps most importantly, trust evolved out of a sense of accountability, from seeing that others follow through on what they say they will.

Trust is based on positive, ongoing experiences. The length of existence a team has been together impacts the level of trust. In the ACI team, positive, ongoing experiences with one another led to a high level of trust. Pam, an ACI team member, reveals, "I'd say right now there's a high level of trust among each other. I believe that part of our trust is the length of time we have worked with each other and that it has developed and has worked better over the years to the degree that we have been better about confronting conflict with each other."

Trust is based on a belief in one another's expertise. Trust is also based on a belief in each team member's experience, expertise, and judgment in his or her particular area of specialty. For members of the design engineering team, an individual team member's expertise and experience were critical in establishing trust in the team. Dana of the AutoMax team relates the following in her high creativity story. "I guess trust depends on your experience and how often you've worked with a team. Like with my team, they pretty much trust my judgment, if I say this or that. If you've got the experience, and you've worked on a project for a long time, and they know it, then you get a lot higher trust."

For teams that never meet face-to-face, belief in one another's level of expertise may be more difficult to establish and, as a result, trust is more problematic. In the WN–Religion Forum team, where face-to-face interaction was nonexistent, the perception of trust across team members varied. One team member stated that trust was only at a task level, not at an interpersonal level. Another WN–Religion Forum team member stated that he did not trust other team members because he had never met them face-to-face. "I don't know the other assistants. I don't know them personally. I don't know about their background. I have not been able to build a trust with them simply for the lack of contact."

Trust is based on a sense of accountability. Virtual team members suggested that trust within their teams was based on interactions with one another in which they witnessed the accountability of others. Stories of high creativity illustrated experiences in which team members were accountable for their contribution to the joint creative effort. Barbara, of the ACI team, talks about this level of accountability:

> I think that in our particular situation we do have a great degree of trust in all levels. It came about by people living up to what's expected of them. Even though we've dropped the ball a few times on meeting deadlines, that still hasn't violated the trust that we have for one another. We can be very frank with each other and we can call each other because of it, kind of that nudge role.

We can say, "You didn't do such and such." We try not to beat people to a frenzy over it, try not to berate them, but just say, "This process didn't work because X person didn't do Y."

For some, creating work online increases accountability, and as a result, trust, because records and documentation are kept. Thus, accountability is easily visible. The ability to see the accountability of others freed up individuals to be creative on their own portion of the creative effort.

On the other hand, in the low creativity stories shared by the virtual team members, the level of trust waned, was lost, or did not exist at all. The most frequently mentioned reason for a decline in the level of trust was low accountability, team members not carrying through on their designated work, or not "pulling their weight." For example, in the ACI team, all of the team members interviewed referred to the "Manual from Hell" project in their low creativity stories. As Barbara of the ACI team recounts, lack of accountability was a key factor in why the team members felt the experience was low in creativity:

> We were working on a project for a client and trying to come up with a manual that spelled out the steps that they had to go through in this process. It was a new process for us and so we were having to create something from the ground up. At the beginning of the "Manual from Hell," the process was divvied up to different people to do different things. That didn't work well because some of the people didn't do their part by the deadline that they agreed to do it. That caused the process to be pushed out. It caused the envelope to be pushed because we did have a deadline that we had to have this to the client. The problem was everyone not getting their piece ready.

The creative process in virtual teams often involves core team members interacting with peripheral team members or individuals external to both the team and organization. For WN–Current Events team members, trust was solid within their team. However, low creativity stories revealed a lack of trust in individuals outside of their immediate team. The key issue, again, was lack of accountability. Cindy, a member of the team, says, "I trust my team. I'm more leery of people outside of my team. I know someone in my team will send me something on deadline, regardless if I just e-mail them once. I can trust them

and I don't feel like I have to go back and harass them about it. But if it's someone outside of the team, and I e-mailed them, and maybe I don't hear back from
them, and the deadline keeps coming closer, then maybe I start to wonder, 'Is
this their style or are they going to just blow me off? Are they actually going to
make the deadline?'"

Assessment Tool: Gauging the Level of Task and Interpersonal Connection

To assist virtual team managers, team leaders, and team members in assessing
the current level of task and interpersonal connection within their virtual teams,
a series of questions are provided for reflection. Answers to the following questions will provide virtual team members with an understanding of the dimensions of connection their team is currently strong in, and what dimensions the
team may need further improvement in. As a result of this newfound understanding, team members should work jointly to create action plans to guarantee maintenance of areas of strength, and to further develop areas in need of
improvement. (If you need to before beginning, revisit the guidelines for using
chapter assessment tools described in the Introduction.)

Task Connection

*Dedication/Commitment—a sense of dedication, intense involvement, and
commitment to the work; the ability to work hard on difficult tasks and problems and
to persevere.*

1. To what extent are team members dedicated to the team's work? Are
   there certain types of work that elicit high levels of dedication from team
   members? Why? (This may be something that is best first answered by
   each of the team members individually, to assess the likes and dislikes
   of each.)

2. To what extent are team members self-driven and committed to the
   team's work? Are there certain types of work that elicit high levels of
   commitment from team members? Why? (This may be something that
   is best first answered by each of the team members individually, to assess
   the likes and dislikes of each.)

3. To what extent are team members able to persevere on difficult, challenging tasks?

4. Are there projects in which the level of commitment has differed among the members working on it? How are these situations handled? What actions may need to occur to assist in gaining consensus of commitment on key projects?

Goal Clarity—*clearly defined, developed goals (through constant clarification and feedback) shared by all members.*

5. Is there a disciplined procedure for team members to clearly develop and define team goals?

6. To what extent are team goals shared by all team members? Are there certain goals that persistently cause disagreement and contention? What mechanisms are in place for dealing with a lack of shared consensus?

7. How strongly are team members committed to team goals? Which team goals do members appear strongly committed to? Which ones tend to elicit lower levels of commitment?

8. Are there procedures integrated into the team's work to allow for clarification of and feedback about team goals once they have been defined? How effective are these procedures?

9. Does the team suffer from indecision and/or wasted time in pursuing team goals? Why? What can be done to avoid this?

10. Is there a process in place for revisiting and updating team goals periodically? How effective is this process?

11. Do team goals get dropped or forgotten? Why? Which types of goals frequently get dropped or forgotten?

Interpersonal Connection

Information Sharing—*regular communication; sharing the results of one's efforts; providing needed information; timely updating of information.*

12. What types of communication systems are in place to ensure regular and consistent sharing of information? How effective are these systems?

13. Is there a forum for members to share the results of their efforts in the pursuit of team goals?

14. How current is the information provided to team members? Is information timely and updated on a regular basis?

15. Is there an agreed-on set of norms for communicating with one another? Do all team members adhere to these norms? What norms might be needed to ensure better and more consistent information sharing among team members? (See Chapter Seven for a discussion of norms and protocols that assist in achieving effective communication in virtual teams.)

16. What actions does the team currently take to ensure effective sharing of information? What actions of the team currently interfere with effective sharing of information?

Personal Bond—a personal connection among team members; a "family-like" feeling; a sense of connectedness that goes beyond common goals and commitment to the work to a bond in which team members are also committed to one another and care for one another.

17. To what degree do team members feel personally bonded to other members of the team?

18. What current activities does the team engage in that encourage a sense of team identity and personal connection between members? What current activities interfere with members feeling close to and bonded with one another?

19. How is face-to-face contact used to assist in building a personal connection between team members?

20. Check the behaviors your team currently uses to assist in building a personal bond among team members:

Team members:

_____ Have opportunities at least a few times yearly to get together face-to-face

_____ Create and participate in team games to establish and maintain team identity

_____ Take the time to share things of interest with one another

_____ When appropriate, share humorous stories and are playful with one another

_____ When appropriate, share personal issues and crises with other team members

_____ Function as a support network for one another

Trust—*a sense of trust that team members will do their designated tasks within the designated time frame; trust in the accurateness of the information provided by other team members; trust that team members will give honest and constructive feedback on ideas, thoughts, and creative efforts shared electronically; trust in one another's expertise and ability to do the work effectively; and trust that team members will hold ideas shared in confidence if requested.*

21. Is there a disciplined procedure in place to guarantee accountability? How effective is this procedure?

22. For the most part, would you characterize team member interactions as positive? Why or why not?

23. Is there a forum for team members to offer constructive and honest feedback to one another?

24. Rate how much you agree or disagree with each of the statements below. Use the following scale:

Strongly disagree   1   2   3   4   5   Strongly agree

_____ Team members are accountable for delivering their work on time.

_____ Team members provide one another with accurate information needed to do their work.

_____ Team members provide one another with honest, constructive feedback on their work.

_____ Team members trust the expertise and ability of their fellow team members to do the work effectively.

_____ Team members trust that if they ask for information to be kept in confidence, that request will be honored.

Final Thoughts

In this chapter, the stories shared by the virtual team members stress how essential the human side is for creativity while working together virtually. It is crucial that team members be connected on both a task and interpersonal level when they are pursuing creative work. This connection cannot be ignored, but rather must be actively encouraged by virtual team leaders, managers, and the team members themselves as well. The human side of teams does not go away just because members are interacting electronically. As Jason (of the ACI team) shares:

> I don't think that people should get it in their head that "Because I'm working at a distance with somebody that the human side and the human issues go away." They don't. All of the personality or what people call personality issues, all of the communication issues, all of the need to respect and be conscious of the other person's feelings and where they're coming from, all of that is still there. Whether you're in the same office building and conference room together, or whether you're on the other end of a telephone or a computer terminal, the person doesn't go away in a virtual team. What we have had to do is to work very hard to keep this a very personal relationship. You have to respect the fact that it's another human being who has feelings and emotions, and ups and downs, and assumptions and lenses. That doesn't go away when you are working at a distance. You have to find ways to manage all of that if your team is going to be successful.

Interpersonal skills are simply just as important, if not more so, in virtual working arrangements as they are in teams that are co-located. Training members in active listening, nonverbal communication, responding with empathy, resolving conflict, establishing interpersonal trust, and cross-cultural communication may need to be crafted differently in a virtual work environment, but they still need to be emphasized. Efforts have already begun to address how to build interpersonal skills in a virtual environment. For example, Holton (2001) conducted a research project to test the applicability of standard team-building tools used to build trust and collaboration in face-to-face teams to the unique needs and environment of a virtual team. Holton concluded that "Standard team building tools can be an excellent place to start the process. These and other techniques can be borrowed from the face-to-face environment and adapted to virtual work. As we continue to construct our virtual future, new tools will no doubt be developed specifically for the virtual team environment" (p. 46).

Clearly the path is open for practitioners and researchers to team together to explore how to most effectively build interpersonal skills in virtual teams. To ensure the needed deep sense of connection among virtual team members for high levels of creative behavior, these interpersonal skills are critical. Chapter Four offers a set of team member and management conditions, and related competencies and interpersonal skills needed for high levels of creativity to occur while working virtually.

Points to Remember

- High creativity experiences are characterized by the following:
  - Team members with a robust sense of dedication, intense involvement, and commitment to a project or task
  - Goals that are clearly outlined and communicated to all
  - Procedures that are put in place to ensure regular and consistent information sharing
  - A strong personal bond or family-like connection among team members
  - A high level of trust among team members, based on members' beliefs in the expertise of their fellow team members; positive, ongoing experiences with one another; and a sense of accountability from seeing that other members follow through on what they say they will
- Low creativity experiences are characterized by the following:
  - Differing levels of commitment among team members
  - Unclear goals that lead to misunderstandings, faulty assumptions, and indecision
  - Unclear or ignored norms for communication, or, in some cases, no norms
  - A superficial, or lack of, personal bond among team members
  - Low levels of trust due to a lack of accountability; team members delivering substandard or late work
- The human side of teams does not go away just because members are interacting electronically. Building connection cannot be assumed or ignored, but rather must be actively encouraged by virtual team leaders, managers, and the team members themselves.

CHAPTER 4

Developing Appropriate Team Member and Management Conditions and Competencies

I think because virtual teaming is a comparatively new organizational approach that it definitely adds challenge, and adds stress. I think a lot of companies, mine included, are rushing rather headlong into an embrace of the virtual concept. And I must say, even though I am a proponent of an aspect of virtuality and this community business, I do have some reservations about whether people will be able to accommodate the new framework of the virtual workplace as rapidly as management expects it to.

Richard, OfficeTech

I N A PROVOCATIVE CHAPTER ENTITLED, "Is America Neglecting Her Creative Minority?" Toynbee (1962) stresses the value of encouraging the creative potential of individuals for the benefit of society. He writes, "To give a fair chance to potential creativity is a matter of life and death for any society" (p. 4). Toynbee warns that "potential creativity can be stifled, stunted and stultified by the prevalence in society of adverse attitudes of mind and habits of behavior" (p. 4). As Toynbee's warning implies, creativity can be enhanced by a work environment or climate conducive to and supportive of creativity. As early as 1954, Carl Rogers talked about the conditions for creativity and the importance of creating an environment characterized by psychological safety and freedom, high internal motivation, and the absence of external evaluation to allow creativity to flourish. Since that time, the literature investigating the influence of the work environment on creativity has further demonstrated the importance of and elaborated on the appropriate factors necessary for enhancing creativity. One key element needed to have a climate that fosters creativity while working virtually is to select, develop, and train managers, leaders, and team members in the appropriate competencies and skills, and situational requirements supportive of creativity.

The first part of this chapter describes the team member and management conditions that emerged from the high and low creativity stories shared by the nine virtual teams I interviewed. In the second part of the chapter, a series of related team member and management competencies necessary to develop and maintain the appropriate conditions for creativity are outlined. Along the way, assessment tools and other activities are included for virtual teams to gain a better grasp and understanding of team member and management conditions and competencies that allow for high levels of creativity.

Team Member and Management Conditions

Six team member and management conditions form the situational requirements necessary for a climate for creativity within virtual teams. Each condition is briefly described in Table 4.1 and further illustrated in this section, with excerpts from the virtual team members' high and low creativity stories.

Table 4.1 Appropriate Team Member and Management Conditions

Acceptance of ideas and constructive tension—Ideas and input are encouraged, valued, and accepted by all members of the team without unnecessary criticism; a high degree of honesty among team members exists, leading individuals to feel comfortable not only in sharing their own ideas, but in giving open and honest feedback to one another as well; constructive tension emanates from a mix of differing views and opinions.

Challenge—A sense of challenge arises from the intriguing and enjoyable nature of a problem or task presented to the group, from the urgent needs of a particular situation, or from the desire to push for something new and move away from the status quo.

Table 4.1 Appropriate Team Member and Management Conditions, Cont'd

Collaboration—The ability to pull together and work closely and comfortably to complete an interdependent task, pursue a mutual interest, or pursue an intriguing idea.

Freedom—The freedom to decide how to do the work; freedom to do the work at one's own pace; freedom from evaluation, surveillance, or having to meet someone else's constraints.

Management encouragement—Management that is encouraging, enthusiastic, and supportive of new ideas and new ways of doing things.

Sufficient resources and time—Sufficient information, human, and technological resources; sufficient time to creatively think about a project and to experiment and try things in new and different ways.

Acceptance of Ideas and Constructive Tension

For creativity to flourish, ideas and input need to be encouraged and respected by all team members. Punitive and unnecessary criticism can kill the seed of a creative idea. However, not all disagreements should be avoided. Constructive tension, in which team members bounce differing ideas and opinions off of one another, may lift a team to high levels of creative thinking. Each of these elements is described below.

Acceptance of Ideas and Input

In highly creative situations, team members said they felt their ideas and input were encouraged, valued, and accepted by all the members of their team without unnecessary criticism. In these situations, there was a high degree of honesty, as team members felt comfortable not only in sharing their ideas, but in giving open and honest feedback to one another as well.

On the one hand, some team members felt that virtual communications positively impacted the degree of acceptance of ideas. For these individuals, ideas and input were more readily offered and accepted electronically. They felt more at ease, comfortable, and less threatened when generating ideas electronically than when doing so face-to-face. Todd of JSC describes how communicating electronically has made idea exchange more comfortable among the members of the team.

> In one sense it's made the sharing of idea easier because people feel more comfortable. If they don't like something that you said, they just fire you back an e-mail. You are responding individually,

and as opposed to, if you're in a room with everybody and you're not the first one to respond, and it looks like the whole group is going in another direction, you may be less likely to share your opinion. But in e-mail, it's like, "hey, I don't agree with that," and you blast it off and you don't have to suffer the repercussions of all these people glaring at you. It's a forum in which it is much easier to express your own feelings and opinions without the peer pressure.

However, others felt being virtual had little to do with how accepting of ideas team members were. The key to acceptance was, rather, understanding and appreciating different team members' work styles. Three of the teams I spoke with (all of the organizational consulting teams) felt strongly about educating team members about one another's work styles, and they invested time and money in training members in how others in the team worked, with the ultimate goal of achieving a mutual level of understanding.

Constructive Tension

An atmosphere that encourages acceptance of ideas also may encourage constructive tension, an unusual mix of differing views and opinions (Ekvall, 1983). Several team members mentioned constructive tension as a positive influence in their team's highly creative experiences. Creativity arose from the tension, conflict, and differing opinions of team members. Larry (of AutoMax) describes the constructive conflict in his team. "In some of the meetings, there was always a conflict. There were always different thoughts, different opinions, but they were all stated constructively. I believe that nobody was not listened to; nobody was taken for granted as far as their expertise."

Some acknowledged that constructive tension may slow the creative process down, but that tension was necessary to arrive at the appropriate solution, rather than a faster, but wrong, outcome. Indeed, constructive tension was so valued by some of the teams that they actively sought to create it in order to achieve high levels of creativity. For example, Chad (of the Jacobs/Taylor team) shares how team members with different perspectives are actively selected to ensure creative tension in his team. "We believe that creativity arises from having differences amongst the team members. That sets up a creative tension so we're not subject to Groupthink. We will go out and attract people who agree on this basic set of beliefs, but have a different perspective, [who are] from a different technical specialty, or from a different culture, or something. That creative difference in the team helps us be creative."

What Happens When Acceptance of Ideas and Constructive Tension Is Low?

In the stories team members shared about low creativity experiences, it was evident that the dismissal of ideas by management or other team members quickly squashed the motivation to be creative. Some team members spoke of frustrating experiences in which ideas were initially solicited and then abruptly dismissed. Lisa, a member of the WN–Current Events team, shares an example of one of these frustrating experiences.

> A low creative experience . . . a project that I worked on recently I didn't feel as good about because I didn't have as much creative input. I was called and asked by one of the people in publicity if I could help with the project. They were going to be doing this big chat and asked could I help to promote this. And I said, "Sure I can." So, I'm out there looking at various places, finding places to post things, and sending e-mails to various different category and forum managers that I already know I can count on because I know them well. Well, what it really came down to was that they weren't sure how much they wanted us to be involved. Truly at the last minute they said, "You know what, never mind, we don't want to use them [category and forum managers] as hosts." So at the last minute I had to send e-mails to all these people that I got to volunteer to host and say, "Thank you, but never mind." My expertise and ideas, they were asked for, I volunteered them, and then they were turned down.

Stories of low creativity also revealed that not all differences lead to constructive tension. In particular, differences in the values held by team members created unconstructive tension, which led to disorganization, confusion, misunderstandings, and, in one case, members leaving the team. Several ACI team members shared comments about a period in their history when they experienced unconstructive tension, and, as a result, some consultants left the firm. In this case, unconstructive tension arose from differences in values centered around the core nature of the business. For other teams (AutoMax; Jacobs/Taylor), unconstructive tension resulted from team members' different values and cultural backgrounds.

Diversity has been found to be an important dimension in nurturing creativity; diversity tends to create a sense of excitement and creative tension. The trend toward globalization in the workplace offers a new level of diversity that can potentially lead to high levels of creative excitement. However, an awareness of the different values that occur with global team membership, along with strategies for dealing with these differences appear to be necessary.

Challenge

Challenge was a major theme in high creativity events shared by team members. A sense of challenge arose from (a) the intriguing and enjoyable nature of a problem or task presented to the team or individual, (b) the urgent needs of a particular situation, or (c) the desire to push for something new and move away from the status quo.

Nature of the Work

Work that was stimulating, engaging, and most of all fun sparked creativity. Melissa of VTG offers an example of a creative project for her team, a training workbook that the team enjoyed designing. "I think that was the most creative just because it was so fun. It involved a lot of layout work and design work. It had a lot of fun text and cartoons; it wasn't dry. When our work can be fun for our clients and fun for us, that's when we get the most enjoyment. And that's when it seems like creativity comes the easiest."

Demands of the Situation

Team members also indicated that creativity was high in situations where they felt they were *working against the odds*. In demanding situations (e.g., a tight time deadline), the team felt driven to prove they could meet the challenge. In a high creativity story told by Eric of AutoMax, the sense of accomplishment that results from creatively and successfully meeting the challenge from a demanding situation is evident.

> We went through the whole design review, and suddenly we were hit with some serious major changes very late in the program. Basically the team sort of sat down and said, "Can we really meet these requirements and still meet the manufacturing dates?" This is

very important because if you don't meet the manufacturing date, then the customer may not get the car, or you may miss the marketplace. We went through the design and I had about two weeks to meet everyone's requirements and get the board out before my holiday. Actually achieving it was really a big boon because not only did it please me, because I've got something out the door and I could go away on holiday and not worry about it, but everyone else was pleased because the timing was still on target and requirements had been put in. It really was against the odds.

Pushing for Something New

In high creativity stories, team members spoke of the desire to push themselves as a team. Emphasis was placed on creating new ways of doing, rather than relying on old material or previously established templates. Rob of ACI gives an example. "We were pushing ourselves into areas where we didn't have any off-the-shelf materials. We were having to, in a way, make up the response. We had to take our practices and principles and apply them in a new arena. And this was our first proposal to this client. When they read it, it basically woke them up to a lot of stuff that they hadn't even thought about."

What Happens When Challenge Is Low?

When there was little challenge or joy in the work, creativity within the team was low. In these low creativity experiences, team members simply said they did not enjoy doing the work (for example, administrative tasks). In addition, sometimes differences in the perception of challenge among team members of certain tasks limited team creativity. Jason of ACI shared that since all his team members did not have the same level of interest or gain the same level of enjoyment from writing, the team had never effectively been able to create company newsletters or marketing material.

In other low creativity situations, the work was quite simply tedious. Laura of ELC spoke of a period in which the team was focused on changing over to a new, shared database. "The period where we were doing hardly any creative work was during the time we had to change over our system. Very tedious, time-consuming, and hard work. It wasn't very creative but we worked together and accomplished what we needed to do. It took a lot out of us because it was so hard. It certainly wasn't creative."

One possible reason creativity was low in these situations may be because it was simply not needed. Previously, I emphasized the importance of creativity for organizational survival. However, I would be remiss if I did not acknowledge that a creative response is not always the most appropriate response. (Chapter Seven elaborates on the importance of establishing norms to distinguish between routine and creative work.)

Collaboration

Virtual team members stressed collaboration as a key characteristic of high creativity situations. Collaboration was characterized as the ability to pull together and work closely and comfortably together to complete an interdependent task, pursue a mutual interest, or pursue a jointly held intriguing idea.

In high creativity stories, team members shared how they effectively "coordinated things," how the team possessed "an extremely high level of cooperation," and how the situation required them to be "very, very tightly strung together." Team members also felt "tuned in" to each other, or that they had "just immediately clicked" with one another. Jason, an ACI team member, shares how his team members being tuned in with one another sparked creativity within the team.

> We just kind of sat there and we talked and we talked and we said, "Let's try this." One of us would have an insight, and the other would build on it, and lo and behold, by the end of the meal or the third glass of wine we had the design for tomorrow, and poof, it seemed to work. It's moments like that where you are with another person and you just play off of each other to create the right thing for the client at this moment in time. There's a creativity there, a spark or an intuition. We were really tuned in with each other in terms of what our response was and it just came out.

Interdependency between team members creates the need for collaboration. Collaboration then results from the team members' common goals, commitment to those goals, and mutual interest in the outcome of their creative efforts. Working together becomes a means to a win-win end. Everyone works together and everyone benefits from the common result.

Freedom

Freedom plays a crucial role in allowing for creativity in virtual teams. When describing highly creative situations, the virtual team members I spoke with said they felt free to work at their own pace and to decide how to do their work. Team members also felt free from unnecessary evaluation, surveillance, or other individuals' constraints. Additionally, when virtual team members were asked what they liked about working in a virtual team, freedom was the most frequent response. They particularly valued flexibility of schedule, work pace, and lifestyle. Nicole of VTG succinctly summarizes a view of freedom that many virtual team members share. "What fosters the creativity? For me, the freedom, the independence to work at my own pace with my own timing. Being trusted to produce the results, [being] given the responsibility and rising to that." Each of the three major types of freedom identified by team members—freedom to work at one's own pace, freedom to decide how to do one's work, and freedom from surveillance and excessive evaluation—are discussed in more detail below.

Freedom to Work at One's Own Pace

In the highly creative stories, team members shared about how they felt free to work at their own pace. Schedules were flexible and adaptable to individual team members' "creative biorhythms" and lifestyles. As one team member put it, "We are not being forced into a nine to five creative box" [Pam, ACI]. Flexibility of schedule also alleviated stress and allowed for a better balance between personal and work lives. Freedom with respect to scheduling afforded team members the opportunity to work at times when there were fewer distractions. Julia, a Jacobs/Taylor team member, describes how virtual teaming has allowed her freedom to effectively balance work-related and personal responsibilities.

> Virtual teaming has created a tremendous amount of freedom for me. I will work at 11:00 at night or get up at 6:00 in the morning and have half a day's work done if I need to. It's great, you have uninterrupted time. On the flip side, I will be in the office and I will take care of a lot of personal things because that's when people are available, during the quote unquote workday. My personal life spills over into the office as well as my office work spills over into my personal life. Having the virtual team has really made that happen very effectively.

Freedom in How to Do the Work

Team members also felt free in highly creative situations to decide how to do their work. The modular approach (described in Chapter One) used by many virtual teams allows for work to be parceled out to individual team members. Team members, then, have control over their section of the creative product and the freedom to accomplish their section as they see fit. Elaine of JSC describes the freedom she has to accomplish her own system of tracking finances. "When I started three years ago, we didn't really have a system set up. So I set up how we track the finances, what letters we send out, how we track the companies and all of that. I never felt that I had to go through the group to set up a system. However, I did share with them the forms that we were using and when other team members gave me feedback, I modified the forms accordingly."

Freedom from Surveillance and Unnecessary Evaluation Pressure

Freedom from unnecessary evaluation helps to establish a relaxing environment in which virtual team members can pursue creative work. On-line exchanges are particularly useful in freeing individuals from the negative effects that surveillance can have on creativity. As Lisa of WN–Current Events shares, "I guess it's the part of being relaxed, there's time to think about something. There isn't the immediacy of somebody sitting in front of your face expecting you or even having the perception that somebody expects you to have an immediate answer. Being on-line lets some of the pressure off."

What Happens When Freedom Is Curtailed?

In the stories in which members spoke of low creativity, *constraint*, or the lack of freedom in deciding what to do or how to do the work, was stressed. For these virtual team members, constraint came from autocratic managers requesting unnecessary changes and from inflexible or over-controlling team members. I found the following story, from an ACI team member who described a low-creative experience, particularly illustrative. "I'm working with another consultant right now who has about the flexibility of the distance between two fly wings. And I don't like it. Oh, it's very difficult. It impacts the ability to do the work, impacts what you're willing or not willing to put on the table, impacts the creativity; it downright stifles it" [Pam, ACI].

Management Encouragement

When managers and team leaders are encouraging, enthusiastic, and supportive of new ideas and new ways of doing things, creativity within virtual teams (or any type of team for that matter) is fostered. How management encouragement occurred in the teams I interviewed is shared below.

Supportive and Empowering

Members of two teams, the VTG and WN–Religion Forum teams, specifically referred to the encouragement and support they felt from team leaders in their highly creative stories. Scott of WN–Religion Forum describes how the team's leader, Eryn, is supportive of team member creativity.

"Our team leader, Eryn, is receptive to all good ideas. That creates the opportunity for creativity; it is ever-present. It's up to the initiative and the ideas of the person generating it to push it forward because we have a highly receptive team leader to put ideas to."

Nicole, a VTG team member, explains how important being empowered by her team leader is for both individual and team creativity to occur. "There is a high level of support for each individual to take initiative and be, you know the buzz word now, 'empowered.' But there's truth in that. And so, each individual was empowered to take on his or her area and develop it. Then we came back, we reassessd. We tweaked and fine tuned. It became a very creative process, both individually and blended in with a team."

Another VTG team member suggested that management encouragement had actually increased since the team had become virtual. The ease of electronic communication helped to increase the frequency with which the firm's managing partners gave recognition, praise, and feedback.

Management encouragement was not mentioned as frequently as some of the other dimensions, perhaps because several of the virtual teams were leaderless, or because leadership was rotated among team members. However, a related theme, acceptance of ideas among all team members (discussed earlier), was prominent in the high creativity stories.

Reliance on the Status Quo

Opposite of management encouragement and support of new ideas is an emphasis or *overemphasis on the status quo*, on doing things the way they have been done in the past. Previous research has found that an overemphasis on the status quo undermines individual and organizational creativity and innovation (Amabile and Gryskiewicz, 1987; Havelock, 1970; Kanter, 1983). In these studies, management's focus was on resisting innovation, keeping things the same, not wanting to take risks, avoiding controversial ideas, and, in general, taking a conservative course of action. In the interviews I shared with virtual team members, emphasizing the status quo was mentioned in some of the low creativity descriptions. However, emphasizing the status quo was not motivated by a desire to avoid controversial ideas or resist innovation. Rather, in these particular situations, it was simply more convenient and efficient to do so. Some teams used templates or frameworks as a starting point in approaching problems to increase efficiency. Lianna, the WN–Current Events team leader, describes how the reliance on old ways of doing, initially set up to automate production of the online publication during her absence, carried over after her return. Although production became more efficient, she did not consider it a creative period.

> I think one thing you had asked earlier that I didn't answer was about times where there's not creativity. One thing I've noticed in our team is that when I was gone for two weeks, I did a lot of work to set them up so that they could kind of automate things. So that they wouldn't have to think about, for example, how to fill a certain page with promotions. I would say "Okay, here's a whole list of them and you can just run them." It was only for when I was gone. But now since I did that, everything is automated. It's easier to do your work because you don't have to think about it. But it definitely loses the creativity that comes when you sit down and you say, "Okay we have to have the leads for tomorrow."

Sufficient Resources and Time

It is true that people can be inspired to high levels of creativity with a shortage of resources. As the saying goes, they can "do more with less." However, a common reason for a lack of creative accomplishment is the mere unwillingness of individuals, teams, and organizations to allocate sufficient resources. In James Adams' (1986) book *The Care and Feeding of Ideas*, he emphasizes the importance of sufficient resources for high levels of creativity. He writes, "Many people I know try to be creative on the side. That is OK, unless one's expectations cause one to judge oneself according to world-class standards. If that is the case, one needs to allocate world-class resources to that task" (p. 120).

Resources are necessary to accomplish anything worthwhile, even in business-as-usual situations. For creativity, it is not just resources one needs to consider but the allocation of these resources within an organizational or team setting that emphasizes risk-taking over efficiency. Resources come in many forms—adequate and proper information (discussed in Chapter Three), suitable technological resources (discussed in Chapter Five), ample staff and people to accomplish the work, and enough time to be able to think in creative ways. The amount of funds devoted to sponsor a creative effort may impact whether resources are sufficient or not. (Although certainly the most creative projects are not necessarily the ones that cost the most.) Perhaps the most crucial resources are time and individual or team effort allotted to do a task. Sufficient time, or the lack of time, was a common thread occurring in the stories shared by the virtual team members.

The Time to Think

In highly creative situations, team members said having the time to think creatively about a project and the time to experiment and try things in new and different ways was key. For example, Cheryl of ACI, shares an experience where having sufficient time allowed her to think in highly creative ways. "I think the first one where it worked so well, we were not under a time crunch, and I had time to really think about things and really be creative, and put some graphics in. For me, time makes a big difference. Some people work better under real time restraints. I need time to think about things." Julia of the Jacobs/Taylor team provides further evidence that sufficient time is crucial for high levels of creativity to occur.

"We worked on a proposal for a client in New York back in January. It worked well for a couple of reasons. I think the main reason it worked well is that we actually had a couple of weeks where we could sit down and really work through it. January was a slow month for us and we actually had a couple of weeks where we could sit and work it through, and take the time to e-mail it to our other teammates, and sit on the phone with them and go through it.

As might be expected, not having enough time hindered creativity in these virtual teams.

What Happens When Time Is Limited?

Although for some team members, deadlines and time crunches provide a sense of challenge that leads to high creativity, it still appears that teams need sufficient time to be able to think creatively about a project and to try new and different things. Without this time, creativity suffers, as team members scramble simply to get projects completed on time. Cheryl of ACI describes a situation in which a lack of time not only hampered her team's creativity, but also created tremendous stress for herself as well.

"It was just such a time crunch. As far as I'm concerned, there was no creativity for me. It was like, I'm going to spell check this, and if it looks like the sentences read okay, then it's going in. And we were handing Matt the binders on his way out the door, and he had 20 minutes to catch a flight. It was just about as stressed as I've ever been without there being a death involved [laughter]."

An Abundance of Human Resources

Networked virtual team members saw themselves as having abundant human resources available for creative work. One virtual team member suggested that the *only* plus technology brought to the creative process was its ability to link individuals who could not otherwise be there. Electronic links, then, widen the creative pool of human resources. Peripheral team members and individuals external to both the team and the organization can be electronically connected when needed. One of the product designer engineers (from the AutoMax team) comments.

> Probably we have more resources at our disposal, just because of the fact of who is networked. When you have multiple people that you're working with and you need to get things accomplished, or pushed through, first of all you have buy-in of the whole team. So, if it went to any of our areas, we knew for sure that we had committed people to do the necessary testing or studies to make it happen. Then, outside of our team, different people are connected differently within our organization network. You know different people who know different people [and] know about different areas within the team. Each team member knows different sets of individuals. That increases available resources probably tenfold. [Larry, AutoMax]

What Happens When Access to Resources Is Problematic?

It seems ironic that the same type of team design that offers team members an abundance of resources can also limit the resources available. However, it turns out that most of the resource problems in the low creativity stories arose from not being able to *gain access* to available resources. Some of the more frequently-mentioned difficulties were technological, such as (a) computer system failures, (b) broken fax and answering machines, (c) lost e-mail, (d) slow computers and unsophisticated hardware and software, and (e) computer systems that were incompatible. Technological difficulties not only limit the ability of the teams to accomplish creative work, but any work at all. And, as Cindy of WN–Current Events, shares, the difficulty need only be with one virtual team member for the entire team to be affected. "I have great access to the tools that I use to build our online publication and [publish] to the Internet. The only difficulty or problem comes in with the fact that these are kind of fragile tools and a lot of times they break. And when one person's tool breaks, the work of the entire team slows down."

Assessment Tool: Understanding the Appropriate Team Member and Management Conditions

To what degree do virtual team leaders and team members realize the importance of the appropriate team member and management conditions described? How can virtual teams assess their current level of functioning with respect to these situational requirements? A series of questions are provided for reflection. Answers to the following questions will provide you with an understanding of the appropriate conditions within your virtual teams. Which areas are your teams strong in and what elements may require improvement? As a result of this newfound understanding, you and your team should work jointly to create action plans to further develop areas in need of improvement and to maintain areas of strength. (If you need to before beginning, revisit the guidelines for using chapter assessment tools described in the Introduction.)

Assessment Questions

Acceptance of ideas means that ideas and input are encouraged, valued, and accepted by all the members of your team without unnecessary criticism. There is a high degree of honesty among team members leading individuals to feel comfortable not only in sharing ideas, but in giving open and honest feedback to each other as well. *Constructive tension* emanates from a mix of differing views and opinions.

1. What actions does your team take to actively encourage ideas from all team members? What systems are in place that allow for that?

2. To what extent do team members feel your ideas or input are valued by the other members of the team?

3. How would you characterize the degree of honesty among team members (high, moderate, low)? To what extent are team members comfortable in giving open and honest feedback to each other? And to what extent are team members receptive in receiving constructive feedback?

4. To what extent do team members understand and appreciate each other's individual work styles?

5. What actions does your team take to actively encourage constructive tension and the expression of differing viewpoints and opinions? What might your team do differently to further the appropriate use of constructive tension?

Challenge arises from the intriguing and enjoyable nature of a problem or task presented to the group, the urgent needs of a particular situation, or the desire to push for something new and move away from the status quo.

6. What types of work do you and your team members find intriguing and enjoyable? What types of work do you find less enjoyable? (Your team may want to assess this individually for each team member, since people generally prefer different types of work. With this information, you may want to assign work according to preference and also create balance among assigned tasks that are enjoyable and not enjoyable.) Consider also, how could your team redesign unenjoyable tasks to increase interest?

7. What elements of your team's work are fun? How can your team actively integrate a sense of play and fun into your work?

8. What situations does your team generally face that create a sense of urgency and "working against the odds"? How does your team currently react in these urgent situations? What actions might your team take to further instill a sense of urgency to stimulate creativity within the team?

9. To what extent do team members push each other as a team to do something new? In what situations is it appropriate for the team to develop new ways of working and doing? In what situations is it appropriate to rely on old material and previously established templates? (For more information on how teams can assess when creativity is necessary or when it might be preferable to rely on previous templates, refer to Chapter Seven.)

Collaboration is the ability to pull together and work closely and comfortably to complete an interdependent task, pursue a mutual interest, or pursue a jointly held intriguing idea.

10. To what degree are team members interdependent on each other to accomplish their work?

11. For the most part, would you characterize team members as able to work closely and comfortably together? Why or why not?

12. To what extent are team members "tuned in" to each other?

13. What current activities does your team engage in that encourage a sense of cooperation? What current activities interfere with team member cooperation?

14. Do individual team members benefit from the end result of your team's work? What might be done to enhance the individual rewards team members receive from your team's joint outcomes?

Freedom can be broken down into three different types—freedom to decide how to do the work, freedom to do the work at one's own pace, and freedom from evaluation, surveillance, or someone else's constraints.

15. To what extent are individual team members given the freedom to decide how to complete their tasks? For what particular tasks is it appropriate for individual team members to freely execute their tasks? For what particular tasks does the team need to have more joint control over the process?

16. To what extent do team members have the freedom to determine the pace of work? (This may vary according to the particular role a team member plays on the team and from project to project.)

17. To what extent does management allow team members freedom in executing their work?

18. Are unnecessary constraints placed on team members? Why? What causes these constraints? What actions might the team take to alleviate or be rid of these constraints?

Management encouragement means that management is encouraging, enthusiastic, and supportive of new ideas and new ways of doing things.

19. To what extent does top management encourage and support new ideas and new ways of doing things?

20. How receptive is your team leader to new ideas shared by team members? What actions does your team leader take to ensure support for new ideas generated within the team?

21. How does your team leader balance the need for efficiency and for creativity?

Sufficient resources include sufficient information, human, and technological resources. *Sufficient time* includes time to creatively think about a project and to experiment and try things in new and different ways.

22. For the most part, do project schedules and deadlines allow time to experiment and think creatively? If not, what actions might be taken to further ensure this?

23. In general, does the team have sufficient human resources (core and peripheral team members, relevant people external to the team) to effectively accomplish creative tasks? What projects might require additional human resources?

24. What issues tend to block access to needed resources (e.g., lack of funds, lack of political clout, or technological difficulties)?

Team Member and Management Competencies

To achieve the conditions just reviewed, virtual team members, leaders, and managers need to develop and practice a special set of competencies. The eleven competencies that virtual team members and leaders need to possess are as follows:

1. Developing self- and interpersonal awareness

2. Supportive communication

3. Cross-cultural communication

4. Conflict resolution

5. Problem solving and decision-making

6. Stress management

7. Time management and personal productivity

8. Developing and motivating others

9. Positive political skills

10. Knowledge management, data gathering, and information access skills

11. Career Advancement

Table 4.2 relates the competencies listed above to the conditions previously reviewed; in other words, what competencies do virtual workers need in order to develop and maintain each of the appropriate team member and management conditions for creativity in virtual teams?

Table 4.2 Conditions and Related Competencies

Condition	Related Competencies
Acceptance of ideas	• Develop self- and interpersonal awareness • Supportive communication
Constructive Tension	• Conflict resolution • Cross-cultural communication • Positive political skills • Problem solving and decision making • Supportive communication
Challenge	• Career advancement • Develop self- and interpersonal awareness • Developing and motivating others • Stress management • Time management and personal productivity

Table 4.2 Conditions and Related Competencies, Cont'd

Condition	Related Competencies
Collaboration	• Develop self- and interpersonal awareness • Conflict resolution • Cross-cultural communication • Problem solving and decision-making • Knowledge management, data gathering, and information access • Supportive communication
Freedom	• Develop self- and interpersonal awareness • Stress management • Time management and personal productivity
Management Encouragement	• Cross-cultural communication • Developing and motivating others • Positive political skills • Supportive communication
Sufficient Resources and Time	• Conflict resolution • Knowledge management, data gathering, and information access • Positive political skills • Time management and personal productivity

Certainly there have been several comprehensive books already written on what competencies and skills are necessary for effective teamwork and collaboration (Johnson and Johnson, 1997; Whetten and Cameron, 1998, and others). My intent is not to be exhaustive in my review, but rather to pull together information on those competencies relevant to virtual teams. As you read this section on necessary team member and management competencies, you may feel that these competencies are necessary for any team member, virtual or not. And you'd be right. You may recall my earlier comments on how virtual teams are first and foremost teams. However, some of the competencies to be discussed differ somewhat for virtual team members as compared to traditional team members. In the following section, you will be able to experience and assess in yourself and your team the competencies required for pursuing creative work in the virtual world.

Developing Self- and Interpersonal Awareness

For centuries, self-awareness has been at the core of human behavior. Philosophers throughout time have espoused the importance of "knowing thyself." Probably the most cited quote on the self is Polonius' advice in Shakespeare's tragedy *Hamlet*, "To thine own self be true, and it must follow, as the night the day, thou canst not then be false to any man." Those who study human behavior have long known that self-awareness is essential to one's personal and professional functioning and to the ability to sympathize and empathize with others. Self-awareness also leads to higher levels of personal growth and creativity. Thus, developing an awareness of who you are remains vitally important in the contemporary workplace and is especially important for virtual team members striving for higher levels of creativity. You may have been taught as a child that to love another, you must first love yourself. The same tenet holds for working creatively with others. Before you can accept ideas in others, before you can know how to work creatively with others, you must first know who you are as an individual.

If teams (and their leaders) actively encourage their members to "know themselves" and to exchange those personal insights with one another, self-awareness can also lead to interpersonal awareness. Interpersonal awareness is particularly critical for virtual team members who must form relationships quickly and through media low in information richness and social presence. Many virtual teams come together rapidly to respond to urgent customer, client, or marketplace needs. As a result, most virtual teams do not have the luxury of going through the commonly regarded traditional stages of team or group development—forming, storming, norming, performing, and adjourning (Tuckman, 1965; Tuckman and Jensen, 1977). Knowing oneself and being able to understand others' styles affords one the ability to form team relationships quickly and effectively. Virtual team members must come on board already knowing who they are, already asking questions to help the team get organized, and already showing an interest in other team members. Interpersonal awareness gives virtual team members the ability to quickly identify their teammates' preferred work styles and adapt accordingly.

Self-awareness involves an exploration, understanding, and appreciation for your own personality traits, personal values, cognitive style, interpersonal orientation, and attitude toward change (Whetten and Cameron, 1998). Carefully read through this section, experience the exercises, and learn more about who you are. Then share that information with your teammates—and have them share their self-awareness insights with you.

Personality

Personality is generally defined as an individual's consistent and distinctive set of enduring and lasting traits. These personality traits vary from person to person. Research into personality has revealed several broad factors known as the "Big Five" that make up the human personality (Digman, 1990).

1. *Extraversion* is the amount and intensity of preferred interpersonal interactions. Extraverts tend to be energetic, friendly, outgoing, and to spend much of their time enjoying relationships. Introverts tend to be more reserved, passive, have fewer relationships, and to be more comfortable with solitude than extraverts.

2. *Neuroticism* is the degree to which an individual demonstrates emotional maladjustment and instability. People high in this trait are inclined to poor adjustment and psychological problems, including anxiety, anger, depression, insecurity, and self-consciousness. People low in this trait are more emotionally stable, more adaptive, more realistic, tolerate frustration better, and are calm, enthusiastic, and secure.

3. *Openness to experience* is the degree to which a person actively seeks out and appreciates experiences for their own sake. People high in this trait are curious, imaginative, unconventional, and fascinated by novelty and innovation. People low in this trait are more conventional, conservative, rigid in their beliefs, and find more comfort in the familiar.

4. *Agreeableness* is the degree to which a person compassionately connects with others. Highly agreeable individuals are good-natured, trusting, cooperative, and helpful. They value harmony more than they value having their way. Antagonistic (low in agreeableness) individuals are suspicious, irritable, sometimes vengeful, and focus more on their own needs than on the needs of others.

5. *Conscientiousness* is the degree of organization, self-control, and persistence a person shows in pursuing goals. Highly conscientious individuals are hardworking, ambitious, responsible, persistent, dependable, and achievement oriented. They focus on fewer goals, but do so in a purposeful way. Less conscientious people tend to be easily distracted, to pursue many goals, and to be negligent and more hedonistic.

Use the Personality Trait Scale that follows to do a quick assessment of your own Big Five personality traits. (For developing interpersonal awareness, have all team members complete the Personality Trait Scale and share the results with one another.)

Using the scale below, circle the number that best corresponds to your self-rating on each personality dimension.

1	2	3	4	5	6	7	8	9	10
Low end of scale							High end of scale		

1. *Extraversion:*

Introverted   Extraverted

1	2	3	4	5	6	7	8	9	10

2. *Neuroticism:*

Emotionally stable   Neurotic

1	2	3	4	5	6	7	8	9	10

3. *Openness to experience:*

Closed to experience   Open to experience

1	2	3	4	5	6	7	8	9	10

4. *Agreeableness:*

Antagonistic   Agreeable

1	2	3	4	5	6	7	8	9	10

5. *Conscientiousness:*

Irresponsible   Conscientious

1	2	3	4	5	6	7	8	9	10

Enter your score for each trait:

1. Extraversion: _____
2. Neuroticism: _____
3. Openness to experience: _____
4. Agreeableness: _____
5. Conscientiousness: _____

Personal Values

Personal values are peoples' beliefs and/or standards that help them define what is good and bad or right and wrong. Values signify the importance a person attaches to something. Values are the most stable and enduring characteristics of individuals. They form the basis for one's personal and work-related life decisions and are the foundation upon which attitudes and personal preferences are formed. Personal values can assist in holding a team together or in splitting it apart. Recall how in the section on Constructive Tension, ACI team members shared their thoughts on a prior time in the team's history where differences in team members' personal values (centered around the core nature of consulting) caused several members of the team to split off on their own.

Values are impossible to see (we see only the resulting actions) and even more difficult to discuss. Yet they are a powerful influence on behavior and they drive interpersonal effectiveness. It is important to one's own self-awareness to clarify personal values. And since interpersonal conflicts driven by values are the most difficult to resolve, it is also essential to have others on the team understand, appreciate, and respect your values as well. Having this appreciation for one another's values may decrease misunderstandings that occur when working virtually. Here is an exercise you might try to better understand your own personal values. (Try also having each of the members of your team do this individually and then exchange answers to lead to better interpersonal awareness and to define a core set of team values.)

Values Exercise. Draw a timeline of the most important events in your life. Start with birth and then work your way to the present. Then anticipate what will happen in the next five years. Look at your timeline and consider the following questions:

- What personal values were reflected in the events you considered important?

- Which values most influenced you to take risks?

- Which values assisted you in making your life decisions (both the worst and best)?

- Come up with a list of five values most important to you right now. Write them down and keep them handy. Use them to guide your day-to-day and future decision-making.

Cognitive Style

Cognitive style refers to the mental processes we use to perceive and judge information. According to Carl Jung (1923), the way that people gather and evaluate information determines their cognitive style. Typically, there are two major dimensions of cognitive style: gathering information and evaluating information. Within each of the dimensions, there are also two characteristic styles. The dimensions combine to produce four cognitive styles: sensing and thinking; intuitive and thinking; sensing and feeling; and intuitive and feeling. The styles are described in Table 4.3.

Table 4.3 Cognitive Dimensions and Styles

Dimension	Style 1	Style 2
Gathering information	*Sensing* individuals prefer routine and order, are rational, and conduct a thorough search for precise details when gathering information to solve a problem. They seek out established facts, rather than new information.	*Intuitive* individuals focus on the big picture, on commonalties and overall categories. Intuitive thinkers often have preconceived ideas as to what information is relevant, and look for information consistent with these preconceptions. They enjoy solving new problems, dislike routine and prefer to look for possibilities rather than work with facts.
Evaluating information	*Thinking* individuals rely on reason, objective data, and intellect to evaluate problems and they use a systematic, logical plan with specific sequential steps. Emotions are downplayed.	*Feeling* individuals evaluate a problem on the basis of a gut feeling or internal sense of how to respond. Problems are defined and refined, and methods for solving problems are based on trial and error rather than logic and reason. Feeling individuals also have a need to conform and adapt to the wishes of others. They may try to avoid problems that might result in disagreements.

Source: Adapted from material in DuBrin, 2004; Whetten and Cameron, 1998.

Jung's analysis of cognitive style provided the framework for the widely used Myers-Briggs Type Indicator. If you and your team members have the opportunity to take the Myers-Briggs test and to share that information with one another, you may develop a deeper understanding and respect for various team members' cognitive styles.

Interpersonal Orientation

Interpersonal orientation refers to an individual's *tendency* to interact and behave in certain ways in relationships with others. It is not the actual behavior displayed in relating with others, but rather one's underlying tendencies to behave regardless of the other individuals or situation. Schutz (1958), well-known for his theory of interpersonal orientation, pointed to three interpersonal needs. For each need, there are two tendencies, a desire to express the need and a desire to receive the need from others.

- *Need for inclusion*—the need to maintain a relationship with others, to be included. Individuals differ in how much they want to be included by others or to include others.

- *Need for control*—the need for power and influence over others. Individuals differ in their need to control or to be controlled by others.

- *Need for affection*—the need to form close relationships. Individuals vary in their need for expressing affection toward others and for wanting affection to be expressed toward them.

Use the following exercise to see which tendency is strongest for each of your three interpersonal needs.

Understanding Your Interpersonal Orientation. For each interpersonal orientation need—inclusion, control, and affection—two statements are presented. Check which of the two statements you prefer most.

Need for Inclusion

Check the statement you most prefer:

_____ I want to join in and be included by others.

_____ I like to be the one to include others.

Need for Control

Check the statement you most prefer:

_____ I take charge and influence others.

_____ I prefer for others to lead me and give me directions.

Need for affection

Check the statement you most prefer:

_____ I like to give affection to others.

_____ I prefer others to give me affection.

For a deeper understanding of your interpersonal orientations, you and your teammates may wish to take the Fundamental Interpersonal Relations Orientation–Behavior (FIRO–B) instrument, developed by Schutz (1958). Virtual team leaders and members can use this information to tailor their communication behavior to meet individual team members' interpersonal needs.

Attitude Toward Change

Virtual teaming generates significant changes to established processes, behavior, and individual work habits and performance. Participants on virtual teams must be open to change. Attitude toward change refers to the methods an individual uses to cope with change, and it identifies the adaptability of individuals to new experiences and ambiguity. One's attitude toward change is an important prerequisite for coping with change. Two dimensions that are particularly relevant in assessing one's attitude toward change are tolerance for ambiguity and locus of control. *Tolerance of ambiguity* is the extent to which individuals are comfortable with and can cope with situations and problems that are novel, unclear, complex, and difficult to solve. *Locus of control* indicates where people place control in their lives. Individuals with an internal locus of control view themselves to be the cause of occurrences in their lives. People with an external locus of control view outside forces, such as luck or chance, to be responsible for their actions.

What is your attitude toward change? And how do the members of your team feel about change? Answer the following to find out.

Attitude Toward Change Scale

Check which of the two you most agree with:

1. _____ I prefer ambiguous, unclear tasks.

2. _____ I prefer routine, structured tasks.

Check which of the two you most agree with:

3. _____ I enjoy trying out different and novel things.

4. _____ I prefer to have things remain the same.

Check which of the two you most agree with:

5. _____ Some things in life are just too hard to solve.

6. _____ There is no problem that I cannot solve.

Check which of the two you most agree with:

7. _____ The bad things that happen to me are out of my control.

8. _____ When things go wrong in my life, it's mostly because I have made mistakes.

Check which of the two you most agree with:

9. _____ Individual effort and hard work are the keys to my personal success.

10. _____ Success depends on being in the right place at the right time.

Check which of the two you most agree with:

11. _____ I can change anything if I try hard enough.

12. _____ Fate and luck play a huge part in how my life turns out.

Interpretation: Items 1, 3, 6, 8, 9, and 11 indicate an openness to change. Items 2, 4, 5, 7, 10, and 12 indicate less of a tolerance for change.

In the long run, the knowledge that comes from learning more about yourselves pays off in team members developing a higher level of interpersonal awareness. To develop interpersonal awareness, Duarte and Snyder (1999) suggest team members need to keep the following strategies in mind:

- Be aware of their team members' interpersonal styles and their impact on others.
- Collect and be open to feedback on one's own interpersonal style from other team members.
- Discuss one's interpersonal strengths and weaknesses with other team members and provide them with appropriate feedback on theirs.
- Plan for and take action that leads to improvement in one's interpersonal style and way of working with others.

Supportive Communication

As one of the virtual team members shared with me, "Without communication, without information sharing, the team does not exist" [Eryn, WN–Religion Forum]. Communication is the sending, receiving, and understanding of messages. But for teams doing creative work, that communication has to be supportive. Creativity means taking risks, sharing the seeds with one another for later creative outcomes, and working through the ambiguity of the creative process. Individuals' creativity will be stunted if their ideas are criticized, squashed, or if they are made to be on the defensive.

Perhaps one way to understand supportive communication is to review what it is not. Jack Gibb (1961) developed six pairs of defensive and supportive communication categories, which are presented in Table 4.4. The left-hand column lists behaviors that may arouse defensiveness on the part of the listener. Behaviors in the right-hand column are interpreted by the listener as supportive and reduce defensive feelings.

Table 4.4 Behavioral Indicators of Defensive and Supportive Communication

Defensive Communication	Supportive Communication
• *Evaluation*: Evaluating and discounting others' ideas; implying others' ideas are wrong or invalid.	• *Description*: Opposite of judging; genuine request for information about ideas in an open, honest attempt to understand them more fully.
• *Superiority*: Communicating that one is superior; arrogance; implying others cannot be right because of their inadequacies. There is no interest in collaborative problem solving or reciprocal feedback.	• *Equality*: Treating others as equals, with respect and trust. Although individual differences may exist, the communicator attaches little importance to them.

Table 4.4 Behavioral Indicators of Defensive and Supportive Communication, Cont'd

Defensive Communication	Supportive Communication
• *Certainty*: Communicating in a manner that implies you know all the answers and alternatives (except for the "bad" ones that the other person is coming up with); you don't need additional information.	• *Provisionalism*: Investigating issues rather than taking sides; seeing alternative perspectives; being willing to accept others' input and ideas even if they are different from your own.
• *Control*: Trying to direct, change, or influence others' behaviors or ideas by imposing your set of values or beliefs on them.	• *Problem-orientation*: Communicating a desire to focus on mutual problem solving rather than placing blame or manipulating. Seeking information with no predetermined solution or attitude.
• *Strategy*: Using deception, hidden motivation, or false emotion with another to maneuver a change.	• *Spontaneity*: Straightforward, being honest, and free from deception.
• *Neutrality*: Communicating a lack of interest or concern for the feelings or welfare of the other person; implies that others' perceptions or ideas are of little importance.	• *Empathy*: Reflecting the feelings and ideas of the other person; identifying with the other's problems and feelings.

Source: Adapted from J. Gibb, Defensive Communication, *The Journal of Communication*, 1961, *11*(3), 141–148. Used by permission of Oxford University Press.

Supportive communication focuses on problems, not on persons. The intent of communication is to describe and understand (and as a result take action), rather than to judge or evaluate. Supportive communication validates the feelings of those involved, rather than making individuals feel invalidated or discounted. Supportive communication is specific and useful, rather than too broad and useless. Particularly relevant to electronic communication (e-mail, chat rooms) is that supportive communication should be conjunctive (jointed to previous messages), not disconnected. And supportive communication requires skills on the part of the listener as well, so that it is not just a one-way message delivery. This is particularly problematic for virtual team members, who often feel caught in a one-way, back-and-forth e-mail exchange. The traditional communication skills that virtual team members (or any team member) need to become proficient in include sending effective messages, giving and receiving appropriate feedback, and actively and empathetically listening to others. Each is discussed in the next section.

Sending Effective Messages

Virtual teams may select from a variety of communication tools to send and receive messages. (Specific types of communication tools are reviewed in Chapter Five.) However, no matter which method is selected, team members still have to practice the basic principles of sending effective messages. Following are a few tips on how to send effective messages:

1. Clearly own your messages by using first person. Use statements like, "I feel . . .," rather than "You make me feel . . ."

2. Make your messages complete and specific. Unclear, incomplete, and general messages are a potential time waster for virtual team members. Lacking the ability to go down the hall to clarify the message's intent, virtual team members may be left trying to figure out what to do.

3. Make verbal and nonverbal congruent. There are times when virtual team members communicate through methods with both visual and audio links. Make sure what you say is consistent with what you are demonstrating nonverbally. This is particularly relevant for face-to-face meetings and desktop video or videoconferences (when the camera is on you).

4. Be redundant. Send the message more than once or through more than one communication mode. (Follow your team's established norms for acknowledgment of messages. See Chapter Seven for more detail on acknowledgment norms.)

5. Make the message appropriate to the receiver's frame of reference and expertise level.

Giving and Receiving Feedback

Feedback is crucial to improving the performance of any team, whether virtual or not. Feedback is any communication to an individual that gives him or her information about some aspect of his or her behavior or its effect on you (Mill, 1976). In a virtual environment, day-to-day encounters with teammates are rare, so feedback is essential. A good way to avoid the potential misinterpretations or misunderstandings characteristic of virtual exchanges is to ask for feedback from your colleagues as to what they thought you said—and to solicit their thoughts as well. Table 4.5 outlines suggestions for giving and receiving effective feedback.

Table 4.5 Giving and Receiving Feedback

To Give Effective Feedback	To Receive Effective Feedback
Feedback should occur immediately after the behavior is observed.	Feedback is more likely to be understood if the receiver listens actively.
Feedback should describe specific behavior.	Feedback is more likely to be understood if the receiver paraphrases back what he or she has heard.
Feedback should reveal one's reaction to another's behavior without making moral or ethical judgments.	Feedback does not necessarily require the receiver to change his or her behavior.
Feedback is more meaningful when it comes from several people, not just one.	The receiver can learn whether the feedback represents only one person's opinions or a consensus by checking with others.

Active Listening

Active listening differs from passively absorbing information (like a tape recorder). An active listener attempts to grasp both the facts and the feelings in the message being sent. To apply this skill, listeners need to listen in the following ways:

- With intensity—concentrate, tune out miscellaneous mind wandering
- With empathy—understand what the speaker is saying rather than what you want to hear or understand
- With acceptance—listen objectively without initial judgment
- With a willingness to take responsibility for completeness—strive to get the full intended message (Rogers and Farson, 1976).

The following behaviors should be followed when actively listening to a fellow team member:

- Really listen until the message is complete. Avoid interrupting or preparing an answer while another person is talking. Strive to spend 20% of the time talking and 80% of the time listening. And when you do talk, aim for smooth transitions between the speaker and the listener.
- Make and maintain eye contact (but don't stare the speaker down). In a face-to-face conversation, look intently at the individual who is talking.

In a videoconference, try looking at the camera to indicate contact with an individual who is talking.

- Show interest. Use head nods, appropriate facial expressions, or phrases like "mmh" or "uh-huh" to indicate interest or agreement.

- Avoid distracting gestures, actions, or mutterings.

- Ask open-ended questions to encourage an individual to talk. Ask clarifying questions to check assumptions about what you thought was being said.

- Paraphrase or repeat back the content and feeling of what the speaker said to make sure you understood the message and to validate the sender's feelings.

- Note all cues (verbal and nonverbal), if all cues are available. You may do this in electronic modes of communication as well, but don't fall into the trap of "reading between the lines" which may lead to misunderstandings and false assumptions.

- Interpret emotional words appropriately; do not overreact.

- Avoid trying to change the speaker's thinking.

- Avoid responding to a speaker's demand for decisions, judgments, or evaluations.

- Integrate what is being said. Use your spare time while listening to better understand the sender's ideas or thoughts.

- Be natural. Don't try to overdo facial expressions, eye contact, asking questions, or showing interest.

One thing I learned from interviewing thirty-six virtual team members was that my own listening skills evolved and became better with practice. Try the listening interlude below with a fellow teammate to sharpen your listening skills. If possible, conduct this exercise with one of your co-workers face-to-face and also during another form of synchronous communication (such as a telephone call, audioconference, synchronous computer meeting). Note any differences in your listening skills. For example, do you check e-mail while listening to team members during an audioconference or a telephone call, because no one can see you?

Sharpen Your Listening Skills

Select an issue or problem (currently unresolved) that is important to your team at the present time. Ask your teammate to share his or her views on this issue or problem. Have a third person sit in (or listen in). That person serves as an observer and assesses your active listening skills. Have the observer use the sheet below to record your listening behaviors. A checkmark should be placed next to the behavior every time the observer sees or hears you (the listener) performing this behavior. Behaviors one through four indicate active and empathetic listening, and behaviors five through ten should be avoided when listening actively.

Active Listening Observation Sheet

Behavior	Check Marks	Comments
1. Appropriate nonverbal behavior (eye contact, head nods, supportive facial expressions, phrases indicating interest).		
2. Paraphrasing the content of the message.		
3. Paraphrasing the feeling embedded in the message.		
4. Asking questions to clarify for understanding or to check perceptions and assumptions.		
5. Interrupting the speaker.		
6. Talking too much.		
7. Being judgmental.		
8. Minimizing or diffusing the problem.		
9. Giving unwanted advice.		
10. Self-referencing (switching the conversation to discuss your similar problems).		

And Much More: Communication Skills
Specifically for Virtual Team Members

Virtual team members and leaders will need to know the traditional communication skills just covered and much more. A list of specific communication requirements for virtual team members to develop and practice follows.

- Proficiency in written communication skills to effectively communicate through e-mail and other collaborative software systems.

- Ability to present in videoconferencing and desktop video systems.

- Ability to communicate in synchronous computer meetings.

- Proficiency in processing auditory information because of the high degree of telephone contact that may occur between virtual team members.

- Knowledge of guidelines and norms about when to see people face-to-face and when to use all the other communication tools available for virtual exchanges. (Chapter Five and the section on communication behavior norms in Chapter Seven provide further information about how to acquire this knowledge.)

Cross-Cultural Communication

Cross-cultural communication skills are so important to members of virtual teams that they are addressed separately from forms of supportive communication. Susan Fritz and her colleagues (1999) view cross-cultural communication as one of the key sets of skills for leaders in the twenty-first century. They write, "The ability to appreciate diversity, communicate effectively, and interact with individuals from different cultures are valuable skills in today's world" (p. 274). The workforce today has and is continuing to become more diverse. The nature of business has become more global. As a result, it is imperative that virtual team members develop the ability to communicate with members who possess diverse backgrounds and cultures—who may live and work across the globe.

First, it is necessary for virtual team members to cultivate an awareness of their own cultural biases and how they may potentially impact their team. Diversity in a team is a valuable resource that can and should be used to increase a team's performance. In addition, research has shown that diversity leads to higher levels of team creativity (Ekvall, 1983). However, there are a number of barriers to effective communications between diverse individuals, including prejudice, stereotyping, and cultural clash. Knowing more about yourself as a diverse individual (through developing self-awareness) and about the other diverse individuals on your team can reduce those barriers and set the stage for recognizing and valuing the diversity within the team.

Research has revealed that individuals are usually more comfortable and at ease communicating with those who share similar experiences, lifestyles, and cultural values. To successfully communicate with others from different cultures and backgrounds, it is important to recognize and appreciate the differences, while also searching for common ground that transcends culture. Suggestions for improving cross-cultural communication include the following:

- Know the dimensions of your own cultural makeup. Challenge your own biases; avoid stereotyping and prejudice.

- Know, understand, and respect the individual differences that exist on your team. Develop cultural sensitivity through actual interaction, trust, and candid discussion.

- Although you value the individual differences within your team, also focus on the commonalities within the team, such as common team goals, a superordinate team identity that transcends individual differences, and a pluralistic set of team values.

- Use supportive communication skills (discussed in the prior section), including sending effective messages, encouraging and providing feedback, and actively and empathetically listening to others.

- Respect one another. Take seriously the different opinions, perceptions, and experiences of others. Listen with a motivation to learn about others, rather than to blame or accuse.

- Be sensitive to cultural differences in nonverbal behavior and etiquette. Although many of the standard nonverbal indicators (eye contact, touch, proximity, gestures) may not be problematic for electronic communication, virtual team members should be sensitive to: (1) how diverse individuals may vary in degree of directness (for example, Japanese negotiators may mean no when they say "We'll consider this"); (2) appropriate subjects or topics to discuss (such as, asking personal questions of a colleague in Great Britain may be an improper ice-breaker to start a team meeting as the British tend to protect their privacy); or (3) emotional expressiveness (some cultures value stoicism while others encourage open expression of feelings).

A real benefit that organizations with heterogeneous, diverse team members have is the potential for higher levels of creativity. Each diverse team member brings a potentially different way of viewing a situation or problem. However, as teams become more and more diverse, so too does the potential for conflict. When conflict does arise as a result of cultural differences, approach the conflict as an opportunity to learn. Conflict, and how to resolve it when working virtually, is the next competency to be discussed.

Conflict Resolution

Conflict is inevitable in human relationships when individuals, teams, or organizations are interdependent. Interpersonal conflict exists whenever two or more people disagree. Some conflict is constructive and can result in needed change and growth and in enhanced productivity and commitment. However, for many teams conflict can be destructive, leading individuals to harden their respective positions. In some cases, this can even lead to a team being divided into camps, with each side supporting a different position. Destructive conflict may result in a decline in team member satisfaction, commitment, and overall productivity. Virtual teams are no different from traditional teams in this regard. They can and do suffer from conflict between team members. What is different, however, is that destructive conflict may be more difficult to detect in a virtual setting. And since virtual team members don't have the advantage of face-to-face rich interaction, resolving conflicts may be particularly challenging.

There has been much written on how to manage or handle conflict. Perhaps one of the most widely cited theorists on conflict-handling strategies is Kenneth Thomas (1976), who outlined five conflict-management styles. For Thomas, how you behave in handling any given conflict depends on two concerns: how important your goals are to you and how important you perceive your relationship to others to be. Given these two major concerns, five basic strategies may be used to manage conflict. See Table 4.6.

Table 4.6 Five Conflict-Management Strategies

1. *Collaboration*: Because both your own goals and the relationships you have with others are important to you, you use problem-solving negotiations to resolve conflict. Solutions are sought that will ensure that both you and the other individuals involved will fully achieve your goals.

2. *Compromising*: You are moderately concerned with your own goals and with maintaining relationships with others. You give up part of your own goals and sacrifice part of the relationship with others to reach agreement. It is a meeting in the middle.

3. *Accommodation*: The relationship you have with others in the conflict situation is more important to you than your own goals. Thus, you give up your goals to maintain your relationships with others.

4. *Competition*: You have a high concern for yourself and see your goals as very important. On the other hand, you have a low concern for others and maintaining a relationship with them is not important to you. You attempt to win and have others in the conflict situation lose. People who use this style try to overpower others by forcing them to give in.

5. *Avoidance*: Your own goals are not that important and neither is maintaining the relationships you have with others. Sometimes withdrawal is used initially to step back from the conflict situation until you and the other person are able to calm down and gain control of your feelings.

Source: Description of Thomas' model adapted from Thomas (1976).

To be effective at resolving conflict, one must be competent in using each of the five strategies. Be sure to establish when each of the strategies is and is not appropriate to use. Susan Fritz and her colleagues (1999) provide a set of circumstances in which each of these strategies should be used. See Table 4.7 for details.

Table 4.7 Appropriateness of Conflict-Management Strategies

Conflict Management Style	When to Use	When Not to Use
Collaboration	• Others' lives are involved. • You do not want to have full responsibility. • There is a high level of trust. • You want to gain commitment from others. • You need to work through hard feelings, animosity, and the like.	• Collaboration may not be the best strategy when time is limited, or when trust is not high among the conflicting parties.
Compromising	• The goals are moderately important but not worth the use of more assertive strategies.	• Compromising does not generally work well when initial demands

Table 4.7 Appropriateness of Conflict-Management Strategies, Cont'd

Conflict Management Style	When to Use	When Not to Use
Compromising	• People of equal status are equally committed. • You want to reach temporary settlement on complex issues. • You want to reach expedient solutions on important issues. • You need a backup strategy when competition or collaboration does not work.	are too great from the beginning and there is no commitment to honor the compromise.
Accommodation	• The issue is more important to the other person than it is to you. • You discover that you are wrong. • Continued competition would be detrimental and you know you cannot win. • Preserving harmony without disruption is the most important consideration.	• Accommodation should not be used when the issue at stake is very important to you and needs to be addressed immediately.
Competition	• You know that you are right. • You need a quick decision. • The other individual is a steamroller type and you need to stick up for your own rights.	• You should consider, however, that competition will certainly not enhance a team's ability to work together and will reduce cooperation among members.
Avoidance	• The stakes are not that high and you do not have anything to lose. • You do not have time to deal with the problem. • The context is not suitable to address the conflict; it is not the right time or place. • More important issues are pressing. • You see no chance of getting your concerns met. • You would have to deal with an angry, hotheaded person. • You are totally unprepared, taken by surprise, and you need time to think and collect information. • You are too emotionally involved and the others around you can solve the conflict more successfully.	• Avoiding may not be appropriate when the issue is very important and postponing dealing with the conflict will only make matters worse.

Source: Fritz, Susan M.; Brown, William F.; Lunde, Joyce Povlacs; Banset, Elizabeth A. *Interpersonal Skills for Leadership*, 1st Edition, 1999. Adapted by permission of Pearson Education, Inc., Upper Saddle River, N.J.

If one word could capture the advice for virtual teams in dealing with conflict, it would be "clarify." Clarify tasks, roles, deadlines, expectations, and even clarify what conflict strategies your team considers appropriate to use and when. Take some time as a team to discuss when each of the five strategies for resolving conflict are appropriate for your team. Then distribute the results to all members of the team, perhaps publishing conflict management norms on your team's Intranet Web page, along with other relevant team norms. (See Chapter Seven for more information on establishing team norms.) Complete the following exercise in your next face-to-face or synchronous meeting.

Team Activity: Clarifying Conflict Handling Strategies

Complete the following activities as a team.

1. Revisit the guidelines offered in Table 4.7 by Fritz and her colleagues (1999) as to when each of the strategies for resolving conflict is appropriate to use.

2. Discuss each of the five conflict strategies and when they would be appropriate to use in the context of your team.

3. Construct a set of guidelines for when to use each strategy. Capture the ideas generated, using the chart that follows.

4. Document and publish your team's conflict-management guidelines. Make sure every member of the team has a copy.

Your Team's Conflict-Management Guidelines

Use Collaboration when	Use Compromising when	Use Accommodation when	Use Competition when	Use Avoidance when

As virtual teams move to resolve conflict, a simple procedure may prove invaluable. Consider the following steps for conflict resolution:

1. *Establish team norms and ground rules*—Before actual conflict resolution can occur, spend time outlining appropriate team norms and ground rules for working through the conflict situation (for example clarifying conflict strategies to use and specifying appropriateness of various communication tools).

2. *Collect and gather relevant information*—Collect data on what the conflict is about and reflect on the causes and effects of team members' differing positions in the conflict situation.

3. *Information sharing*—Team members share the information they collected on the causes of conflict with the entire team. Using appropriate supportive communication skills, team members probe and ask open-ended questions to clarify and ensure mutual understanding. Out of this dialogue, team members work toward discovering what is of common interest.

4. *Solution generation and action planning*—Outline specific solutions to deal with issues causing conflict. There may be a prolonged period of negotiation, where the emphasis should be on suggesting partial solutions or compromising, but still emphasizing common goals. After agreeing upon a solution, discuss what actions need to be taken to implement the solution. Then review, summarize, and confirm areas of agreement for action.

5. *Action is taken and progressively reviewed*—Evaluate actions for how well they resolved the team's problems. Meet periodically, if necessary, to ensure a smooth transition after the actions are taken.

Effective conflict resolution in virtual teams requires that team members take the initiative to be open, communicate supportively, understand one another's conflict management strategies, and clarify ambiguous situations or messages. For virtual teams, additional tips are as follows:

- Use appropriate technology tools to deal with conflict. Do not attempt to settle differences through e-mail. A preferable method would be to use the telephone or meet with the person face-to-face.

- Address and deal with conflicting loyalties and agendas between team members and between the team and others inside and outside of the organization.

- Have the team leader and team members jointly take an active role in clarifying ambiguous tasks.

- Use professional and organizational codes of ethics, if needed, to resolve conflicts of interest.

- Use appropriate conflict-management strategies (spelled out in team norms).

- Realize that conflict is a normal fact of life and focus on the task, not on the person.

- Because destructive conflict may be difficult to catch in a virtual setting, continually survey the feelings of the team to ensure that conflict produces only positive tension. Don't let tensions build or fester.

- Deal with the "out of sight out of mind" mentality that may occur in virtual teams by assertively (rather than aggressively or passively) reminding your colleagues about your ideas or concerns.

Problem Solving and Decision-Making

When conflicts arise in virtual teams—and they will because of the functional, organizational, or cultural differences, and possible different agendas of team members—those involved need to be able to solve problems and make decisions. Team problem-solving or decision-making is the process of reaching a solution or judgment about something (a task, agenda, crisis, issue, problem) based on the input, ideas, and feedback from more than one individual. Virtual team members need to be able to collaboratively solve problems and also to independently solve problems and make decisions. Because virtual team members typically work on their own, they need to be able to make effective decisions on their own. Differences in time zones and the inability to access one's team members easily may not support consultative decision-making processes. This does not imply, however, that everyone on a virtual team is off on their own making decisions without consulting their team members. Virtual teams need to have honest discussions about what decisions can and should be made independently and what decisions require input from subsets or the entire team. Some suggestions for solving problems and making decisions in your virtual team follow:

- Clarify the team's purpose, vision, goals, and interests. Publish and give this information to all members and use this information to make decisions.

- If you are working independently and need advice to make a decision, agree on what procedure you will use and how to get in touch. For example, you may agree to contact the project team leader first; if the project team leader is unavailable you may agree to then contact the managing senior partner.

- Clarify who has authority to make what decisions, and what will happen if you can't agree. (See Chapter Seven for more information on project review, revision, and final approval norms.)

- Don't try to push your opinions on others. Present your position as clearly and rationally as possible, but listen to other members' feedback and carefully consider others' input before you move on.

- Avoid changing your mind only to reach agreement and avoid conflict. Only support solutions that you find agreeable.

- Seek out differences of opinion, even to the point of possibly soliciting input from outside the team. Try to involve all team members in the decision because they represent a wide range of information and opinions. This can help the team to reach a higher-quality solution.

- Decipher and discuss underlying assumptions through listening carefully to one another and encouraging the participation of all members.

To accomplish creative tasks, individuals and teams need to be able to effectively solve problems and make decisions. Some researchers even suggest creative thinking and problem-solving are really one and the same. (For more information about techniques to develop creative thinking, see Chapter Six.) There is some truth to that. Linear creative techniques do require problem-solving. And, of course, decisions need to be made throughout a team's creative process.

Stress Management

Stress is a reality in the "anytime, anyplace global workplace" (O'Hara-Devereaux and Johansen, 1994). The days of nine to five office hours have been uprooted by a new generation of ultra-portable devices that make it easy to access individuals no matter where they are or what time of day it is. (For a discussion of the importance of setting availability norms, see Chapter Seven.) As teams have become more global in composition, the work day has expanded to meet the needs of varying time zones. It is not uncommon for individuals to attend audio or desktop videoconferences in the wee hours of the morning (although good team leaders balance this inconvenience among all the members of the team). As the boundaries of a typical work day get pushed, team members' stress levels may rise. In addition, many virtual teams are brought together quickly to meet pressing marketplace needs, and as a result, members may be faced with tight, sometimes unrealistic deadlines. The result is stress, caused by the new burdens of working in a virtual environment. Stress causes anxiety, which prevents individuals from working effectively and from possibly taking any further action. Stress also hampers creativity. Emotions that result from stress, such as anxiety, anger, and depression, are blocks to creative thought (Miller, 1987, 1999).

But stress is not always a negative force. There can be beneficial consequences to stress, including increased motivation, better problem solving or decision-making, higher levels of challenge and personal growth, and even increased creativity. For virtual team members, being adept at stress management is a necessity. A list of strategies for coping with stress follows:

- Determine what the stressor is, and select an appropriate action to deal with the stressor. Virtual team members tend to be task-oriented by the very nature of working in a modular work design approach (see Chapter One). Applying a modular work design model when dealing with stress is probably the most effective way to respond to stress.

- Utilize standard time management techniques. (See the next section on time management and personal productivity for specific suggestions on how to manage time.) Also, use calendaring and scheduling programs to help manage and organize time and resources.

- Rely on the kindness and support of others. As discussed in Chapter Three, virtual team members can experience high levels of personal bonding. Use the support network of your team members to seek out help, talk out issues, or release pent-up emotions.

- Cognitively restructure negative thinking. Challenge your catastrophic thinking. If you are feeling something cannot be done, ask why? Ask what you might need to make it happen. Then focus on making it happen. Positively reinterpret a stressful event; search for the good in the bad.

- Use humor. Send out amusing stories or jokes if team norms permit this.

- Distract yourself by taking a break to alleviate stress or to refresh your thinking. However, be careful not to avoid work or let personal issues interfere with your productivity, especially if you are working at home.

- Use relaxation techniques, such as exercise, meditation, visualization, and rest. I've even heard of a virtual team beginning an anticipated stressful videoconference with a team meditation moment.

Time Management and Personal Productivity

Because there is less on-site daily direction and less visibility of what individual team members are doing, virtual team members need to exhibit high levels of personal initiative and self-management. Virtual team members must be able to achieve personal productivity with minimal direction. They must be able to set goals, prioritize tasks, manage projects, and effectively manage the use of their time. In addition, they must be flexible and take the initiative to make changes when needed and follow-up by communicating those changes to team members.

In Chapter Three, we saw how accountability is essential for building trust within a virtual team. Virtual team members who cannot manage their time appropriately run the risk of not accomplishing important tasks on time or of completing them haphazardly. Late, shoddy, or less-than-thorough performance causes team members to doubt others' accountability and, as a result, impacts trust within the team. Since most virtual teams utilize a modular work design approach and rely on each member completing his or her portion of the project, when even one team member does not adequately manage his or her time, the entire team may suffer. A list of standard time management strategies follows:

- Break down a task into manageable chunks. Set priorities for which chunks need to get done first.

- Streamline your work and focus on important tasks first. In doing so, make sure you concentrate on only one important task at a time. If you can, try to complete that one task before moving on to something else.

- Distinguish between what is important and what is urgent. Then spend time on important matters, not just on those that demand your attention.

- Chart out a time log to help you identify on what tasks or activities you are using your time and pinpoint those tasks or activities you can eliminate. Make sure you review this log often so you can eliminate tasks that really don't need to get done.

- Prioritize actions daily. Establish your own criteria to prioritize, which may include your own feelings and degree of interest, the importance of the task to you and others, and the sense of urgency of the task for you and others.

- Find out when your most productive time of the day is and schedule your most important activities for that time. And protect that time; don't let other less important tasks or issues distract you.

- Make sure to give yourself some personal time daily.

- When possible, delegate.

- Say no without guilt.

The following time management and personal productivity techniques are more specific to those working out of a virtual office:

- Act as if you work in a traditional office. Set regular hours, get dressed, have a separate office, if possible, establish a clear workspace at home and let others in the house know you cannot be disturbed.

- Stay in touch with teammates to make sure you get all necessary and important information.

- Minimize conducting personal life issues at the same time you are working. For example, do not watch television while working.

- Set regular times for meals, snacks.

- Use the technology you have at home to send and receive information and project files.

- Make a commitment to others. It is especially useful if you make that commitment in written form. For example, promise a report on a certain date in an e-mail message. The fact that you have committed to something in written form (even if it is not a formal contract) makes it psychologically official. However, be sure when you are making a deadline commitment that you can realistically accomplish that task within the timeframe specified.

- Manage information and knowledge. Control the amount of paperwork and electronic work you need to go through. (For more details, see also the Knowledge Management, Data Gathering, and Information Access section further in this chapter and the section on project and task management norms in Chapter Seven.)

Source: Some of the above strategies were adapted from DuBrin, A. (2004). *Human Relations: Interpersonal, Job-Oriented Skills.* 8th ed. Upper Saddle River, NJ: Pearson Educational Inc./Prentice Hall.

In managing time, it is important to focus on both efficiently using time each day and on effectively using time over the long term. Many of the strategies just reviewed focus on ways to use time more efficiently. However, efficiency without effectiveness is futile. To make sure you are effectively using your time, you must match the use of your time with your core goals, values, or interests.

Developing and Motivating Others

Managers and leaders are generally regarded as those individuals responsible for motivating the members of a team. This no longer holds, as all members of a virtual team are today responsible for developing and motivating others. Why has this change occurred? First, as mentioned in Chapter Two, virtual team members are being asked to play both the role of team leader and team member simultaneously. Second, virtual team members typically have more freedom and autonomy than their traditional cohorts and, as a result, develop personal strategies to motivate and improve their own behavior, such as self-reward, self-punishment, self-goal setting, and positive self-talk. Lastly, virtual team members are likely to interact with a variety of peripheral team members (such as customers, clients, suppliers) in addition to core members of the team. Even in these peripheral interactions team members need to practice the competency of motivating others. Recall in Chapter Three the quote that Cindy, a member of the WN–Current Events team, shared revealing a sense of trust with core members of her team, but a lack of trust with peripheral team members or individuals external to both the team and organization: "I trust my team. I'm more leery of people outside of my team." In short, the competency of developing and motivating others, once assigned only to team leaders and managers, is now a skill that all virtual team members need to acquire and own.

There are four elements to developing and motivating others from afar—supporting, coaching, empowering through delegating, and recognizing and rewarding team members. In reality, these are the same strategies used to develop and motivate team members in traditional teams. However, implementing these strategies frequently requires different approaches in the virtual world.

Supporting

After setting goals, the most critical factor in developing and motivating others is to create a supportive and encouraging environment. This means supporting team members by showing acceptance, consideration, and concern for their individual needs and feelings. The skills of supportive communication (previously discussed) are an important element in achieving an encouraging work environment.

Coaching

Coaching involves giving advice to a team member to help improve his or her specific skills. Coaching is a day-to-day, hands-on process of helping workers to grow and improve their job competence by providing suggestions and encouragement. A coach analyzes work performance, provides insight as to how performance can be improved, offers leadership and a supportive climate, and provides instruction, guidance, advice, and encouragement. However, coaching changes when you do this from a distance. Fisher and Fisher (2001) offer the following tips for distant coaching:

- Start by clarifying goals and measures. Do this with a lot of communication and employee involvement. Then, create accountability systems, based on these goals and measures. Strive for shared accountability, which creates a real feeling of partnership.

- Use Socratic coaching techniques. Ask questions instead of giving answers. This builds in virtual team members the ability to make decisions independently, something they need to be able to do.

- Be a proactive coach. Do more than just address problems or accomplishments as they arise. Coach along the way, and also at specific assessment points, such as at the end of projects, assignments, and tasks.

- Respond to subtleties and nuances. Watch for clues that signal the need to step in and coach.

- Implement a peer feedback process. One technique involves asking all team members to share with one another behaviors they would like them to *stop, start,* and *continue* doing.

- Establish regular one-on-one coaching sessions with each team member.

- Coach to improve performance. When performance issues warrant it, develop and use a structured improvement plan. The plan should primarily be developed by the employee, but the coach should be clear about expectations and elements that need to be included in the plan. Along the path of achieving the plan, provide regular coaching to ensure success.

Source: Constructed from Fisher, K., and Fisher, M. D. (2001). *THE DISTANCE MANAGER: A Hands-On Guide to Managing Off-Site Employees and Virtual Teams.* New York: McGraw-Hill. Reproduced with permission of The McGraw-Hill Companies.

Empowering Through Delegating

Empowerment means sharing power with subordinates and pushing down decision-making and implementation power to those most affected by the decisions made. It involves sharing relevant information and knowledge to allow employees to do what is needed to meet team and organizational goals. Team leaders and managers who empower are facilitators who guide their teams using knowledge and experience, rather than using coercive influence. One of the main advantages shared when I asked the virtual team members what they liked about this type of work was flexibility of schedule. But to develop and motivate others, team members need to be empowered to do more than merely adapt their schedules. They need to have (as mentioned earlier in this chapter) freedom to do the work as well.

A primary way to empower others is through delegation. Some tips for successful delegation are as follows:

- *Allow team members to participate and be involved in the delegation of tasks.* Ensure subordinate acceptance of responsibilities. Involve people in making decisions that affect them. Take into account individual differences in motivation and skills. Provide team members with a variety of experiences. Delegate both pleasant and unpleasant tasks.

- *Make the delegation assignment clear.* Provide clear goals and guidelines regarding expectations and limitations. Specify responsibilities clearly. Clarify the assignment of the work task; determine what is to be delegated and to whom. Specify limits of discretion and reporting requirements and inform others about the delegation.

- *Provide support and resources.* As a task is delegated, provide necessary support and resources (i.e., time, training, information, and advice) needed to complete the task. Remove bureaucratic constraints and unnecessary controls. Express confidence and trust in team members, and provide coaching and advice when requested (see earlier tips on distant coaching).

- *Monitor and provide feedback.* Keep track of progress and provide feedback during and after task completion. Establish systems of accountability.

- *Delegate to different followers.* Delegate tasks to those who are most motivated to complete them, as well as to those who have potential but no clear track record of performance yet in that area.

- *Treat mistakes as a learning experience.* When problems surface, if they do, solicit input or recommendations from the team member.

Source: Some of the tips were adapted from Yukl, G. (2002). *Leadership in Organizations.* 5th ed. Upper Saddle River, NJ: Prentice Hall.

Rewarding and Recognizing

A key thing to understand when motivating others is that people are primarily motivated by *what's in it for them.* Offering rewards, praise, appreciation, and recognition for effective performance, significant achievements, or important contributions are some of the ways we can help to communicate to others what's in it for them. Virtual team leaders need to develop the ability to give rewards that support virtual collaboration. Although traditional reward and recognition programs can be used for virtual teams, there are additional ways to reward and recognize virtual team members. For virtual teams, reward and recognition can come in the way of celebrating milestones. Fisher and Fisher (2001) offer the following tips for celebrating at a distance:

- Celebrate both team and individual accomplishments.
- Celebrate milestones (not only the big finish).
- Include face-to-face celebrations.
- Hold an annual or semi-annual goal achievement review activity.
- Respect personal preferences when deciding how to celebrate. What may be a reward for one person may not be for another.
- Create a place on your Intranet for posting best practices.
- Celebrate the small stuff, such as personal milestones, birthdays, anniversaries, childbirths, and so on.
- Use portable parties. Put together a party kit and send to all members during a teleconference or videoconference.
- Use e-gift certificates.
- Include others (perhaps senior managers, executives, and other interested co-workers) in the celebration, either electronically or face-to-face.
- Invest personal time to make celebrations and recognition more meaningful.
- Ask the team members how they would like to celebrate.

Source: Constructed from Fisher, K., and Fisher, M. D. (2001). *THE DISTANCE MANAGER: A Hands-On Guide to Managing Off-Site Employees and Virtual Teams.* New York: McGraw- Hill. Reproduced with permission of The McGraw-Hill Companies.

Good team leaders, managers, and members get things done with the assistance of others. Whether you are a virtual or traditional team member, the same holds true. You can get a lot more work done by developing and motivating those who work with you.

Positive Political Skills

Because of the boundary-crossing composition of virtual teams, individuals who are virtually working together may and often do have different agendas, different ideas for how resources should be used, and different suggestions for new actions to take. It is a fact of organizational life that some individuals or teams within an organization are more powerful than others. Power is generally defined as the ability or capacity to influence others, to get them to do what you want.

Politics is power turned into action. Politics involves using one's power to influence others. Politics relates to who gets what, when, and how. Although politics is normally viewed in a negative light (and certainly there are instances in which politics can be illegitimate, extreme, or can violate what is ethical), there is a side to politics that can be useful. Positive political skills (DuBrin, 2004) are normal everyday politics that can be used to ensure better performance and more support for your team's creative efforts.

Positive political skills help build good relations with others, which in turn can help you and your team accomplish your work and lead to career success. Few individuals, even in traditional teams, can achieve success without having at least an awareness of the political forces that surround them and how to use them. If you have a good relationship with relevant others, you are much more likely to have them on your side, influence them, and ultimately gain power.

For virtual teams, whose members are often dispersed from the central "corporate" setting, and who lack day-to-day rich interactions with teammates, it is hard to know and read the political forces within an organization. You may recall in Chapter Two the quote the leader of the OfficeTech team shared about the definite advantage it was for his team that he (as the leader) was located at the corporate office. It allowed him to stay politically connected, to understand the political landscape of the organization, to champion the team, and, if needed, defend their actions as well. Positive political skills are made up of three elements:

- Impression management—managing the impression you display for others

- Using positive political strategies to improve interpersonal relationships,
- Avoiding hazardous political mistakes

Impression Management

Impression management is a set of behaviors directed at enhancing one's image by managing the impression you display to others. This is not an easy task for individuals who rarely see each other face-to-face and who may have only occasional auditory exchanges as well. If interpersonal interaction within the team is text-based and electronic, people are more likely to misread what is being shared or get the wrong impression. In addition, when others do misread each other and get the wrong impression in a virtual setting, there may not always be the opportunity to "make it right." What follows are some tips for managing your impression in the virtual workplace:

- Before you send any electronic message off, take the time to review what you have written. Put yourself in the receiver's shoes and try to see how he or she might interpret what you wrote. Never send an angry e-mail right away. Always reread it and send it later after you have had a chance to calm down and, as a result, tone it down.
- Think about silence as well; no response (even to e-mail messages) is sometimes seen as rude.
- Make sure you allow time for face-to-face meetings and attend social gatherings when possible.
- Traditionally, impression management has been equated with clothing and appearance. For virtual team members, what is more important (at least when these individuals are dispersed) is how you tell others about your accomplishments. Company, team, and individual Web pages, sharing personal e-mail messages, keeping in touch, and sending thank you notes with praise are all good ways to publicize your accomplishments.

Using Positive Political Strategies

Political strategies you may use to gain more power and influence for yourself and your team within the organization include the following:

- *Be assertive, not aggressive*—Since there are fewer opportunities for direct communication in virtual work than in regular office settings, virtual team members must take advantage of opportunities for direct communication when those situations occur. Learn how to be assertive and stand up for your best interests in an interpersonally effective way. To do this, speak clearly and own your feelings. Avoid confrontational language. Maintain eye contact and a firm body posture. Speak with a pleasant but firm tone.

- *Use reason to persuade*—Use logical arguments and factual evidence to persuade others that a request is viable and likely to attain task objectives.

- *Supplement reason with appeals*—Emotional appeals use language that touches others' emotions. With inspirational appeals, an individual makes a request that arouses enthusiasm by appealing to others' values and ideals. Personal appeals involve asking someone to carry out a request out of friendship or as a personal favor.

- *Network with influential people*—Develop contacts with people who can influence others in your behalf. Networking can occur inside and outside of an organization or team.

- *Volunteer for assignments*—Especially volunteering for assignments that may not fit nicely into your job description displays your initiative.

- *Flatter influential others*—The old saying, "You can get more flies with honey than vinegar" applies in organizational life. Seek to get individuals in a good mood or to think favorably of you by flattering them before asking them to do something. Build good relationships by flattering people sensibly and credibly. Another way to flatter is to listen with interest. This makes others feel important.

- *Acquire information power, and use it*—Being the source of needed information gets you more power. Controlling vital information includes knowing how to gain access to useful information that others do not know how to retrieve. (See also the competency of Knowledge Management, Data Gathering, and Information Access described later in this chapter.)

- *Stay (or at least appear) cool under pressure*—Losing your cool or showing signs of panic under pressure may damage your reputation with influential people. In contrast, appearing to be in emotional control under pressure gives the impression you are worthy of more responsibility.

- *Express constructive disagreement*—If you disagree with an influential superior or co-worker, use carefully worded, inoffensive statements to convey disapproval, disagreement, or discontent. Accurately and constructively express your feelings. Be diplomatic.

- *Sell the benefits*—Sell the benefits of a prospective idea, program, or suggested action. Mask your self-interest by presenting how it will benefit the organization. Develop the ability to convince your supervisor that an issue that is important to you is also important to the team and organization.

- *Exchange favors*—Every parent knows the value of developing a buddy system. ("I'll pick up your child from school one day, if you pick up mine another.") The same philosophy holds in organizations. Here, an individual makes a promise that you will receive rewards or tangible benefits if you comply with a request, or reminds you of a prior favor to be reciprocated. Reciprocal logic requires that you do something for others if you want them to do something for you.

- *Increase visibility*—As a virtual team member in an electronic world, one of the key things you can do is to keep yourself and your efforts visible. This means you should expand contacts, make presentations, join task forces, send personal notes, and the like. The team should also keep its work visible to the organization.

- *Ensure your credibility*—You are more likely to be able to persuade people if others trust and have confidence in you. To earn that trust and confidence from others, be competent at what you do and have worthy and ethical intentions about what you are doing.

Political strategies do not have to be used in a deceptive or covert manner. Virtual teams benefit from holding discussions on what strategies they find most useful and when to use them, and what strategies they want to avoid. Defining team norms for how to influence others, especially outside of the team, can lead to more successful influence attempts.

Avoiding Hazardous Political Mistakes

Gaining power and influence is like losing weight. It is hard to do, but can be ruined with one big meal or political blunder. To avoid losing the power you have accumulated, it is critical that you avoid making political blunders.

DuBrin (2004) suggests that, to avoid political blunders, you should avoid the following actions:

- Criticizing your team leader in a public forum
- Bypassing your team leader
- Being openly disloyal to the team and/or organization (i.e., making it known you are looking for another job)
- Being a pest or overly persistent in asserting a request
- Being perceived as a poor team player
- Burning your bridges or creating ill will among former employers

Knowledge Management, Data Gathering, and Information Access

As a virtual team member, you have probably experienced a time (or perhaps many) when you have had a question or needed some information and could not get in touch with the person who had the answer to that question or get access to the relevant information. Virtual team members will not always be able to contact who they need, when they need to, nor will they have access to all relevant information when they need it. They will need to be able to sort through the knowledge, data, and information they do have and to be able to analyze information in order to make decisions. Skills to develop in this competency include the following:

- *Proficiency with technological tools*—The virtual team member must be proficient in a variety of tools and technologies, including e-mail, collaborative software systems, the Internet and Intranet, desktop and standard videoconferencing systems, and audioconferencing. Virtual team members need to know when specific technological tools are appropriate and when they are not. They also need to observe proper etiquette or protocols for each technology. (A good way to begin acquiring this knowledge is to make sure you have read Chapter Five and the section on communication norms in Chapter Seven.)
- *Critical thinking skills*—Virtual team members must be able to analyze and judge the relevance of information, as well as acquire knowledge to make decisions. Thinking critically also helps you to influence others and decide

whether to be influenced yourself. Strategies for critical thinking include being able to analyze assumptions, recognize cultural values, recognize when evidence is needed to support a claim, recognize fallacies, and understand the rhetorical tools available to you when you create an argument.

- *Library and Internet search skills*—Although virtual team members generally do not need to be experts in conducting research, they should be proficient at searching for the most current information and knowledge.

- *Ability to access and manage project data, schedules, and assignments*—A virtual team member must be able to plan and organize individual work so that it corresponds to the team's work. (See the section on project and task management norms in Chapter Seven.)

- *Ability to sort through and deal with information overload*—To control information overload, virtual team members need to make choices about what information to share with whom and by what media, and to be able to sort through and filter out unnecessary, irrelevant, or less pressing information. (Again, see the section on project and task management norms in Chapter Seven.)

Career Advancement

For nearly 20 years, I worked as a film editor in a freelance capacity. To be able to survive in the freelance market, one has to quickly develop an appreciation for and the ability to advance your career. Virtual team members need to know the same, as more and more companies are outsourcing and using contract workers, many of which are virtual teams. Some virtual team members, especially telecommuters, believe that opportunities for promotion are considerably less as a "virtual" member of the organization due to their autonomy and lack of day-to-day contact with their manager and other key business leaders. Further, many virtual teams are fluid in nature with ever-changing membership, which may also affect a virtual team member's ability to advance in a particular setting. Thus, virtual team members have to actively work to advance their careers.

There is a reason why I chose to talk about this competency last. One of the most important things an individual can do to advance his or her career is to develop and practice all of the competencies previously discussed. For example, developing self-awareness helps you to understand where your creative interests and passion lie. Developing an interpersonal awareness, supportive communication, and cross-cultural communication skills leads to better relations with others. Stress and time management help you to be more personally productive. Finding and working with the right distant coach can help to further your job performance and subsequent career success. Positive political skills help you to gain support from influential people. And so on.

You may find the following strategies helpful in advancing your career:

- *Find out where your passion lies and be passionate about what you are doing.* Research has shown that when you are doing what you are passionate about and are highly intrinsically motivated to do your work, you will also be highly creative as well (Amabile, 1983). As Peter Drucker (1985) says, "To succeed, innovators must build on their strengths" (p. 138).

- *Keep growing through continuous learning and self-development.* Strive to stay on top of your particular area of expertise and your technological skills. Develop depth and breadth. Participate in the creation of knowledge by writing articles or books and making presentations. Document your accomplishments. (See Chapter Eight for more information on how your team can continually learn and assess itself.)

- *Work with a mentor.* Find someone you trust and whose career you would like to emulate and develop a mentoring relationship with him or her. Listen to your mentor, work with him or her, and learn what you can.

- *Build a network of influential people around you and don't be afraid to rely on them.*

- *Take sensible risks.* Doing something new shows others you have the ability to handle extra responsibility. However, pursuing only those risks you see as sensible assists in avoiding potentially damaging risk-taking experiences.

- *Learn about the organization you work for and make sure it is a good fit for you.* Take the initiative to learn about the organizations in which you work. Learn about the culture that guides behavior, the standard ways of operating, the mission and vision that drives your organization, and the leadership styles of those who lead you. Learn who is powerful, who can provide you with crucial information, who is supportive, and who is not so supportive. Then realistically assess how the organization fits with your own professional and personal values and goals.

Assessment Tool: Analyzing Personal Strengths and Gaps in Team Member and Management Competencies

Here I offer an assessment tool that members of your virtual team can take independently to assess their level of functioning with respect to the competencies just discussed. An accurate assessment of these competencies should allow for the fact that *not all competencies may be of equal importance to every virtual team.* With this in mind, I have designed this instrument to allow the members of your team to assess both how they currently stand with respect to each of the competencies discussed and how important they feel each of these competencies is to their team. This yields an individualized assessment of the necessary competencies for each virtual team member. Action plans for future growth should probably focus around individual team members' pronounced *gaps* (competencies an individual is performing at a "fair" or "poor/undeveloped" level that are "somewhat important" or "very important" to the team), and *areas of strength* that can be further developed (competencies individuals are performing at a "very good" level that are "somewhat important" or "very important" to the team).

Following is a list of all the competencies discussed. On the *left*-hand side of a particular competency, assess your *current* performance level with regard to the specific competency listed. Use the following scale:

1 = Poor or undeveloped

2 = Fair

3 = Very good

4 = Excellent

On the *right*-hand side of a particular competency, assess the *importance* of a particular competency to the overall performance of your team. Use the following scale:

1 = Not at all important

2 = Seldom important

3 = Somewhat important

4 = Very important

Current Level	*Competency*	*Importance to Team*
_____	Awareness of One's Personality Traits	_____
_____	Awareness of One's Personal Values	_____
_____	Awareness of One's Cognitive Style	_____
_____	Awareness of One's Interpersonal Orientation	_____
_____	Awareness of One's Attitude to Change	_____
_____	Interpersonal Awareness	_____
_____	Sending Effective Messages	_____
_____	Giving Feedback	_____
_____	Receiving Feedback	_____
_____	Active Listening	_____
_____	Cross-Cultural Communication	_____
_____	Conflict Resolution	_____
_____	Problem Solving and Decision-Making	_____
_____	Stress Management	_____
_____	Time Management	_____
_____	Distance Coaching	_____
_____	Empowering Through Delegating	_____
_____	Rewarding and Recognizing	_____
_____	Impression Management	_____
_____	Appropriate Use of Political Strategies	_____
_____	Avoidance of Political Mistakes	_____
_____	Proficiency with Technological Tools	_____
_____	Critical Thinking	_____
_____	Library and Internet Search skills	_____
_____	Ability to Manage and Access Project Data, Schedules, Tasks	_____
_____	Ability to Manage Information Overload	_____
_____	Career Advancement	_____

Final Thoughts

Part Two of this book has dealt with the dimensions necessary for a climate for creativity within virtual teams. Now you might be wondering how the climate necessary for creativity in virtual teams compares to that needed to support creativity in more traditional face-to-face teams. There has been much research looking at what is needed in the work environment to foster creativity, both for individuals and groups. In reviewing this line of research, what I have concluded is that even though virtual teams are composed of individuals who interact across organizational, geographical, and time boundaries, the conditions necessary for creativity to be realized are strikingly similar to those needed to support creativity in co-located groups. Many of the creative climate conditions I have found important through my conversations with virtual team members echo the findings of earlier researchers who investigated co-located groups and organizations. For your information, those references are provided in Table 4.8.

Table 4.8 References on Creative Conditions for Traditional Groups and Organizations

Condition	References
Goal Clarity (Chapter Three)	Amabile, 1988; West, 1990
Trust (Chapter Three)	Rogers, 1954; West, 1990
Constructive Tension (Chapter Four)	Ekvall, 1983; Runco, 1994
Challenge (Chapter Four)	Amabile & Gryskiewicz, 1987; Amabile & Gryskiewicz, 1989; Amabile et al., 1996; Ekvall et al., 1983; Nemiro, 1997; Pelz & Andrews, 1966; Runco, 1995
Collaboration (Chapter Four)	Amabile & Gryskiewicz, 1987; Ekvall, 1983; Kanter, 1983; Nemiro, 1997; Pelz & Andrews, 1966; Steiner, 1965
Freedom (Chapter Four)	Amabile & Gryskiewicz, 1987; Andrews, 1975; Ekvall et al., 1983; Nemiro, 1997
Management Encouragement and Support for Creativity (Chapter Four)	Amabile & Gryskiewicz, 1987, 1989; Andrews, 1975; Baran, Zandon, & Vanston, 1986; Daft & Becker, 1978; Ekvall, Arvonen, & Waldenstrom-Lindblad, 1983; Steiner, 1965; VanGundy, 1987

Two creative climate conditions that emerged in my research that have not been directly addressed by prior creativity researchers are information sharing and establishing a personal bond (described in Chapter Three). Perhaps because previous creativity researchers considered these dimensions to be obvious prerequisites for creativity, they did not explicitly highlight these factors in their investigations. For the virtual teams, however, information sharing and establishing a personal bond are not considered obvious. Even so, they are crucial elements in a climate for creativity, and teams have to work hard to establish and maintain both. Without communication, exchange of information, and a personal bond, a virtual team simply will not exist. In fact, Handy (1995) suggests that without a personal bond or sense of belonging, virtual organizations, of which virtual teams are often a part, are destined for a precarious future. "A sense of belonging is something humans need if they are to commit themselves to more than simple selfishness. . . . Without some real sense of belonging, virtuality looks like a very precarious state and a perilous base for the next phase of capitalism, whatever the economic and technological advantages" [p. 8]. Nevertheless, it is not surprising that both virtual and face-to-face teams require a similar climate for creativity. When the virtual team members I spoke with were asked to define a virtual team, they overwhelmingly responded that they were a *team first.*

Now it may seem that all one has to do to establish a climate for creativity within a virtual team is to eliminate practices that hinder creativity and put in place those practices that foster creativity. This approach, however, may be simple-minded and somewhat impractical. A more realistic approach would be to strive to establish a "delicate balance" of the necessary conditions (Amabile and Gryskiewicz, 1987). For example, *acceptance of ideas* is important for a creative climate, but all ideas cannot be totally accepted. In the practical business world, new ideas need to be assessed, evaluated, and sometimes dismissed. The most realistic and appropriate ideas are pursued. For another example, consider that the amount of *freedom* afforded teams in pursuing their creative tasks needs to be balanced with periods of constraint. This seems especially crucial in a virtual team, where the potential for going off into unproductive independent thought is real. One team member explains that the "efficiency of the communication in most virtual team situations may lead to some good independent thinking, some good independent effort, but it can also possibly cause people to just polarize, split off, and become disconnected" [Scott, WN–Religion Forum].

As the quote at the top of this chapter indicates, management in many contemporary companies is "rushing rather headlong into an embrace of the virtual concept" [Richard, OfficeTech]. However, management cannot assume that they can move workers into their homes and simply leave them there to do work. On the contrary, virtual team leaders and managers will need to actively develop in themselves and their virtual followers the appropriate team member and management conditions and competencies discussed in this chapter to be able to establish a climate supportive of creativity in virtual teams. Interestingly, in a working arrangement that some have referred to as "working without context" (O'Hara-Devereaux and Johansen, 1994, p. 150), context for the virtual team members I have shared discussions with was not non-existent. The climate dimensions discussed in the last two chapters form the "context" in which creativity can be realized in a virtual working arrangement. However, even with a climate supportive of creativity, teams still need appropriate and sufficient resources to produce creative work. Part III offers two chapters that describe the resources virtual teams may utilize when communicating and creating together. These resources include communication and creativity software tools, and creativity enhancement techniques.

Points to Remember

- High creativity experiences are characterized by the following:
    - Team members who feel their ideas and input are encouraged, valued, and accepted
    - A high degree of honesty among team members in sharing ideas and giving open and honest feedback
    - An understanding and appreciation of different team members' work styles
    - Constructive tension, conflict, and differing opinions of team members
    - A high-level of challenge arising from the intriguing, enjoyable nature of a problem or task, the urgent needs of a particular situation, or the desire to push for something new and move away from the status quo
    - A strong sense of collaboration allowing team members to work closely and comfortably together
    - Team members who are given the freedom to work at their own pace and to decide how to do their work
    - Supportive and encouraging management
    - Sufficient information, human, and technological resources, and time to think creatively, experiment, and try out new ways of doing things

- Low creativity experiences are characterized by the following:
    - The abrupt dismissal by management or other team members of proposed ideas
    - Unconstructive tension arising from differences in team members' cultural backgrounds, values, and belief systems
    - Work that is unenjoyable, tedious, and does not challenge team members
    - Constraint or a lack of freedom in deciding what to do or how to do the work
    - An overemphasis on the status quo, on doing things the way they have been done in the past
    - Inability to obtain appropriate and sufficient resources
    - A lack of time to think creatively and experiment with new ways of doing things
- Virtual team members require many of the same competencies that traditional, co-located team members need to establish the conditions for creativity. However, some of the competencies may differ somewhat for virtual team members. In general, virtual team members and managers need to observe the following guidelines:
    - Be aware of who they are and how they impact others
    - Supportively communicate with others
    - Be sensitive and respect the diverse individuals they work with
    - Effectively resolve conflict
    - Be able to solve problems and make decisions, both independently and with the members of their team
    - Manage stress and make effective use of their time
    - Develop and motivate others through supporting, coaching, empowering through delegating, and celebrating as a way to recognize and reward contributions and achievements
    - Use positive political skills to gain and maintain power and influence

- Be able to access and manage necessary knowledge, data, and information to accomplish their creative work

- Advance their individual careers

- The climate for creativity for virtual teams is strikingly similar to that needed to support creativity in co-located groups. This similarity makes sense when we consider that when virtual team members were asked to define a virtual team, they overwhelmingly responded that they were a team *first*.

- It is important to strive for a realistic balance of necessary team member and management conditions.

- Context is not non-existent. The dimensions described in Chapter Three and Four form the "context" that is supportive of creativity in virtual teams.

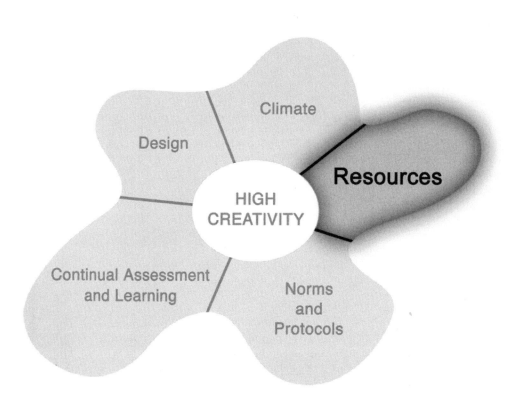

Climate

Design

Resources

HIGH
CREATIVITY

Continual Assessment
and Learning

Norms
and
Protocols

PART III

Resources

TRADITIONAL FACE-TO-FACE COMMUNICATION is declining as more and more companies are outsourcing, making use of tele-commuters, or creating virtual teams. Even in organizations where members are located in the same physical worksite, use of electronic communication is becoming prevalent. In Jessica Lipnack and Jeffrey Stamps' (1997) book on *Virtual Teams*, they describe the fifty feet rule of collaboration. They write, "The probability of people communicating or collaborating more than once a week drops off dramatically if they are more than the width of a basketball court apart. . . . Increasingly, the people we work with are no longer within shouting distance" (p. 6). Thus, even individuals in the same organizational setting, if located more than fifty feet apart, are more apt to communicate with one another electronically. So selecting appropriate communication tools is just as important for members of companies who reside in the same city as those who are dispersed across the globe. Chapter Five discusses the types of communication tools available for virtual teams and assesses which tools are most effective for each stage of the creative process. *Resources* for supporting creative work include tools to help teams communicate and also techniques to help stimulate individual and team creativity. Chapter Six describes a series of linear and intuitive creativity techniques and software tools that virtual teams may use to further stimulate ideas and enhance their creative process.

CHAPTER 5

Selecting Appropriate Communication Tools to Support the Team's Creative Process

I don't feel a whole lot of gaps in terms of what we can't do because of separation. Even the creative planning work, we seem to find ways to do that by Fax and file sending and phone combinations and conference calls. We're able to do that well. Somebody will initiate and send it out to others, get a response, get a working document, get three people on the phone, figure out where we're going with that, and that is how it works.

Matt, ACI

Usually the ideas, the sort of bigger ideas, are discussed in person. It seems like we haven't had the germination of those big ideas over the Internet or over e-mail. But the implementation and the finalization of those things are definitely done through e-mail. You know, it may be a phone call or two. We've had a couple of instances where we've had a mini-conference call with three of us, but really it seems like the big ideas have been presented to the group. So it's really verbally, in a group setting more often [than] face-to-face, that the team comes up with the big ideas.

Melanie, Job Search Consortium

I N COLLABORATIVE AND CREATIVE WORK, communication is essential. If there is faulty or no communication or inadequate information exchange, team creativity is hampered. Accomplishing creative tasks collaboratively can become particularly problematic when the very team members who are attempting to achieve the creative results are geographically dispersed throughout the globe in a virtual team. This chapter highlights the communication tools available for doing creative work.

First, the major communication tools available to virtual teams will be covered. Then, these tools will be placed in a model outlining which tools might work best for each stage of the creative process. Suggestions will be made for tools for talking (in a shared meeting place); for generating ideas; for doing (developing and designing in a shared workspace); for saving (storing and building a content repository); for finalizing and bringing closure to creative work; and for evaluating (reviewing, assessing, and learning). Then an assessment tool to help teams select appropriate communication tools to utilize during their creative process will be presented.

Communication Challenges for Virtual Teams

Each member of an effective team possesses a needed element to contribute. Effective communication behavior pulls in all these elements so that problems are collectively solved. Communication is the vehicle for creating synergy and for keeping a team together and moving it forward. However, communicating with one's team members can become problematic when those team members are geographically dispersed throughout the globe, reside in different time zones, possess different levels of technological proficiency, and come from different cultural backgrounds. Thus, one of the key challenges facing virtual teams is how to effectively communicate with one another across the miles.

Why is it difficult to communicate and exchange information virtually? One answer might be the rate or speed at which communication flows. People who are able to send electronic messages at a rapid speed may not take adequate time to clearly encode and process their thoughts and messages. In addition, because electronic information can be exchanged so quickly, information overload is a danger for those on the receiving end. As virtual team members attempt to deal with information overload, they may block out potentially important communication exchanges. In addition, much communication between virtual team members is asynchronous (not at the same time). Feedback and confirmation, then, may be delayed, leading to potentially disruptive misunderstandings and miscommunications and to time not well spent. Finally, a key answer to why communication poses such a challenge for virtual teams lies in the difficulty of transmitting complete messages and multiple cues, and offering immediate feedback through the electronic communication methods often used by virtual teams, methods that are limited in information richness (discussed in detail later). Face-to-face communication is considered the richest form of communication, but for virtual teams, where face-to-face interaction is not frequent and, in some cases, non-existent, the inherent limited richness in communication exchanges can lead to further misunderstandings and miscommunications among team members.

Thus, there is a *real need for virtual team members to learn how to be active and effective communicators and to design and utilize an effective communication plan that supports and does not detract from their creative process.* Indeed, the very survival of virtual teams depends on individual team members' ability to exchange critical information despite the challenges of time and place.

The Dimensions of Time and Place

Information technology supporting communication between virtual team members is frequently categorized along the two dimensions of time and place (O'Hara-Devereaux and Johansen, 1994). The dimension of *time* refers to whether the communication tool supports communication that occurs synchronously (at the same time) or asynchronously (at different times). Communication that is *synchronous* allows members to communicate with one another simultaneously or at the same time, as in a face-to-face conversation, telephone call, videoconferencing session, or chat room discussion. For computer-mediated communication to be synchronous, computers must be linked together in real time. *Asynchronous* communication occurs when communication between team members is not simultaneous and does not occur at the same time. Common asynchronous forms of communications are e-mail, shared database systems, and bulletin boards (an electronic notice board where users post notices). The dimension of *place* refers to whether the tool allows for co-located (same place) communication or dispersed (different places) communication. Combining these two dimensions together yields four separate categories in which some common technologies used by virtual teams can be classified, as shown in Table 5.1.

Table 5.1 Dimensions of Time and Place

Same Place and Same Time:	Different Place and Different Time:
• Face-to-face meetings • Computer meetings	• Audioconferencing • Videoconferencing • Chat technology (IRC)
Same Place and Different Time:	**Different Place and Different Time:**
• Bulletin board • Shared databases • Web pages	• Voice mail • E-mail • Intranets • Threaded discussions

For most individuals, communicating at the *same time* in the *same place* is the most comfortable type of interaction, as in face-to-face meetings. Virtual teams may incorporate varying amounts of face-to-face interaction, especially early on to develop a sense of trust among team members before they begin working together at a distance. However, this mode of communication is not the predominant form of communication for virtual teams. Thus, virtual team members may also communicate with one another at *different times* and at *different places* (for example through e-mail, voice mail, fax machines, computer conferencing, and shared database systems). They may also interact at the *same time* but from *different places* (for example, company meetings or training programs with team members or trainees in different locations linked together at the same time through audio, video, or computer conferencing). In addition, although team members may work in the *same place,* they may be physically present at *different times* through shared workstations.

At the juncture of same time and same place and different time and different place interactions is communication that can be engaged in *anytime* and *anyplace.* The key to establishing an anytime and anyplace workplace is mobility, consisting of portability and connectivity wherever one is (O'Hara-Devereaux and Johansen, 1994). Technology that supports portability and connectivity includes lightweight laptop computers, modems, and cellular phones. In their book *Global Work: Bridging Distance, Culture, and Time,* O'Hara-Devereaux and Johansen (1994) suggest that users may need to "prepare to go to work in the anytime/anyplace office with (indeed probably wearing) a wide range of portable, task-specific computer devices capable of performing such on-the-road jobs as calendaring and note-taking, document reading, or voice and text communications" (p. 88). Chad, a member of the Jacobs/Taylor organizational consulting team, explains how portable communication tools are key for the members of his team.

> I actually wear a fishing vest because it's got all the pockets and I can have everything stuffed in it, my PDA [personal digital assistant] in one pocket and cell phone in another. I don't have to think about it. I just put it on, get on the plane and I go.

The Dimensions of Social Presence and Information Richness

Available communication tools can also be evaluated according to the degree of social presence and information richness each technology offers. As teams select their communication tools and decide for what purposes each will be used, they will need to consider the degree of information richness and social presence that each communication tool offers. *Social presence* refers to the degree to which a specific type of technology facilitates warmth, sensitivity, and a personal connection with others. Face-to-face meetings have a high level of social presence, allowing for facial expressions, touch, posture, and other nonverbal cues to be communicated along with the verbal message. E-mail and other forms of written communication have far less social presence. Despite the fact that we can add emotions in our written messages by way of a variety of emoticons (i.e., sad or happy face icons), it is still much harder for a virtual team member to feel a high level of involvement or sense of interpersonal dialogue in this medium. E-mail is more of a one-way communication answered by another one-way communication, rather than a two-way personal dialogue exchange. Whether communications are synchronous or asynchronous also adds to the degree of social presence experienced. Synchronous communication tools, such as face-to-face, audio conferences, and videoconferences, have more social presence than asynchronous communication tools, such as e-mail or voice mail.

The concept of *information richness* was developed by Daft and Lengel (1984) to explain information processing behavior in organizations. Richness was defined as "the potential information-carrying capacity of data" (p. 196). More specifically, communication channels differ in their ability to handle multiple cues simultaneously, facilitate rapid feedback, and be personal. Rich communication methods are highly interactive and rely on a great deal of information, thereby reducing confusion and misunderstanding. Face-to-face communication is the richest channel because it provides for the maximum amount of information to be transmitted during a communication exchange. Multiple cues (such as words, posture, facial expression, gestures, and intonations) and immediate feedback (both verbal and nonverbal) can be shared. Lean or less rich communication methods are static or one-way and convey much less information. Computer-mediated communication is a lean channel, because no nonverbal cues are present. Moderately rich forms of communication include videoconferencing, audioconferencing, and telephone conversations. Written letters and memos are the leanest forms of communication. Table 5.2 categorizes some of the common communication tools available to virtual teams according to whether they are rich or lean and whether they offer high or low social presence.

Table 5.2 Dimensions of Information Richness and Social Presence

Tools That Are Rich and Offer High Social Presence	Tools That Are Lean and Offer Low Social Presence
Face-to-face meetings or discussions	Shared database systems
Synchronous computer conferencing (with audio and video links)	Bulletin boards
	Intranet Web pages
Videoconferencing	E-mail
Audioconferencing	Voice mail
	Fax; standard or express mail

Communication Tools Available for Collaborative and Creative Work

Although virtual teams may need electronic communication tools more than traditional co-located teams, in reality, team members who live in the same city need the appropriate communication tools just as much as team members who are dispersed across the globe. In this section, some of the more common tools available for communicating virtually are described. The tools are classified in Table 5.3 according to whether they support synchronous or asynchronous interaction.

Table 5.3 Synchronous and Asynchronous Communication Tools

Synchronous Communication Tools	Asynchronous Communication Tools
Face-to-face meetings	Asynchronous computer meetings
Synchronous computer meetings	Bulletin boards and Intranet Web pages
Videoconferencing	E-mail
Audioconferencing	Group calendars and schedules
Telephone	Voice mail
	Fax; standard or express mail

Synchronous Communication Tools

Face-to-Face Meetings

The most obvious and yet least-used method for communicating is the face-to-face meeting or discussion. Virtual teams may need to use these meetings as well. In fact, the majority of the virtual teams I spoke with had some face-to-face contact, even if only a few times a year. Face-to-face meetings for virtual teams are generally needed early in the team's creation to assist team members in sorting out what their roles will be, what goals the team will pursue, what norms will govern the team's behavior, and to develop the needed trust and personal bond to sustain them in their future of working virtually together. Common uses for face-to-face meetings are listed below.

Face-to-face meetings in virtual teams are
commonly used for the following reasons:

- To conduct strategic planning sessions and discuss the overall direction of the business

- To assess the previous year's efforts and establish goals for the upcoming year

- To conduct idea generation or brainstorming sessions

- To make creative decisions on current work

- To assess and review prior and current work projects

- To prepare team members for work assignments by establishing agendas, assigning roles and tasks, and setting goals

- To celebrate team success

- To establish, solidify, and maintain human bonds
- To address sensitive issues such as personnel and performance issues and talk through potential solutions
- To maintain client relationships
- To communicate when there are technological problems with other methods
- To respond to team members' personal crises

Most people think of face-to-face meetings as having little or relatively simple technology (such as a blackboard, flipchart, or whiteboard). However, technology can and does enter into face-to-face meetings as well. Technology that enhances face-to-face meetings may include overhead projectors, videos, computer display systems, electronic whiteboards that allow team members to save dry-erase marker notes made on the board to a connected computer, and integrated software packages shared through each participant's computer workstation. These types of technological products can help virtual teams to plan strategically, brainstorm and generate ideas, and evaluate their ideas. Technology used in these meetings can also assist in documenting and providing an electronic record of the face-to-face meeting for later reference.

Synchronous Computer Meetings

When it is not feasible to hold a meeting face-to-face, holding team meetings via a computer network is a workable option. And if these computer meetings are synchronous and have the capability to include text, audio, and video links, they can come quite close to possessing the levels of information richness and social presence that exist in face-to-face interactions. In these synchronous meetings, team members can transfer and send one another text and data files. A variety of tools may be incorporated into a synchronous computer meeting.

Team members may, for example, share typed conversations in *electronic chat rooms.* Internet Relay Chat (IRC) technology is basically an on-line equivalent of a conversation in real time. However, the chat occurs through a keyboard. For creative work, setting up separate, dedicated chat rooms to discuss different ideas, topics, or projects may be useful. On-line chat rooms also give team members the opportunity to find others outside their team who share similar interests or can offer assistance, advice, or relevant information. An added benefit to IRC technology is that it automatically creates a transcript of each chat session, which participants may review.

Instant messaging (IM) is similar to a chat room except it is between two people (not an entire team) and one does not have to enter the chat room to converse. Through an Internet Chat Query (ICQ), a team member can see if another team member is on-line. The IM chat box pops up on the screen, allowing team members to talk through text in a live, synchronous conversation. Some wireless phones are now also capable of instant messaging so team members can be reached by IM even when they are offline.

Electronic chat rooms may be combined with *interactive whiteboards* that display shared documents and allow users to sketch thoughts or ideas. Interactive whiteboards are extremely useful for virtual teams doing creative work. They allow team members to generate ideas and to write and sketch designs or diagrams in a shared whiteboard workspace for all team members to see and collaborate on. One example is The SMART Board™ (designed by SMART Technologies Inc.), which turns the computer and projector into a powerful tool for collaborating. (The SMART Board can be used as an electronic or interactive whiteboard, with or without a projector.) With a computer image projected onto the board, individual team members press on the large, touch-sensitive surface to access and control applications. Using a pen from the SMART Pen Tray, team members can draw, record notes, or highlight important information. All notes can be saved to a computer file to be printed, e-mailed, or posted to the Web.

Desktop video systems are useful in allowing team members to transmit and share either still visual images or full motion video. In addition, *desktop audio links* allow for real time, parallel voice discussion about the shared work. Sometimes referred to as Internet telephony, team members speak to one another via computer microphones and speakers.

Synchronous computer meetings require that all team members have computer, video, and audio capabilities and specialized groupware software. Although the more sophisticated multimedia synchronous conferencing systems can be costly and require all team members to have compatible systems, these systems can be an asset to virtual teams doing creative work. In addition, these systems provide an electronic record of the meeting so that absent members may later attend the meeting or so the team may have a record for future use and learning. Common uses of synchronous computer meetings are listed below.

Synchronous computer meetings are commonly used to do the following:

- Brainstorm and generate ideas
- Generate and evaluate alternative solutions
- Sketch or draw ideas, preliminary designs, prototypes, or concepts
- Display relevant data for problem solving
- List and subsequently prioritize ideas, options, or potential solutions
- List, discuss, and share opinions on certain topics
- Gain team input on initial product design
- Gain team consensus and agreement on later stages of product design
- Maintain team member involvement in complex and long-term projects
- Gain input from a variety of stakeholders on complex projects
- Capture information in meetings that would otherwise be captured on a flipchart
- Create an archive of meetings for later review

Videoconferencing

Videoconferencing supports synchronous communication of both audio and video. Dispersed team members get a sense of their colleagues' social context and physical environment. Videoconferencing requires members to use specialized video facilities, which usually requires members to communicate from a specialized room. The effectiveness of a videoconferencing session, however, varies greatly depending on the quality of video picture, which may differ in terms of motion quality (jerkiness) and resolution of the image. When the video quality is high, videoconferencing can be a good alternative to more expensive face-to-face meetings. Video rooms are often superior to desktop video links (discussed previously) because they provide higher quality images. Common uses for videoconferencing are listed below.

Videoconferencing sessions are commonly used for the following reasons:

- To conduct strategic planning sessions
- To discuss and define problems
- To list, debate, and prioritize potential solutions
- To make straightforward (not complicated) decisions

- To state and discuss opinions on specific topics
- To provide a forum for large keynote meetings (such as speakers or company state-of-the-union addresses)
- To celebrate team success

Audioconferencing

In an audioconference, all team members are simultaneously connected via a telephone call. Conference calling works well for small groups, while for larger groups a bridge is used to connect different phone lines. Audioconferencing is a relatively inexpensive and yet still effective alternative to face-to-face meetings for remote team members. It is especially useful for meetings that do not require team members to focus on a document or other visual image (unless the document or image can be shared electronically via a desktop). However, the structure and preparation required for an effective audioconference are much greater than for a face-to-face meeting. (See Chapter Seven for more information on specific protocols to be followed for preparation.) Common uses of audioconferences are listed below.

Audioconferences are commonly used for the following reasons:

- To generate ideas
- To assess and review current work
- To review previous work
- To raise new issues or concerns

Telephone

In spite of all the sophisticated communication tools available to assist teams in doing collaborative and creative work, the telephone still remains one of the more common forms of communication for those who are working across time and geographic boundaries. Of the nine virtual teams I interviewed, the telephone was the second most frequent method used, second only to e-mail. And with the advent of cell phones, people are more accessible by phone than they have been in the past. Some organizations are finding it helpful to combine cell phones, pagers, and voice mail so that if someone leaves a message, the voice mail system calls out the pager and relays the message. Then the team member can use his or her cell phone to return the message. Common uses of the telephone are listed below.

Telephone calls are commonly used for the following reasons:

- To get input, feedback, or a second opinion about how to proceed
- To ask project related questions and get answers
- To share ideas or discuss important information
- To touch base, keep in touch, or establish personal contact
- To communicate when there are technological problems with other methods
- To respond to individual team members' personal crises

While the telephone is an effective method, it is difficult to record or document a conversation for future review. Often, outcomes and actions taken after the session depend on individual memory and any notes taken.

Asynchronous Communication Tools

Asynchronous Computer Meetings

There are a variety of groupware software tools (such as Lotus Notes®, Teamware®) that allow virtual team members to work on projects asynchronously through shared database systems or shared files. *Shared database systems* allow team members to transform textual documents and e-mail messages into databases and create fields that can be searched and indexed. Information is frequently distributed on servers, and individual team members have the ability to search the database and transfer information to their personalized databases and tailor it for their own use. More sophisticated systems have the capability to store a variety of data, including multimedia information. Shared database systems provide virtual teams with the following benefits:

- Access to reference materials and stored knowledge from other teams
- A place to store the work of individual team members
- A way to review and ensure that all work in progress is updated to the latest edition and available to all members
- A place to store the team's experiences, lessons, and products for future use

Team members can access *shared files* anytime from any Web browser. This is an ideal way for remote-located or traveling team members to create and collaborate. For security purposes, access to shared files can be limited to only team members. However, with the use of shared database systems and shared files, document management becomes critical so that files are not accidentally deleted or overwritten. (See Chapter Seven for more information on project management norms and how to work effectively with shared files.) Common uses for asynchronous computer meetings are listed below.

Asynchronous computer meetings are commonly used for the following purposes:

- To brainstorm and generate ideas
- To generate ideas for plans and ideas about products
- To comment on products
- To collaboratively author written documents
- To collect data and discuss trends

Bulletin Boards and Intranet Web Pages

Bulletin board tools provide shared space for the posting of messages and ideas and for asynchronous discussions about questions or issues that do not require immediate answers. Discussions can be structured as linear or threaded. In a linear discussion, responses are added to the end of a linear chain of messages. In threaded discussions, a response can be attached directly to any message, so a discussion can potentially branch out infinitely. In general, threaded discussions seem better for question and answer applications (for example, technical support), while linear structures are more useful for extended conversation on deeper issues. Bulletin boards allow participants to become involved at their own convenience rather than having to match the schedule of others. One can take as much time as needed to read and digest what others have to say and to compose a response before posting a reply. However, it may take a lot of calendar time to complete a bulletin board discussion, and it can be difficult to reach consensus on a decision because it is hard to tell when everyone has had their say.

Many teams use the power of their company's Intranet to set up *team Web sites*. An Intranet is a network of computers within an organization that are accessible to all team members. Unauthorized access from outsiders to the network is prevented with the use of firewalls. In essence, the Intranet is like a protected neighborhood of computers within a larger city of the Internet. Intranet team Web pages provide an ideal medium for teams to publicize their efforts within an organization. If the team desires, it may make the Intranet Web pages accessible to relevant stakeholders, such as adjunct team members, vendors, clients, or customers. However, firewalls may also be used to limit the access of specific audiences to certain sections of the team's Web site. For example, a potential customer may be able to access a list of products available, but not access files on work-in-progress products that are not deliverables yet. Common uses of bulletin boards and team Intranet Web pages are listed next.

*Bulletin boards and Intranet Web pages
are useful for the following purposes:*

- Providing a quick overview of where a team and its projects are at
- Giving pertinent information to stakeholders, such as customers
- Orienting new members of a team
- Gathering large amounts of information about specific topics from diverse groups of individuals outside of the team
- Allowing team members to brainstorm
- Planning and generating ideas for product development
- Building on and commenting on the ideas of others
- Storing or archiving specialized topic databases to be used by team members in their shared work
- Collecting data and discussing trends

E-mail

E-mail is a destination address where an individual can be reached virtually, regardless of geographic address. E-mail is the most common and best understood form of information technology used for work from a distance. Most members of virtual team members view e-mail as a necessity. Many e-mail systems also offer access to a variety of mail protocols, mailboxes with a flexible folder structure, and interfaces to instant messaging services. E-mail can also be merged with other collaborative technologies (for example, audio and video links) to provide higher levels of information richness and social presence.

Studies have shown that e-mail is used for two main purposes: task-related use (such as routine information exchange, status updates, broadcasting requests, coordinating project activities, scheduling meetings) and socio-emotional, non-task related use (such as taking a break from work, keeping in touch) (Steinfield, 1986). E-mail is an excellent way to communicate about simple and straightforward issues and to share and pass along information. It is useful for sending quick, short messages that keep conversations, project pieces, and information moving forward. It can also be used to exchange and review documents using file attachments. And it may function as a stress reliever and relationship builder through the exchange of humorous jokes, inspirational stories, and other personal messages.

E-mail is freeing in that it removes the boundaries of location and time. Team members are no longer bound by rigid schedules or traditional modes of communication. Team members may communicate and interact with individuals across the globe, individuals they may never have been able to communicate with before.

E-mail is best suited for one-to-one communication and sometimes group messaging or copying others. It is not the best choice if you are expecting fast turnaround time, unless norms are in place for when team members should respond. (See Chapter Seven for discussion of availability and acknowledgement norms.)

As with any text-only tool, it is easy for misunderstandings and faulty assumptions to develop through e-mail exchanges. Without the richness of the added cues of voice, eye contact, and body language, an e-mail message can be heard much differently from how it was intended. So there are situations in which e-mail is *not* the preferred way of communicating. E-mail is not considered appropriate for issues that require high levels of interaction, such as performance-related discussions, or communicating about sensitive issues that may lead to conflict. Reaching compromises or resolving conflicts cannot effectively be accomplished through e-mail. In addition, e-mail is insensitive to cultural norms and cannot adequately convey situational context. Nevertheless, e-mail has a diverse range of purposes. Some of the more common uses of e-mail are listed next.

E-mail is commonly used for the following reasons:

- To convey routine correspondence and check status
- To update team members on schedule and calendar changes, client status, and other requests

- To make announcements or provide written status to multiple people at the same time
- To exchange comments or preliminary drafts and development work, revise plans and documents, and send documents to team members for review and feedback
- To continue threads of either project development or client contact
- To give and get project-related advice
- To make and answer requests
- To exchange hard data and information
- To document, save, and store a copy of a communication or information passed along
- To engage in a written dialogue with another individual team member
- To broadcast same ideas or messages to all members of the team (with the use of a distribution list) or quickly send out a message to the entire team
- To develop policy and set rules
- To follow up on specific policies or rules
- To keep in touch with other team members
- To build personal connection by sharing humor and personal stories

Group Calendars and Schedules

These software tools assist team members in creating and manipulating information on their individual calendars and in scheduling and coordinating team meetings and requests for resources or information that are shared among team members. Each team member's calendar and schedule can be accessible anytime from any Web browser, which reduces scheduling conflicts. Administrative staff can notify all team members of important events by posting this information to all employee calendars at once. To prevent critical events from slipping through the cracks, reminders can be sent via e-mail or wireless devices for important events and appointments. Common uses of calendars and schedules are listed below.

Calendars and schedules are useful for coordinating the following:

- Team members' activities and schedules
- Team members' use of shared resources

- Virtual teams with members who work in different time zones
- Virtual teams that are somewhat large in size
- Meetings with vendors, customers, and clients outside of the team's boundaries

Voice Mail and Pagers

Most of us are familiar with the benefits of voice mail. We call a colleague, client, or vendor with a question, request, or complaint. The individual is away from his or her desk, and a voice message answers instead. Voice mail is a convenient way to leave a message requesting a return call, instead of having to continually call until you finally find the individual in his or her office. Voice mail also offers a quick way to communicate information at a time that is most convenient for the caller. Although voice mail has definitely alleviated the frustration of being unable to reach individuals in their offices, it is not a substitute for interactive conversation between team members. Of the nine virtual teams I interviewed, the three organizational consulting teams used voice mail most regularly. Team members, often traveling and on location at a client site, would use voice mail as a way to leave a message to touch base with one another. Common uses of voice mail are listed next.

Voice mail is commonly used for the following purposes:

- To convey an urgent message (if the norm of the team is that members check their voice mail regularly)
- To relay information or make a request that is easy to understand
- To provide project status updates
- To communicate simple and clearly-stated action items

Fax, Express, and Standard Mail

When all else fails, one may always send documents, files, or drafts through Fax, Express mail, or standard mail. Some team members may prefer to receive large documents this way. These methods are useful for relaying information that cannot be posted to shared database systems (for example, client contracts), to proof documents, or as a back-up tool when other communication tools have failed (i.e., software or hardware compatibility problems). A facsimile (fax) is a copy of material that is transmitted either in hard copy or through an electronic format, and is received as a paper copy or electronically through the computer. It is useful for sending copies when a hard copy is needed quickly. Common uses for Fax, Express mail, or standard mail are listed next.

Fax, Express mail, or standard mail are
commonly used in the following situations:

- To send important, confidential documents (Express or standard mail only; many Fax machines are in public mail rooms)

- To allow team members to proof nearly completed documents in their final formatted form

- To exchange files when other electronic systems are down, or when members cannot download files due to a lack of compatibility among systems

Overall Trends

We have just reviewed the wide array of communication tools available for virtual teams. Now let's consider which tools virtual teams are really using. What I found in my discussions with virtual team members was that they were using relatively unsophisticated tools to communicate. I asked members of the nine virtual teams to rate how frequently their team used each of twelve different communication methods: face-to-face, telephone, Fax, mail, voice mail, e-mail, computer conferencing, shared database systems, remote screen sharing, video-conferencing, teleconferencing, and bulletin board services, including list servs. Table 5.4 illustrates the average frequency each of the communication methods were used by the nine teams.

Overall, several trends emerged in how the teams used communication tools.

1. For seven out of the nine teams, *e-mail was the most frequent* method of communication. Six teams (Jacobs/Taylor; VTG; ELC; OfficeTech; WN–Current Events; and WN–Religion Forum) reported using e-mail on a daily basis. Three additional teams (ACI; JSC; and AutoMax) reported using e-mail a few times a week. Clearly, virtual teams communicated frequently with e-mail.

Table 5.4 Mean Frequency of Methods of Communication for Each Team

Method	Org. Cons.			Edu. Cons.		On-line Serv.			Engineers
	ACI	J/T	VTG	ELC	JSC	OfTch	WN-CE	WN-R	AutoMax
Face-to-Face	1.2	2.5	1.3	1.0	1.0	1.0	2.3	1.0	3.3
Videoconferencing	1.0	1.0	1.0	1.7	1.0	1.0	1.0	1.0	1.2
Teleconferencing	1.7	1.5	2.3	1.0	1.2	2.7	3.0	1.0	2.5
Telephone	2.9	**4.5***	3.3	1.7	2.3	4.7	3.7	1.5	**3.7**
Voice mail	2.7	4.0	2.3	1.0	1.8	3.3	3.0	1.0	3.0
Remote screen sharing	1.3	1.0	1.0	2.3	1.0	1.3	1.0	1.0	2.5
Computer conferencing	1.0	1.0	1.0	**5.0**	1.0	1.3	1.7	1.5	2.0
Shared database system	2.0	2.5	**5.0**	4.3	1.5	3.0	3.3	2.0	2.7
BBS and list servs	1.5	1.5	2.3	4.0	1.0	3.3	2.7	2.0	2.0
E-mail	**3.2**	4.0	**5.0**	4.7	**3.7**	**5.0**	**4.7**	**5.0**	**3.7**
Fax	2.7	3.0	2.0	1.0	2.0	2.0	1.0	1.0	1.7
Mail (express or regular)	2.2	2.0	1.7	1.0	1.7	1.3	1.0	1.0	1.2

*The most frequently used communication method for each team is boldfaced. E-mail was the most frequently used method of communication in seven out of the nine teams.

Note: Scale used: 1 = rarely or never; 2 = a few times a month; 3 = a few times a week; 4 = daily; and 5 = several times a day.

Source: Nemiro, J. (2002). The Creative Process in Virtual Teams, *Creativity Research Journal, 14*(1), pp. 69–84. Used by permission of Lawrence Erlbaum Associates, Inc.

2. *Telephone was the next most frequent* method of communication used by the teams. However, some virtual teams used the telephone more frequently than others. Of the nine teams I interviewed, six teams (ACI; Jacobs/Taylor; VTG; OfficeTech; WN–Current Events; and AutoMax) used the telephone frequently. In these teams, phone calls were used to touch base and catch up, to establish personal contact, or to ask questions. For example, Matt, a member of an organizational consulting virtual team (ACI), explains how his teammates used the phone on a regular basis to touch base with each other.

> I don't think we can usually get through a week without phone contact with each of our partners. It'll be a phone call from an airport, "What's going on with, how are you, and let me tell you what's happening." I landed here today and two of my phone conversations have been with my partners, not specifically for anything but catchup. "How are you, what's going on, what's happening with your client, how're things going in your life?" and that's regular.

On the other hand, three teams (ELC; JSC; and WN–Religion Forum) used the telephone infrequently, usually to share information about an emergency. For example, they phoned each other if the computer system failed or if someone had a personal crisis. Laura, a virtual team member on the ELC education team, describes using the telephone when a team member's cat died. "It was a difficult thing, so I called her. As I say, one of the very few phone calls I've made."

3. *The extent of face-to-face (FTF) communication within the teams varied,* with one team (AutoMax) meeting FTF a few times weekly, two teams (Jacobs/Taylor; WN–Current Events) meeting FTF a few times a month, four teams (ACI; VTG; JSC; OfficeTech) meeting FTF a few times a year (rarely), and two teams (ELC; WN–Religion Forum) who had never met one another FTF. As seen here, few virtual teams are 100% virtual. Most teams have at least some scheduled face-to-face opportunities for interaction.

4. Only a *few of the teams regularly used more sophisticated forms of technology,* such as videoconferencing, remote screen sharing, and shared database systems. For example, the VTG team, an organizational consulting firm, used Lotus Notes® for pretty much everything. Face-to-face meetings

were rare for this team, since meetings were frequently held through Lotus Notes®. And since the meetings were asynchronous, members did not need to attend these meetings simultaneously. Melissa, a VTG team member, shares,

> Everything that we do is done through Lotus Notes®. Every proposal we send, every interaction, every project everybody is working on gets posted to Lotus Notes®. And basically all of our meetings are held through Lotus Notes®. We don't often need to get together face-to-face to have a meeting. Lotus Notes® holds the meeting and we participate as we feel like it, as we log in and log out. I mean, it's pretty amazing.

5. Overall, the *most* frequently used methods of communication were *e-mail, telephone, shared database systems, and voice mail*. Overall, the *least* frequently used methods of communication were *face-to-face exchanges, mail, and videoconferencing*.

I must admit I was surprised that these teams, many of whom were parts of much larger organizations with access to a variety of sophisticated networking tools, did not use some of the more sophisticated methods of communication more frequently when collaborating. In their book on *Virtual Teams: Reaching Across Space, Time and Organizations With Technology*, Lipnack and Stamps (1997) found the same phenomenon in one of the teams they studied (from Sun Microsystems). The co-team leader of that team said that because the team only had fifteen members, a highly-structured project management system (in this case, videoconferencing) would have slowed things down. The teams I interviewed were also relatively small, ranging from three to twelve members. And, in fact, the smaller teams (OfficeTech had 3 team members; WN–Religion Forum had four team members, WN–Current Events had 5 team members, and VTG had six members) relied heavily on e-mail as their standard mode of communicating, while the larger teams incorporated a wider variety of methods into their communication repertoire.

I believe the types of communication tools virtual teams are using are beginning to diversify and will continue to do so as new technologies, such as desktop conferencing with video and audio links, interactive whiteboards, and the Intranet become more available. This trend is already becoming a reality. For example, Poltrock and Sharma (1995) write about the ways in which technology for cooperative work at The Boeing Company has evolved from primarily using electronic mail, voice mail, and videoconferencing, to using a more diverse set of groupware options such as desktop conferencing, shared workspaces, and workflow management systems (which allow team members to receive electronic work instructions and/or automatically-generated e-mail messages telling them a task has been completed). Poltrock, a member of Boeing's Research and Technology organization, works with Boeing project teams to understand their technology requirements, to communicate these requirements to researchers and vendors, to acquire and evaluate emerging technologies, and to transfer them to project teams for use in their collaborative work.

Specific Tools Used During Stages of the Creative Process

As was discussed in Chapter One, virtual teams move through four stages while producing creative work: idea generation, development, finalization and closure, and evaluation. One of the first realizations that evolved from my conversations with virtual team members was somewhat simplistic but nevertheless important. *Not all virtual teams used information technology in the same way and for the same purpose during their creative process.* Table 5.5 summarizes the tools that were used most commonly by the teams in each of the four stages of the creative process. (Only two teams had members who addressed communication methods used in the evaluation stage.)

Table 5.5 Communication Methods Used by Teams in Each Stage of the Creative Process

	Stages of the Creative Process			
Team	Idea Generation	Development	Finalization and Closure	Evaluation
Consultants				
ACI	• E-mail • Teleconference • Phone • Fax • Face-to-face (*infrequent but more enjoyable*)	• E-mail • Teleconference	• Face-to-face	

Table 5.5 Communication Methods Used by Teams in Each Stage of the Creative Process, Cont'd

Team	Idea Generation	Development	Finalization and Closure	Evaluation
		Stages of the Creative Process		
Jacobs/Taylor	• Face-to-face	• Phone • E-mail	• E-mail	
VTG	• Shared databases • E-mail	• Shared databases *(for most development work)* • Face-to-face *(to sort out what is realistic)* • E-mail *(for feedback)*	• Shared databases • E-mail • Face-to-face *(for complex projects)*	
Educators				
ELC	• Computer conferencing • E-mail	• Computer conferencing • E-mail	• Computer conferencing • E-mail	
JSC	• Face-to-face	• E-mail • Phone • Fax • Teleconference	• E-mail	• Face-to-face
On-line Service Providers				
OfficeTech	• E-mail • Phone • Face-to-face	• E-mail • Phone	• E-mail • Phone	• Face-to-face
WN–Current Events	• Face-to-face • Teleconference	• E-mail	• E-mail	
WN–Religion Forum	• E-mail	• E-mail	• E-mail	
Design Engineers				
AutoMax	• Face-to-face • E-mail	• Computer conferencing • E-mail • Teleconference • Face-to-face	• Computer conferencing • Teleconference	

Source: Nemiro, J. (2002). The Creative Process in Virtual Teams, *Creativity Research Journal, 14*(1), pp. 69–84. Used by permission of Lawrence Erlbaum Associates, Inc.

After reviewing the patterns of information technology use and face-to-face contact in the creative process for the nine virtual teams, some interesting similarities and differences across the four stages of idea generation, development, finalization and closure, and evaluation became apparent.

Idea Generation

The balance between the number of teams using face-to-face encounters in the idea generation stage and those teams using electronic forms of communication was intriguing. Four teams relied primarily on face-to-face contact to generate ideas (AutoMax, Jacobs/Taylor, JSC, and WN–Current Events), and five teams relied primarily on electronic forms of communication to generate ideas (ACI, ELC, OfficeTech, WN–Religion Forum, and VTG). Teams that did use face-to-face meetings in this stage felt strongly that ideas could not be effectively generated without face-to-face interaction. For example, some members of the JSC team suggested that without face-to-face communication, synergy was lost; in fact, the only time the team felt creative was when they met face-to-face. Elaine, a JSC team member, shares the following.

> Definitely face-to-face is when the most creativity occurs. When we're e-mailing each other, I don't think that people are as creative. I feel that the physical interaction, when we're in the same room, really generates energy and creativity. We start brainstorming about areas that we want to pursue and we come up with short-range plans and how we're going to pursue that. And then once we leave, we feel like we've been very productive.

The Jacobs/Taylor team believed so much in the importance of face-to-face contact for generating ideas that it built a room intended to encourage just that behavior. Julia, one of the senior consultant members of the team, elaborates on the importance of the team's thinking room.

> The creative process of generating ideas, I've not seen work well over e-mail. Or it can work for me over the telephone sometimes but it always seemed rushed and hurried. I wouldn't say that works well for us remotely. It is difficult to have the same feeling and energy and thoughtfulness electronically. When Chad, Glen, and I get together to work on a proposal or a project for a client, we set aside time. We have a room that we call the thinking room,

and one wall is completely lined with white board. The room gets us away from everything else in our desk, and it's a room that we feel comfortable in and that we believe helps facilitate creativity. So it's not just that we were face-to-face real time, it's that we have a place where we go, and that really helps creativity.

AutoMax team members used informal face-to-face meetings and teleconferencing sessions to generate ideas and gain "buy-in" of initially proposed ideas and designs. In addition, members of the ACI team, although they infrequently generated ideas face-to-face, admitted that it was simply more fun and enjoyable to generate ideas in person.

On the other hand, five teams were able to generate ideas effectively without much face-to-face contact. In fact, some members in these teams felt generating ideas on-line was liberating. They felt less pressure to be creative and felt they could take the time to comprehend ideas and then build on them. Ideas and input were more readily offered and accepted electronically because it was easier, more comfortable, and less threatening than face-to-face contact. The facilitative effect of on-line interaction on idea generation has been supported by research on group decision rooms, a computer-based system used for synchronous and anonymous group idea generation and decision-making. This research has showed that individual group members participate more when these systems are used (Aiken and Riggs, 1993). Team members may participate more in idea generation when it is conducted on-line because they feel less subject to ridicule for possible foolish ideas and less subject to conformance pressure. Members may also have more "air time" to contribute ideas on-line (as opposed to face-to-face). They may also feel more comfortable sharing ideas because all participants are treated equally; discussions are not normally dominated by one or two individuals, as can be the case in face-to-face discussions. (For more information on the benefits of electronic group decision-making tools, see Chapter Six.)

Perhaps there is no one optimal way to generate ideas in a virtual team. Rather, the most effective way may be tailored to each team and may depend on a variety of factors, such as the personalities and working styles of team members, the team's creative climate, the geographic location of members, and the material and technological resources available to the team. Some research has suggested that electronic brainstorming done near the close of a project is much more effective than at the beginning, where team members are trying to develop a shared language (Majchrzak, Rice, Malhotra, King, and Ba, 2000). Nevertheless, it is clear that these virtual teams did generate ideas whether they communicated face-to-face or electronically. Each individual virtual team in this investigation appeared to have found its own optimal way to generate ideas.

Development

Moving from idea generation to development in the creative process of virtual teams, there was a consensus among the teams that on-line communication was more efficient for development work. Only two of the teams used face-to-face communication during the development stage, and even then it was not the primary mode of communication. Development of creative ideas was accomplished through a variety of electronic means: e-mail, teleconference, computer conferencing, shared database systems, phone, Fax, and, on occasion, videoconferencing. Since frequent face-to-face contact was not realistic for most of the teams due to their geographic dispersal, they saved face-to-face contact for the more interactive stages of idea generation, finalization and closure, and evaluation. For some teams (like the Jacobs/Taylor team), initial face-to-face brainstorming sessions were often so vibrant and productive that once ideas were generated, the team found it could effectively accomplish all development work through electronic exchanges. Julia, a Jacobs/Taylor member, explains, "Once we've got the basic idea done, we don't need to meet again. Any kind of material that's created, we electronically mail to each other, and upgrade and pass back and forth, and have telephone conversations. That works very effectively." In addition, the work design approaches (discussed in Chapter One) illustrate how, for many of the teams, work in the development stage was divided up or parceled out, making physical contact during this stage even less crucial.

The product design engineering team (AutoMax) used the most diverse set of tools during its development stage. This team's job was to design circuit boards for automobiles. The team's mission was to develop its products with input from all stakeholders in order to achieve first pass success. To achieve this mission and bring globally dispersed stakeholders into the design cycle sooner, AutoMax used sophisticated methods to communicate. After initial face-to-face idea generation, the team held periodic teleconferences to begin specifying a product design and to gain buy-in from relevant stakeholders. Once enough information was collected and an initial design had been conceived, the team held weekly design review meetings through synchronous desktop video and teleconferencing. During these meetings, team members and stakeholders could review and further develop the design. Larry, a member of the team, shares an example of the team's design process.

> Probably the most complicated of the things that we designed through this system was a revised circuit board assembly. We had a four-layer assembly, a costly design. Initially during design activities, we determined that we needed to move to a less expensive type of circuit board—a two-layer assembly. At that point, it was strictly verbal between the electrical engineers and the designers. At the point where we thought it might be possible, we started teleconferencing with our manufacturing facility basically trying to get their buy-in. As soon as we had enough information to go and make an initial attempt at laying out the board, and we could all look at this design, we moved into the medium where we were all teleconferencing and looking, sharing a computer session together. So the face-to-face and the teleconferencing of the initial portion was to develop ideas and get buy-in from all individual parties that this was something that we could even look at and that nobody had a problem with going in this direction. Then after we had made a design, the group met as a whole and used teleconferencing and shared the computer session.

Dana, another AutoMax team member, further explains how helpful the weekly design review meetings via computer and teleconferencing were.

> Instead of having to fly down to the plant, Fax information, or ship a paper down to the plant and then having them mark it up and bring it back, we can actually look at the circuit board on the computer, and they can say, "We would like to know what would happen if we moved this part over here." They can move the part right in front of my eyes, or I can move it for them. It's really nice. It's just another way to share information basically but it speeds it up a lot.

Finalization and Closure

The teams I interviewed used a variety of communication tools to finalize and close their projects. The ACI organizational consulting team felt the need for face-to-face contact to touch base before finalizing the work. According to Pam of ACI, development work can be done on-line, "but coming to conclusions and gaining agreement and the closure is, I think, more effective when together face-to-face." For the VTG team, another organizational consulting team, finalization and closure usually occur electronically, but members may interact face-to-face when working on complex projects.

Other teams (AutoMax, ELC) used more interactive types of information technology (teleconferencing, computer conferencing, shared database systems) to finalize and bring closure to their creative endeavors. However, the majority of teams (five out of nine) simply used e-mail and the telephone to tie up loose ends and bring closure to the creative process. For example, members of the WN–Current Events team use e-mail to finalize an on-line publication. Team members send in their individual pieces of the publication to one member who assembles the pieces into the final on-line product.

Evaluation

Oddly enough, only two teams (JSC, OfficeTech) directly spoke of an evaluation period in which the creative outcome was assessed after implementation. Although the other teams did not directly mention the evaluation stage in their interviews, most did at least informally evaluate their work. Both teams that held formal evaluation sessions did so face-to-face. Craig, of OfficeTech, comments on his team's creative process and on how the members of his team come together face-to-face to formally assess the strengths and weaknesses of their creative efforts.

> The producing part itself is where a virtual team works well. About the only time the virtual people and home people get together is for the brainstorming. Also, for a lot of projects we have kind of a wrap-up meeting at the end where we discuss the positive and negative aspects of the project and how to improve the process.

In summary, virtual teams generate ideas in any number of ways. Some teams do so primarily through face-to-face brainstorming sessions, while others prefer unstructured electronic exchanges. Most teams develop ideas, and finalize and close their projects electronically. (Although a few teams felt they should be coming together face-to-face to gain closure.) Evaluation is not often formally conducted, but if it is, it is done face-to-face.

Which communication tools should your virtual team use in the pursuit of creative work? The next section presents a model to assist virtual teams in deciding which tools might be best to use in each stage of the creative process.

Criteria for Selecting Appropriate Communication Tools

General Rules and Tips

With the array of technologies available to virtual teams, how do virtual team leaders and members decide which tools to use and under what circumstances? The answer is, *it depends.* Communication tools that offer high levels of information richness and social presence are not always better. Which tool to use depends on the message to be sent and the nature of the task presented to the team. From this perspective, one may either match or mismatch messages and tools, and virtual team members should optimize their selections of communication tools accordingly. When adopting new technologies (or evaluating existing technologies) for use, it is essential to evaluate them critically instead of assuming they are appropriate for the entire range of the team's tasks. A general rule: *First, consider what you are intending to communicate and accomplish. Then, select the best communication tool(s) available to fulfill what you intend.* (One way to start may be to revisit the earlier discussion on common uses for each of the various communication tools.)

Another rule-of-thumb is to *use communication tools high in social presence and information richness to transmit complex, non-routine, and ambiguous messages* (such as brainstorming, resolving conflicts, and strategic planning and direction setting). *More straightforward, routine, and simple messages* (like updating members on project status) *may be transmitted with tools lower in social presence and information richness.* Communication failure may occur when a rich communication tool that is also high in social presence is used to transmit a simple or unambiguous message. As a result, the receiver of the message may get confused or even attach additional meaning to the message that was not intended by the sender. More typically, communication failure may result from using a lean communication tool that is low in social presence to convey an ambiguous message. In this situation, the communication tool does not provide enough cues to capture the complexity of the intended message. Table 5.6 lists some situations that may call for communication tools that are high in richness and social presence and other situations that may call for tools that are lean and lower in social presence.

Table 5.6 Situations for Communication Tools

Situations in need of tools high in social presence and information richness	Situations in need of tools low in social presence and information richness
when new team members need to be introduced to the team	when the team is dealing with a routine situation
when the team interacts for the first time with new customers	when the team is exchanging information or hard data between members
when the team addresses touchy or interpersonal issues (deals with conflict; needs to express emotion)	when team members are working on developing their parts of a creative effort
for initial brainstorming or idea generation sessions	when team members are sharing the results of their creative efforts for review
when the team solves a new problem	
when the team is faced with an ambiguous or ill-defined situation or problem	
when evaluating creative efforts for future growth and learning	

What happens when a team requires a rich communication tool that is high in social presence, but finds that tool is unavailable? (Perhaps the team has no funds or limited travel funds to bring dispersed members together.) Another rule-of-thumb is that *when communication can't be rich or high in social presence, use multiple methods of communication.* Research suggests that in the absence of rich face-to-face interaction, the more methods of communication used, the better (Kayworth and Leidner, 2000).

For Creative Work

Virtual teams doing creative work need to integrate a variety of tools into a workable communication plan. In this section, a model is presented to offer suggestions for which communication tools are most appropriate for use during each stage of the creative process (see Table 5.7).

Table 5.7 Appropriate Communication Tools

Purpose	Appropriate Communication Tools
Talking—These tools provide a shared meeting place for virtual team members to interact anytime during the creative process.	Face-to-face meetings Synchronous computer meetings Videoconferencing Teleconferencing Telephone E-mail and instant messaging systems Bulletin boards
Brainstorming and Generating Ideas—These tools allow team members to jointly share and build on ideas.	Face-to-face meetings Synchronous computer meetings Interactive and electronic whiteboards Teleconferencing Chat rooms Bulletin boards
Doing—These tools support development and design work and offer a shared workspace for development work to occur synchronously or asynchronously.	Synchronous computer meetings Interactive and electronic whiteboards Videoconferencing Asynchronous computer meetings (shared database systems, shared files)
Saving—These tools are used to archive and store creative efforts and to allow these efforts to be reviewed over and over. These tools offer the capability of, as one team member put it, "holding on to the creativity." They assist in building a content repository in which past ways of approaching and resolving client needs or problems are stored. These past approaches then may become frameworks, templates, or outlines later applied to similar client situations.	Asynchronous computer meetings (shared database systems, shared files) Chat room records Audio-link transcripts Interactive or electronic whiteboards (where information is stored to the computer) Bulletin boards Company Intranet Web pages
Finalizing and Closing—These tools allow team members to pull all the elements of a project together and to make final adjustments as needed. They also assist in the process of reaching consensus and closure.	Face-to-face meetings Synchronous computer meetings Shared database systems E-mail Teleconferencing
Evaluating—These tools assist team members in reviewing and assessing creative efforts and outcomes and in capturing these assessments for future learning.	Face-to-face meetings Synchronous computer meetings Videoconferencing Shared database systems (to store team's experiences and lessons for future use)

Assessment Tool: Constructing a Communication Plan to Support the Team's Creative Process

Consider the communication tools reviewed in this chapter, the purposes outlined for each tool, and the model presented in the previous section. Now, as a team, construct a communication plan outlining which tools to use during your creative process. Consider the following three steps as you develop your communication plan:

- Step 1: *Examine* how current communication tools support (or detract from) your team's creative process.

- Step 2: *Match* the intentions of a specific communication message (for example, needs of a specific creative task, particular target audience, appropriate tone) to the appropriate and available communication tools.

- Step 3: *Construct* a communication plan to support the team's creative process.

Step 1: Examine. To begin, as a team reflect on the following questions to understand how current communication tools support or detract from your team's creative process.

1. Track your team's current use of information technology and face-to-face contact throughout your creative process. (Sharing stories about communication methods used to produce a specific creative result may provide insight into commonalities and variations in the use of information technology and face-to-face contact across different types of creative efforts.)

2. In what ways do you feel the communication tools used throughout the creative process support high creativity? In what ways do they block or hamper creativity?

3. If you could design the optimal combination of electronic and face-to-face interaction that you feel would lead your team to high levels of creativity, what would that design be like?

4. Is the technology currently available to your team interactive and sophisticated enough to support your team's creative process? If not, what might be needed?

5. Are there adequate personal opportunities for real time, human contact to support the creative process? If not, what might be needed?

6. How effectively does the current integration of information technology and face-to-face contact during the creative process suit the personalities and working styles of each individual team member? (To gain insight into team members' individual needs, you may find it helpful to have everyone answer this question independently, and to then have individual team members share results with the group.)

Step 2: Match. Next, use the following items to help you match the intentions of a specific communication message with the appropriate and available communication tools.

1. Clarify the nature of the creative task(s) presented to the team.

2. With each communication, consider what you need to accomplish (for example, build relationships, share information, design and develop, finalize, or evaluate).

3. Weigh any potential limitations that may inhibit the proper use of a specific communication tool. (Limitations could include lack of time, team member comfort level or needs, and technological competence.)

4. Specify the target audience (for example, all team members, just some team members, team leader, or individuals outside the team) for each communication.

5. Decide on the appropriate tone you want to set in a specific communication. (For example, a tone could be formal or informal, personal or professional, warm or neutral, fast- or slow-paced, or high or low in interaction.)

Step 3: Construct the communication tools plan. To achieve high levels of creativity while working virtually, a team must carefully select the appropriate technological tool that matches the requirements of the team's creative task and the stage at which that creative product is in. You can now specify what communication tools are practical and available for your team to use to accomplish what you have described (for example, to meet the needs of a specific creative task, to communicate to a particular target audience, and to set the appropriate tone). Use the matrix in Table 5.8 to specify the communication tools that are most effective and available to use during each stage of your team's creative process.

Table 5.8 Matrix for Preferred Communication Tools

Creative Tasks	Preferred Communication Tools
Talking	
Brainstorming and Idea Generation	
Doing and Development (Shared Workspace)	
Saving	
Finalizing and Closing	
Evaluating	

Final Thoughts

An individual can be creative, as can a team and an organization (Woodman, Sawyer, and Griffin, 1993). Team creativity involves more than the sum of creative contributions from each team member. Team creativity involves a synergistic potential, in which the individual efforts of team members result in a level of performance that is greater than the sum of those individual inputs.

Virtual teams pursuing creative work need a variety of communication tools to bolster and sustain their creative process. For creative work, it is key to incorporate into your communication plan periodic face-to-face encounters, or information technologies that simulate real time face-to-face contact, or both. Asynchronous modes of interaction are beneficial, but creative efforts cannot be accomplished without the opportunity for rich, synchronous interactions.

The virtual team members I conversed with agreed. Eryn, the leader of the WN–Religion Forum team, whose team interacted mostly through e-mail, emphasized that sometime during the creative process, verbal and real time interaction needs to take place. Eryn explains.

> I think it is necessary to speak with the people, whether it's on chat or on the telephone, at some point in the process. I don't think creativity can all be done on e-mail. You have to be together at the same moment at some point.

Communication tools and technologies available for virtual teams are evolving. The development of desktop audio and video links, interactive whiteboards, and Internet Relay Chat, for example, has increased opportunities to simulate the richness of face-to-face contact through technology. Incorporating these tools into a team's communication plan will be crucial for high levels of creativity to occur. Scott, another member of the WN–Religion Forum, puts it this way.

> As the technology gets better and you're able to see and hear someone on the screen and get more of a personal attachment and really parallel what people experience in a single building work environment, I think that you have less of a chance of people becoming too independently minded, going off and maybe perhaps being disconnected from the team. When all you have available is e-mail, occasionally calling on the phone, chat rooms, I don't think it promotes the teamwork and the excitement and the physical connection that I think energizes teamwork and working together as a team. It's certainly not preferable to being in a real team where you're in the same room. But the potential is there; it's going to get better.

Virtual teams doing creative work also need access to techniques and software tools developed to enhance team and individual creativity. As will be seen in the next chapter, some of these techniques and software tools have been designed especially for virtual teamwork, while others have been adapted from methods used by more traditional, co-located teams. In either case, these techniques and software tools help to further stimulate creativity in the virtual workplace.

Points to Remember

- Communication is the vehicle for creating synergy, for keeping a team together and moving it forward. However, virtual teams face special challenges in trying to effectively communicate with one another across the miles.

- Communication tools can be classified as to whether they support *synchronous* communication or *asynchronous* communication. Synchronous communication allows team members to interact with one another simultaneously, as they do in a face-to-face conversation, telephone call, videoconferencing session, or chat room discussion. Asynchronous communication allows communication between team members to occur at different times. Common asynchronous forms of communication are e-mail, shared database systems, and bulletin boards.

- Available communication tools can also be evaluated according to the degree of *social presence* or *information richness*. Social presence is a tool's ability to facilitate a personal connection between team members. Information richness is a tool's ability to transmit multiple cues simultaneously and to offer immediate feedback. Face-to-face meetings have a high level of social presence and information richness, while e-mail and other forms of written communication have far less social presence and offer less information richness.

- Virtual teams reported using relatively unsophisticated tools such as e-mail and the telephone more frequently than they used more sophisticated tools. However, the trend is changing, as virtual teams are beginning to use newer technologies such as desktop conferencing with video and audio links, interactive whiteboards, and the Intranet.

- As virtual teams work through their creative process, there is a pattern to the communication tools they use. Virtual teams generate ideas in any number of ways, some doing so primarily face-to-face, while others preferring unstructured electronic exchanges. Ideas are developed, finalized, and brought to closure electronically (for the most part). Evaluation, when formally conducted, is done face-to-face.

- A virtual team needs to take the time to develop a workable communication plan which specifies what tools are most appropriate for use during each stage of the creative process. Following three steps will help virtual teams develop these plans: (1) Examine how current communication tools support (or detract from) the team's creative process; (2) Match the intentions of a specific communication message with the appropriate and available communication tools; and (3) Construct the communication plan to support the team's creative process.

- For creative work, it is key to incorporate into the communication plan periodic face-to-face encounters or information technologies that simulate real time face-to-face contact, or both. Asynchronous modes of interaction are beneficial, but creative efforts cannot be accomplished without the opportunity for rich, synchronous interactions.

CHAPTER 6

Pulling Together a Creativity Toolbox: Creativity Techniques and Software Tools

We'll start off with a database that represents a project, let's say redesigning the Chart seminar. Everybody on the team will put their ideas in there. And as a result of everyone putting their ideas in there, it becomes a very creative process because one idea will create another idea will create another idea will create another idea. Then at some point the individuals on the team who are managing the project sit down and take all those ideas and start to figure out which of them are realistic and which of them aren't. That process we do in person. Those team members will meet personally and spend a day going over the materials. And then whatever they have decided will be electronically sent to Cristina who designs all the graphics and lays out all the materials. Then Cristina electronically passes around her efforts for other members of the team to review and edit. Then, it's ready to print. And then they go do a seminar and see how it goes. And then the feedback from the seminar is electronically distributed to everyone so they can see it. At that time, the team members in charge of that project may get back together again to do more updating of the process. So I would say we find the get-going creativity, the dumping of thoughts, can definitely be started electronically. Then there are sections where people have to meet, the sorting of digital material. Then there are sections where it can go back to electronic again.

Susan, VTG

THIS CHAPTER DEALS WITH THE TECHNIQUES and software programs that can assist or augment creative thought. As the above quote suggests, more and more teams are comfortable generating ideas electronically. In fact, some prefer generating ideas electronically because they can do so anonymously and asynchronously, and without feeling pressure from other team members to respond. In referring back to Chapter Five, it is interesting to note that at least half of the virtual teams I conversed with used electronic tools to generate ideas, and some were quite content to do so. Certainly there has been much written on techniques to stimulate creativity in both individuals and groups. The intent of this chapter is not to be comprehensive in summarizing all creativity techniques. Rather, this chapter's purpose is to review some of the more prominent linear and intuitive techniques for idea generation, and to suggest ways virtual teams may use these techniques. This chapter also describes computer software programs that virtual teams might use to stimulate collaborative creativity and idea generation.

Creativity Techniques

Scholars identify two main approaches to stimulating creativity: linear approaches and intuitive approaches (Miller, 1987, 1999). With *linear* techniques, an individual or team consciously decides to creatively attack a problem using one or more techniques to clarify the problem and generate creative ideas for solving it. Linear approaches for idea generation provide a structure within which one can seek and find alternative solutions. Solutions are arrived at using a logical pattern or sequence of steps. On the other hand, *intuitive* techniques help individuals or teams to achieve an inner state of calmness, out of which unpredictable inspirations or insights may appear. There is little or no sense of a structured path through which to find a solution. Rather, solutions spring forth, often leaving an individual feeling surprised as to where the creative thoughts came from.

In the pursuit of optimal creativity, both linear and intuitive approaches are necessary. A typical pattern is linear thinking or logic preceding and following intuitive insight (Miller, 1987). The following section describes the most commonly used techniques to stimulate creativity. These techniques fall into linear and intuitive categories. Each technique is described, a sample application is provided, and suggestions for how the technique can be adapted for use by a virtual team are provided. Table 6.1 lists the techniques that will be reviewed.

Table 6.1 Linear and Intuitive Techniques

Linear Techniques	Intuitive Techniques
Attribute listing	Imagery
Morphological synthesis	Analogical thinking
Force-field analysis	Drawing
Mind mapping	Meditation (mind clearing)
Idea checklists (e.g., SCAMPER)	
Brainstorming	

Linear Techniques

Attribute Listing

One way to embellish our ideas is to dissect them into parts and think of ways to improve or change each one of the parts. Attribute listing is a specific technique for generating ideas in this fashion. Robert Crawford (1978), the designer of attribute listing, argued that "each time we take a creative step we do it by changing an attribute or quality of something, or else by applying that same quality or attribute to some other thing" (Davis, 1999, p. 179). This technique allows individuals to expand beyond their typical notion of things. It is particularly useful for improving tangible objects. To begin, properties or attributes of a product are listed. The list is then reviewed one at a time with a view toward improving each attribute. Then, for each attribute one may ask the following questions:

- How else can this be accomplished?
- Why does this have to be this way?
- What else is this like?
- What have others done?
- Where could we find an idea?
- What could we copy?
- What has worked before?

A sample attribute list is provided in Table 6.2, which illustrates how one might improve each of the attributes of a picture frame.

Table 6.2 Attributes and Improvements

Attribute	Improvement
Rectangular shape	Round, oval, three-dimensional shape
Covered with glass	Covered with Lucite, plastic film, nothing, a drawn shade
Wooden frame	Aluminum or plastic frame or no frame
Opens from the back	Opening could be a slot inside, hinge to open from front, or no opening at all
Hangs by a wire	Could be attached by suction cups, magnetic holder, or hooks over a ledge

Attribute listing can be used for complex problems or challenges as well. The thinker lists the main attributes (characteristics, dimensions, parts) of the problem, challenge, or process. Good ideas can be selected out of each of the lists. For example, in a creativity class I taught, one of my students had the dream of becoming a comic book writer. To help foster and encourage this student, we took it upon ourselves as a class to create comic book stories. Student teams used attribute listing to generate comic book story ideas (Davis, 1999). Using the grid in Table 6.3, students listed in the first column different types of interesting characters. In the second column, students created a list of goals or objectives (things characters might want to possess or achieve). In the third column, students listed obstacles to accomplishing these goals. Finally, in the fourth column, students listed potential outcomes. One of the grids generated by a student team follows, along with the story the team created based on this grid.

Table 6.3 Attribute-Listing Grid

Characters	Goals	Obstacles	Outcomes
Narcoleptic Man	To be a hero.	Randomly falls asleep.	Goes to medical school and studies ways to stop narcolepsy, to be able to stay awake and fight crime.
Claire Voyant	To read the minds of evil people.	Can hear everyone's thoughts at the same time. It is often hard to decipher the evil stuff.	Partners with narcoleptic man to fight crime.
Evil Doer	Always trying to take over the world.	Unfortunately, good always triumphs over evil.	His plans are squashed. He escapes and goes off to a deserted island to prepare plots for more evil.
Damsel N. Distress	To avoid being overtaken by evil.	Weak and naive, often unaware of what is going on around her.	Works on developing her beauty to attract someone to protect her from evil.

And here's a brief summary of the story that was created.

> *The Powers of Narcoleptic Man:* Narcoleptic man is a medical student who is studying the disease of narcolepsy. Through his studies, he develops a super potion that gives him super human powers and keeps him awake all the time. Claire Voyant has been seeing a psychiatrist at the same medical school that Narcoleptic

Man attends. Claire wants to better understand the "voices" she is constantly hearing from what others are thinking. Narcoleptic Man and Claire Voyant meet. He reveals his super human ability to stay awake to her, and she reveals her ability to eavesdrop on others' thoughts to him. They form a partnership to fight crime. While fighting crime, they witness Evil Doer trying to capture Damsel N. Distress. Narcoleptic Man and Claire Voyant fight off Evil Doer and save Damsel N. Distress. Narcoleptic Man falls in love with Damsel N. Distress and they marry and have a family of Narcoleptic Damsels N. Distress. Claire Voyant sets up a successful security business in which she is now able to hear the thoughts of evil doers and catch them before they do harm.

Suggestions for Using Attribute Listing in Virtual Teams. While attribute listing can be done individually and the results then shared with the entire team, it is probably more effective, enjoyable, and fun when the entire team participates—or when at least a subset of the team participates. If feasible, face-to-face meetings with a few resources (such as a flipchart or whiteboard) can be used to perform this technique. However, it is certainly not necessary to get together face-to-face to generate some fun ideas in an attribute listing session. Virtual teams may also construct their lists electronically via synchronous computer meetings incorporating the use of interactive whiteboards and audio-conferencing tools. Asynchronous threaded discussions can also be useful in generating ideas for improving different attributes of a product or service. Furthermore, some idea generator software programs (reviewed in detail in the section on creativity software tools) offer lists of questions or idea triggers, or a team can custom tailor its own set of questions to provoke new ideas on product attributes. Outliner software programs (also discussed in detail later) may assist teams in beginning to organize and formulate a structure for the ideas generated.

Morphological Synthesis

This technique is basically an extension of the attribute listing procedure. With morphological synthesis, a team or individual generates creative solutions to complex problems that have many variables to consider in a logical way that is relatively easy to follow. Morphological synthesis involves listing and examining all possible combinations that might be useful in solving a given problem. The process begins with listing specific ideas for one attribute or dimension of a problem along one axis of the matrix. Ideas for a second attribute are then listed along the other axis. Within each matrix cell lies a new idea combination and potential solution to the problem. Morphological synthesis can yield a wide variety of ideas, some practical, some outlandish. Although some of the ideas from this method will be eliminated during evaluation, alternatives that might otherwise have been overlooked may be generated. Even if a particular combination is not an appropriate solution, it may serve as a stimulus for someone to devise a winning idea.

Gary Davis (1999) provides a rather humorous example of morphological synthesis, illustrating how sixth-graders generated ideas for a new type of sandwich using this technique. Variables across the top row of Table 6.4 are ingredients children suggested might be added to sandwiches to add an original flavor. Variables listed in the farthest left column are the children's standard sandwich favorites. Ideas for new sandwiches can be found in each intersection of cells. The first, second, and third top-rated choices by the children for best sandwich are also indicated in Table 6.4.

Certainly, morphological synthesis can also be adapted for more serious business issues as well. For example, to generate new business opportunities, a team may want to list potential markets along one axis and potential products or services along the second axis. The intersecting cells may generate a myriad of opportunities not previously explored.

Suggestions for Using Morphological Synthesis in Virtual Teams. As this technique is closely related to attribute listing, it can be done using the same suggested tools. In addition, since morphological synthesis may take on more of a graphical form than attribute listing, visual outliner programs (described in the section on creativity software tools) and shared workspaces for drawing and sketching such as interactive whiteboards may be particularly useful for this creativity technique.

Force-Field Analysis

This technique was first developed by social psychologist Kurt Lewin to analyze forces influencing situations. Lewin suggested a set of positive and negative forces is constantly pushing or pulling individuals in one direction or another, much like a tug of war. Force-field analysis allows individuals (or teams) to

Table 6.4 Sandwich Flavors

	Celery	Applesauce	Cucumber	Peppers	Tomato	Raisins	Nuts	Dates	Banana	Cottage Cheese	Cranberry Sauce
Egg Salad											
Chicken											
Tuna Fish		2nd choice									
Peanut Butter											1st choice
Jelly											
Sardines											
Deviled ham											
Corned beef										3rd choice	
Salmon											
Cheese											
Liver-sausage											

First choice: Super Goober—Peanut Butter and Cranberry.

Second choice: Charlie's Aunt—Tuna Fish and Applesauce.

Third choice: Irish Eyes are Smiling—Corned beef and cottage cheese.

Source: Adapted from CREATIVITY IS FOREVER, 4th Edition by Gary A. Davis. Adapted by permission of Kendall/Hunt Publishing Company.

visually identify those forces contributing to or hindering a solution to a problem. The steps involved are listed below (adapted from Miller, 1987).

Step 1.   Write a brief, objective statement of the problem or challenge the team is facing.

Step 2a.   Determine the extremes. Describe what the situation would be like if everything fell apart or was an absolute catastrophe, the worst-case scenario.

Step 2b.   Describe the situation as it would be if it were the ideal, the best-case scenario.

Step 3a.   Take the position that you are in the center, and catastrophe and ideal are each playing a tug of war. List the forces that are currently pushing you to a more catastrophic situation.

Step 3b.   List the forces that are pulling you in the direction of the ideal.

Step 4.   Specify actions that may move you closer to your ideal by:
(a) identifying a positive force that can be strengthened.
(b) identifying a negative force that can be weakened or minimized.
(c) brainstorming a new positive force that could be added.

Table 6.5 is an example of a force-field analysis that I constructed.

Table 6.5 Force-Field Analysis

Step 1—Problem Statement How to write a good book on creativity and virtual teams.	
Step 2a—Describe absolute catastrophe. Book is not received well by series editors and publisher and is never published.	*Step 2b—Describe ideal.* Book is well received; insightful feedback is generated from review of the first draft. This feedback leads to an even better book, which is finally published and received well by the intended audience.
Step 3a—Identify negative forces. 1. Limited time left—feeling pushed for time and pressured. Will the allotted amount of time left before delivery of the first draft afford me enough time to pursue all aspects in enough detail and be able to revise accordingly? 2. Other work-related responsibilities that use up my time. 3. Personal responsibilities that take up a major portion of my time.	*Step 3b—Identify positive forces.* 1. Experienced and encouraging team of book series editors, publications and editorial staff, and administrative and editing assistance. 2. Extensive data generated from two years of research on virtual teams. 3. Light teaching load in spring and summer quarters, allowing time to work on book.

Table 6.5 Force-Field Analysis, Cont'd

Step 4a—Actions generated to weaken negative forces.	*Step 4b—Actions generated to strengthen positive forces.*
1. Affirm belief in the creative process. Realize there is and will be time for necessary revisions.	1. Make use of experienced support team. Update them consistently of progress. Utilize their input in subsequent revisions.
2. Perform only essential tasks right now at work until after delivery date of first draft. And *don't* take on any new commitments until after delivery date.	2. While revising the book draft, revisit original interview transcripts again to locate any interesting themes or data that may have been missed. Review additional references pile has been accumulating for content that might be relevant.
3. Seek out temporary help to assist with personal responsibilities until after delivery date. Limit personal commitments until after delivery date.	3. To make use of light load during *spring*:
	• Allot two to four hours daily when on campus to work on the book. Protect this time by avoiding distractions during this period (for example, talking with colleagues or students during this time; taking non-emergency phone calls; checking e-mail). Leave office door closed.
	• Allot three to five hours each night (including weekends) to work on the book.
	To make use of light load during *summer*:
	• Limit other commitments (for example, travel, conferences, and the like) to allot time for revisions.
	• Allot four to six hours daily during the week to work on the book.

Step 4c—New positive force that can be added.
1. Recruit research assistants to help gather additional references and resources.

Suggestions for Using Force-Field Analysis in Virtual Teams. One way to begin the force-field analysis is to have team members create statements describing catastrophic and ideal situations individually at first. This allows for all perceptions of the situation to emerge before the team discussion. Individual statements may be posted to a shared database, put into a shared file, or put on a private section of the team's Intranet Web page. The team can then schedule either a face-to-face meeting or a synchronous computer meeting (with access to interactive whiteboards, word processing, or outliner programs) to process the individually created statements and form a joint description of what is catastrophic and what is ideal. Adding an audio link (through audioconferencing or desktop audio) may also be useful. From this newly-constructed team statement, members may now collaboratively identify forces that are pushing the team toward catastrophe or pulling the team toward the ideal—and generate actions that may move the team closer to the ideal.

Mind Mapping

Mind mapping was formalized as a creativity technique in the 1970s by Tony Buzan, a British brain researcher. In mind mapping, thoughts and associations around a central theme are graphically represented. Mind maps are useful for when you have a central topic (for example a product, market, technology, or process) that you want to build on. The overall picture of a particular problem or challenge is illustrated, as well as the details that make it up. By examining the mind map, one is able to see what is already known about a particular topic and to identify any critical gaps. The procedure begins with writing a central theme and then depicting thoughts and associations (represented by key words) as branches growing out from the central theme. Associations are potentially limitless, as each association may in turn trigger another. A mind map can reach out in any direction and catch thoughts from any angle. After thoughts and associations are mapped out, one can search for unifying patterns and connections, potentially offering a new idea or creative solution to a problem. Moving and synthesizing concepts into new clusters often provokes new ideas. A mind map may also indicate areas where new information needs to be collected. Through the creation of a mind map, one is able to move from the general (central theme) to the specific (different thoughts and associations) and back to the general (creative connections and new ideas) (Michalko, 1998).

A series of guidelines for mind mapping are provided in Table 6.6. These guidelines have been adapted from those suggested by Michael Michalko (1998) in his book, *Cracking Creativity: The Secrets of Creative Genius*.

Table 6.6 Mind Mapping Guidelines

1. *Start with a central theme.* Put a word or short phase that describes the core of your problem on a large sheet of paper (or electronic whiteboard) and draw a circle around it.

2. *Use key words and prompts.* Write down as many key words as you can that you feel are associated with the central theme. Use only key words and ignore irrelevant words. Express only the essentials.

3. *Record key words.* Print out key words (representing thoughts and associations) around the central theme. Express thoughts and associations with a minimum of key words, avoid clutter.

Table 6.6 Mind Mapping Guidelines, Cont'd

4. *Put down everything that comes to mind (without judgment at this point).* Fill the page with as many spontaneous key words as you can, even if they seem ridiculous.

5. *Connect the key words with lines radiating from the center.* By linking the words you are showing clearly how one thought relates to another and you will begin to see relationships that will help you gather and organize the data into clusters.

6. *Make use of graphics.* Colors, pictures, and symbols can be used to highlight important thoughts and show relationships between different areas on the map.

7. *Cluster.* Organize the major clusters into themes. A mind map is a creation on paper that comes close to the way your mind clusters concepts in your brain. Now you can move more into an evaluator role, testing out your associations, missing information, and areas where you need more and better ideas.

8. *Revise.* Continually revise, refine, and elaborate on your mind map as you work your way closer to the ultimate answers.

Source: Reprinted with permission from CRACKING CREATIVITY by Michael Michalko. Copyright © 2001 by Michael Michalko, Ten Speed Press, Berkeley, CA. Available from your local bookseller, by calling Ten Speed Press at 800-841-2665, or by visiting us online at www.tenspeed.com.

An example of a mind map (outlining the uses, benefits, and procedures of the mind mapping technique) is shown in Figure 6.1. This mind map was generated through the *Axon Idea Processor software program* (a creativity software program which will be described later in this chapter).

Suggestions for Using Mind Mapping in Virtual Teams. Mind maps can be done individually or by the entire team. You can mind map in a team by having all members first independently create their own mind maps and then combine efforts, or by working collaboratively as a team to construct a mind map. Mind maps are easily constructed in a face-to-face meeting with relatively few resources (flipchart, whiteboard). Virtual teams may also construct mind maps electronically with help from electronic and interactive whiteboards, or from creativity software programs called visual outliners that are designed to facilitate the mind mapping process. (See section on creativity software tools.) Visual outliner programs attempt to automate and assist in the process of drawing graphical outlines, mind maps, and concept maps. In addition, some Electronic Meeting Systems (EMS) like GroupSystems have features to allow dispersed team members to jointly construct a mind map. (See section on creativity software tools.)

Figure 6.1 Sample Mind Map from Axon Idea Processor

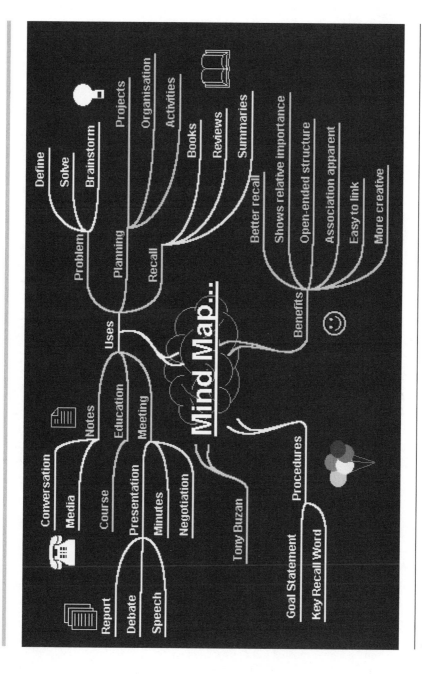

Source: Copyright © 2003 Axon Research. Used by permission of Axon Research.

Idea Checklists

Sometimes new ideas emerge out of being stimulated, challenged, and prodded into creative thinking by a series of structured questions or exercises. The most well-known idea checklist designed for creative problem solving is SCAMPER. In 1963, Alex Osborn, a trailblazer in creativity and idea generation stimulation, developed a list of idea-spurring questions. These questions were later arranged by Bob Eberle into the mnemonic of SCAMPER. (See Table 6.7). The SCAMPER technique is based on the notion that everything that is new is really some addition or modification of something that already exists.

To begin the SCAMPER process, decide on a subject, topic, problem, or challenge your team wants to creatively think about. Then ask and answer the following questions and see what new ideas and thoughts emerge.

Table 6.7 SCAMPER Questions

Substitute? To have a person or thing act or serve in the place of another.

Ask: Who else instead? What else instead? What other ingredient? Other process? Other power? Other place? Other approach? Other tone of voice?

Combine? To bring together, to unite.

Ask: How about a blend, an alloy, an assortment, an ensemble? Combine units? Combine purposes? Combine appeals? Combine ideas?

Adapt? To adjust to suit a condition or purpose.

Ask: What else is like this? What other idea does this suggest? Does the past offer parallels? What could I copy? Whom could I emulate?

Modify? To alter, to change the form or quality.

Ask: New twist? Change meaning, color, motion, sound, odor, form, shape? Other changes?

Magnify? To enlarge, make greater in form or quality.

Ask: What to add? More time? Greater frequency? Stronger? Higher? Longer? Thicker? Extra value? Plus ingredient? Duplicate? Multiply? Exaggerate?

Minify? To make smaller, lighter, slower.

Ask: What can be made smaller? Condensed? Miniature? Lower? Shorter? Lighter? Slower?

Put to other uses? To have a person or thing act or serve in the place of another.

Ask: New ways to use as is? Other uses if modified?

Table 6.7 SCAMPER Questions, Cont'd

Eliminate? To remove, omit, or get rid of a quality, part, or whole.

Ask: What to subtract? Omit? Streamline? Split up? What could be left unsaid?

Reverse? To place opposite, to turn around.

Ask: Transpose positive and negative? How about opposites? Turn it backward? Turn it upside down? Reverse roles? Change shoes? Turn tables? Turn other cheek?

Rearrange? To change order or adjust, different plan, layout, or scheme.

Ask: Interchange components? Other pattern? Other layout? Other sequence? Transpose cause and effect? Change pace? Change schedule?

Source: Definitions of scamper techniques taken from Eberle, B. (1996). *Scamper: Games for Imagination Development.* Used by permission of Prufrock Press, Waco, Texas. Idea spurring questions from Osborn, A. (1963). *Applied Imagination: Principles & Procedures of Creative Problem-Solving.* Adapted by permission of Pearson Education, Inc., Upper Saddle River. NJ.

Try a mini-SCAMPER session on your own or with the members of your team. This activity will help you appreciate and understand the creative potential you can quickly generate with guided linear techniques. If you are like me, you may be tempted to skip ahead, preferring to read rather than do this exercise. I understand the temptation. However, creativity techniques cannot be learned through mere reading. It is in the doing that learning takes place.

Exercise

Think about a product or service that your team is currently producing or offering. Now ask and answer the following questions:

- Can we substitute something in the product or service?
- Can we combine this product or service with something else?
- Can we adapt something to the product or service?
- Can we modify or change the product or service in some way?
- Can we magnify or add to the product or service?
- Can we minify the product or service in some way?
- Can we put the product or service to another use?
- Can we eliminate something from the product or service?
- Can we rearrange the parts of the product or steps in the service?
- What happens if we reverse the product or service offered?

Suggestions for Using Idea Checklists in Virtual Teams. Several software programs designed to help individuals and teams generate and process creative ideas have features offering built-in lists to prod team members into new insights. (See section on creativity software tools.) For example, the Brainstorming Toolbox software program provides thousands of original prompts to spark ideas and offers specialized questions to help problem solvers explore alternative solutions. Features such as Random Word, Random Picture, and the SCAMPER questions are examples of idea checklists that virtual teams may easily access. Another example of an idea checklist is the Creative Whack Pack sixty-four-card series, designed by Roger von Oech (1992) to give individuals or teams a "whack on the side of the head" to be jolted out of habitual thought patterns that undermine creative thinking. Cards are divided into four categories, each of which represent the four roles or types of thinking of the creative process: (1) Explorer—discovers resources that can be used to create new ideas and find new information, (2) Artist—transforms resources into new ideas, (3) Judge—evaluates an idea, decides what to do with it, and lends decision-making advice, and (4) Warrior—turns ideas into action. These cards have now been made available on-line. A problem is typed into the program, and then cards with questions are shown at random (sometimes referred to as whack-surfing) to stimulate one's imagination as to how to solve this problem.

Brainstorming

This is one of the most well-known techniques for stimulating creativity and generating ideas, particularly useful for groups. The birth of brainstorming is typically credited to Alex Osborn, a partner in a New York advertising agency, who formalized a set of ground rules for the practice of brainstorming. These ground rules will be described later in this section. In business, brainstorming has been used to develop ideas for new products, to improve existing products or processes, and to solve marketing, advertising, or personnel problems. Gary Davis (1999) proposes a number of reasons for why brainstorming has become so popular.

- It's intuitively appealing.
- It's simple to learn and implement; not much training is involved beyond a few minutes of clarification of the ground rules.
- It's fun; new ideas are often humorous.

- It's therapeutic; one is asked for ideas and is given the chance to share and speak up.

- It stimulates imagination, flexibility, and creative attitudes.

So what is involved in a brainstorming session? To begin, a problem or challenge is stated and defined (hopefully in neutral terms). It should be a problem that everyone in the team has the potential to be able to solve. Participants then randomly and spontaneously offer ideas for solving the problem. These ideas are offered under specific conditions. Two principles and four ground rules form the basis for these conditions.

Principles

- *Judgment of ideas should be deferred.* It is essential not to judge, evaluate, or criticize ideas as they are being generated. Nothing puts a stop to creativity more quickly than critical, judgmental thinking too early in the creative process. Criticism and harsh evaluation will interfere with flexible idea generation.

- *Quantity breeds quality.* Many times we will produce one or two ideas and proceed as if they are the answers. But creative ideas occur infrequently. The more ideas a team has generated, the more likely the team will discover the best idea to solve the problem. So it only makes sense to produce as many ideas as you can before evaluation and to stretch participants beyond their first automatic and routine responses.

Ground Rules

1. *Criticism is ruled out.* Deferred judgment produces a receptive, encouraging creative atmosphere. New ideas are reinforced rather than punished. Suspend evaluation until all ideas are given.

2. *Freewheeling is welcomed.* Accept all ideas, even the wild ones. In fact, the wilder the ideas, the better. One is more likely to find a creative and workable idea by being wild first and taming it down, rather than criticizing, evaluating, and editing as one proceeds. Stretch for ideas. When you think you have gotten all ideas, go for another round and be even more outrageous.

3. *Quantity is wanted.* Aim for quantity, not quality. The notion is that the more ideas generated, the higher the probability that one will be appropriate

and novel (creative). The purpose of a brainstorming session is to produce a long list of ideas. Probability theory would suggest that the longer the list of ideas, the better the chance one of those ideas will be creative. Typically, ideas produced later in a brainstorming session (after the easy and quick ones are out of the way) will be more imaginative.

4. *Combination and improvement are sought.* To lengthen the list of ideas, those involved in a brainstorming session should build on, embellish, and enrich the other ideas generated, spontaneously hitchhiking on the ideas of others.

Source: Applied Imagination: Principles & Procedures of Creative Problem-Solving, by Alex Osborn, © 1963. Adapted by permission of Pearson Education, Inc., Upper Saddle River, NJ.

People often play different roles in a traditional brainstorming session. A facilitator guides and monitors the process, making sure the ground rules are followed. Record keepers provide a collective memory by recording the ideas generated by the group. Participants actually take part in the idea-generation process of brainstorming and, while doing so, adhere to the principles and ground rules laid out.

In traditional brainstorming groups, participants offer ideas one at a time, leading to a serial processing of information. In contrast, *brainwriting* was developed by Horst Geschka and his associates at the Batelle Institute in Frankfurt, Germany, to allow multiple ideas to be generated simultaneously. There are two major principles: idea generation is silent, and ideas are created spontaneously in parallel sequences. Brainwriting is particularly useful in ensuring that the most vocal voices do not prevail. Table 6.8 provides guidelines for brainwriting (adapted from Michalko, 1998).

Table 6.8 Brainwriting Guidelines

1. Discuss the problem to clarify it; write it out and make it visible to all group members.

2. Distribute index cards to participants and instruct them to silently write their ideas on cards, one idea per card. *Note:* this can be easily adapted for virtual teams with several groupware options.

3. As participants complete their cards, they pass them silently to the person on the right.

Table 6.8 Brainwriting Guidelines, Cont'd

4. Group members read the cards and are either stimulated into thinking of a new idea or modifying the original idea. These new ideas or modifications are then placed on additional cards.

5. After a while, all the cards are collected and displayed. Sets of ideas may be subsumed into larger categories.

6. Then participants evaluate ideas (or larger categories of ideas) and the team reviews trends among the evaluations. *Note:* for virtual teams, tools such as Vote in GroupSystems (discussed later) may be useful for tabulating results of independent evaluations.

Suggestions for Using Brainstorming in Virtual Teams. Not only is brainstorming the most popular technique for idea generation, it is also the most formally developed technique for electronic use, which makes it a viable option for virtual teams. Electronic brainstorming aids fall under the wider umbrella of Group Decision Support Systems (GDSS) and Electronic Meeting Systems (EMS), which refer to electronic systems that help teams and work groups solve problems. (More is shared on EMS later in the chapter.) Typically these software programs aid communication in four areas: generating ideas or plans, making decisions, resolving conflicts, and seeking consensus. Electronic brainstorming fits into the category of generating ideas.

There are a variety of options for performing electronic brainstorming. For example, GroupSystems, an EMS software package, offers several features (Electronic Brainstorming, Topic Commenter, and Group Outliner) to aid dispersed team members in idea generation. In the Electronic Brainstorming feature, the session leader enters a question or issue to provide a stimulus for participants. An electronic "sheet of paper" is automatically distributed to each participant. After a participant enters an idea, the first discussion sheet is exchanged for a new one. This new sheet may display an idea entered by another participant. The participant may then comment on the response or begin a new line of thought. As the brainstorming continues, each discussion sheet yields new ideas to spark additional perspectives and responses. Ideas generated in these sessions can be categorized later with keywords. (See Figure 6.5 later in the chapter for a sample computer screen from GroupSystems' Electronic Brainstorming feature.)

Other communication tools available to virtual teams such as videoconferencing, audioconferencing, synchronous computer meetings with video and audio links, and interactive whiteboards, can also be used to pursue an electronic brainstorming session. These tools are, for the most part, supportive of synchronous brainstorming sessions. Virtual teams may also find asynchronous threaded discussion boards to be valuable tools for generating multiple ideas in parallel sequences, as in the brainwriting technique.

Brainstorming is useful because it creates a cross-fertilization of ideas. However there are three major disadvantages to face-to-face brainstorming sessions: (1) production blocking, withholding ideas simply because only one person at a time can talk; (2) evaluation apprehension, the reluctance to suggest incomplete or poorly-developed ideas due to fear of criticism; and (3) social loafing (free riding), the tendency to invest less effort in group projects because members can sit back and leave the work to others. Research has shown that electronic brainstorming seems to have all the advantages but none of the disadvantages of traditional, face-to-face brainstorming groups.

Intuitive Techniques

While linear techniques structure information and point out where to look for new ideas, intuitive techniques utilize our ability to perceive whole solutions in sudden leaps of logic. Intuition is more fluent in images, sounds, and symbols than in words. The assumption behind using intuitive approaches is that, at some level, one already knows the answer. By developing a sense of inner calmness, an individual can access his or her intuition.

Unfortunately, intuitive techniques are often looked at with doubt in the corporate arena. However, intuition is not unreal or untrustworthy. Intuitive insight is often based on the persistent, linear work one has done previously. William Miller, author of *The Creative Edge: Fostering Innovation Where You Work*, describes the importance of intuition in creative problem-solving: "The logical *without* intuition and emotion is actually irrational, because it is not based on our full capacity for problem solving. Because logic alone is not whole, it cannot produce whole, reality-based solutions or promote the integral, long-term health of any person or organization"(1987, p. 83). Intuition uses information and data that has been stored away by our linear thought processes. Miller further explains, intuition "is our inner, intuitive world that is constantly giving us the guidance and answers to our questions about living and problem solving, *especially* when our logical, linear thinking reaches its limit" (1987, p. 83).

To tune into intuition properly, it is important to note that intuition is not the same as our subconscious (memories, thoughts, emotions that may affect our daily lives). Intuitive wisdom emerges when our subconscious thoughts are quieted and we experience inner calmness. A discussion of four commonly-used intuitive techniques—imagery, analogical thinking, drawing, and meditation (mind-clearing)—follows.

Imagery

Imagery involves using symbols, scenes, or images as windows to creative thought and insight. It has been defined as "an individual's internal mental representations of real objects, scenes, events, or symbols in the absence of the direct, external, observable, concrete experiencing (i.e., sensation) of the objects or events themselves or their symbols" (Houtz and Patricola, 1999, p. 1). Images can be objects, events, or scenes. They can be short-lived or long-lasting. Images can occur spontaneously or be deliberately generated and manipulated. Imagery has often been referred to as "having pictures in one's head." One of the most famous and most frequently-cited examples of mental imagery in creative problem-solving is Kekule's account of his discovery that the arrangement of atoms in the benzene molecule and other organic molecules are closed chains or rings. This discovery resulted from an image in which Kekule visualized a snake biting its own tail. Thinking analogically then, Kekule hypothesized that the carbon atoms in benzene are arranged in a ring fashion. The image of the snake inspired Kekule's analogy, which led to his breakthrough discovery. Kekule's account of the image that came to his mind follows.

> I turned my chair to the fire and dozed. Again the atoms were gamboling before my eyes. The smaller groups kept modestly in the background. My mental eye, rendered more acute by visions of this kind, could now distinguish larger structures, of manifold conformation, long rows sometimes more closely fitted together, all twining and twisting in snake-like motion. But look! What was that? One of the snakes had seized hold of its tail and the form whirled mockingly before my eyes. As if by a flash of lightning I awoke. [Koestler, 1964, p. 118]

Several types of images have been typically associated with creative imagery. Kekule's snake image is an example of a hypnagogic image, an image arising during the drowsy state just before sleep. Other eminent scientists have also reported the use of images in achieving great discoveries. For example, Albert Einstein shared that he always "thought in pictures." Einstein attributed his eventual discovery of the theory of relativity to a thought image he had of himself riding a beam of light (Houtz and Patricola, 1999). The different categories of images (as categorized by Holt, 1964) are described as follows:

- *Thought* images are faint, subjective representations without sensory input; these are the images of memory and imagination.
- *Eidetic* images are greatly enhanced thought images of such vividness and clarity as to seem like actual perceptions. Eidetic images are vivid, strong, and persistent. People experiencing eidetic images may actually believe the images are real.
- *Synesthesia* is cross-modal imagery that involves, for example, hearing colors or tasting shapes.
- *Hallucinations* are images related to a person's beliefs. These images are perceived as reality but they do not really exist.
- *Dream images* are hallucinations during sleep. They may be classified as hypnagogic images, images of great clarity that appear in the drowsy state just before sleep, or hypnopompic images that arise during the drowsy state just before awakening. These images occur during times of imagination and fantasy related to daily problems and challenges.

Sometimes, just in the simple viewing and focusing on an image (a circle, scene from nature, or sound of the wind), the solution to a problem may emerge. This is because through this intense focus the body and mind relax, and one's sense of inner calmness emerges. Why not try an imagery exercise right now? This one is centered around finding the key values you feel should guide your virtual team in pursuing creative work. What are the key elements you feel need to be in place for high levels of creativity to emerge within the team? That is the issue you will be asking your intuition for some insight on.

Exercise

Close your eyes. Relax. Breathe in and out, concentrating only on the *ins* and *outs* of your breath. Whisper internally to yourself the words "in" and "out" on each inhalation and exhalation. Allow yourself to relax. Experience your mind tuning out the daily mental clutter. Feel your body relax. Allow yourself to feel this for a few minutes. Then ask your intuitive self for appropriate images that symbolize the key values you want your team to hold in encouraging creativity. Accept whatever images emerge. (Do not try to edit any out.) Savor those images and look for qualities in them and how they might relate to the values you want your team to hold. Avoid getting caught up in the literal meaning the images evoked. Let yourself experience the creative potential that can be released in the combined power of physical relaxation and intuitive imagery.

You may also choose to do this exercise with all of the members of your team. First, individually generate images. Then, share with one another the images each of you generated. Discuss the qualities in these images and how they relate to the key values you see as important for your team to perform creative work.

Here are some guidelines for using imagery (adapted from Davis, 1999; Michalko, 1998; and Miller, 1987, 1999).

Guidelines for Imagery

- Begin with a problem or challenge you would like some guidance on. Close your eyes and picture this problem or challenge.

- Relax your mind and body through focused breathing, meditation, soothing sounds, or music. It is important to reach a state of relaxation and to block out distracting internal thoughts.

- Ask your intuitive self for appropriate images that symbolically represent your problem or some aspect of it. Accept those images that emerge. (Do not edit some out.)

- Write down or draw the images that come to mind. Look for qualities in the images and how they relate to your problem or challenge. Do not get caught up in trying to figure out the literal meaning of the images. Look for analogies or relationships between your images and the problem or challenge.

- As you become more adept at visualizing images, ideas will emerge spontaneously and effortlessly. If a chain of images emerges, often the first ones are the most significant.

As strange as it may sound, images that offer solutions or creative insights can also come to us in either daydreams or night dreams. In fact, highly creative individuals are most likely to cite dream images as sources of creative ideas (Daniels-McGhee and Davis, 1994). Since childhood, we rarely allow ourselves the freedom or time to daydream. However, daydreams are good windows to creative insight. Daydreams can be invoked by simply thinking about some ideal world or situation you would like to be in. In a course I taught on creativity, I asked participants to daydream for five minutes. I allowed myself to daydream as well. Honestly, I was surprised by where I went in those few minutes. I was also surprised by how helpful the creative insight was in regards to a work-related challenge I was experiencing. Although a few of the participants in the course had difficulty with this exercise, most did not. A few even emerged with insightful solutions to personal or work-related issues. Allow yourself to daydream periodically as well. Try this exercise.

Exercise

For the next five minutes, allow yourself to do something that you most likely have been forbidden to do since preschool—*daydream*. Sit in a relaxed position, close your eyes, and breathe deeply. Now let your mind wander freely—visit other places, see strange images, or hear odd sounds. Then open your eyes and jot down what you experienced. After your daydream, consider the following:

- Where did you go? What did you experience?
- Were you surprised by how far your daydream took you?
- Did you have difficulty with the exercise? If so, why?
- In what ways might your daydream have practical value?
- What stops you from daydreaming more often?

The key to capturing creativity in night dreams (or in periods just before and after sleep) is being willing to write down the images or words as soon as you realize them and make sure they don't slip away. These insights are hard to recapture. Later in the morning after your sleep, you can fill in the gaps of what you wrote and other details as you recall. Look for qualities in the images you experience in dreams. Treat them as metaphors rather than as exemplifying literal meaning. Take a moment to consider how many times you have had an idea just before falling asleep. I leave a note pad next to my bed to capture ideas that emerge during the drowsy period before real sleep. These ideas have ranged from conceptual insights on research projects to ideas for my children's birthday parties. Give it a try when you go to bed tonight. Leave a sheet of paper by your bed and capture any thoughts. If paper does not work for you, believe it or not, technology has also been developed to help individuals have more lucid dreams and also remember more of their dreams. With one such program called NovaDreamer®, you wear a mask with photoelectric sensors over your eyes. The sensors detect eye movement during REM sleep and give you a light or sound cue when you enter REM sleep. This program's developers suggest the cue is just the right brightness or volume to enter your dreams without awakening you, and to condition you to remembering more of your dream.

Suggestions for Using Imagery in Virtual Teams. Imagery is best used for individual work that is later shared with the rest of the team through synchronous videoconferencing, audioconferencing, or computer conferencing. Threaded discussion boards can be another way to discuss and share individually generated images with other team members. If desired, imagery can also be used by the entire team together. Programs that display random images or words, quotations, or affirmations are useful for triggering images and resulting ideas. (The Axon Idea Processor, which will be further described in the section on creativity software tools, has some of these features.) Virtual meditation tools (discussed later) may also be helpful in practicing imagery.

Analogical Thinking

One of the essential steps in imagery is to analogically think how the images generated may apply to a particular problem or challenge. Think analogically, rather than focusing on the literal meaning of the images. Analogical thinking is a valuable technique for achieving new insight on a particular challenge. When we create an analogy, we make the familiar strange and the strange familiar. Analogical thinking involves taking ideas from one context and applying them in a new context. William J. J. Gordon, the originator of the Synectics Methods, identified a series of analogical thinking strategies that creative people tend to use spontaneously (Gordon, 1961; Gordon and Poze, 1972, 1980). Gordon developed these strategies into the teachable Synectics problem-solving methods of direct analogy, personal analogy, fantasy analogy, and symbolic analogy.

To construct a *direct analogy,* think of how related problems have been solved. Then assess whether the approach used to solve the related problem would work in another setting. For example, I asked some of my Cal Poly Pomona students who were coming up on final exam week to consider "How do animals organize several different things?" and to consider how this question might provide ideas for how they could study for all their final exams. The discussion that emerged was entertaining, mostly around how their pet dogs like to organize their world. But out of the humorous discussion came the idea of organizing materials for each exam into piles and of approaching each pile little by little—much like a dog would circle round and round before settling on one spot to sit.

To use a *personal analogy* to gain new perspectives on a problem, simply imaginatively become a part of the problem. Identify with an object or process in order to get a new perspective on the problem. Imagine yourself to be an object or process in the problem in order to stimulate an insider view of the situation and inspire new ideas and insights. For example, to encourage my older daughter to finish her lunch at school, I asked her "What would you be like if you were a lunch that was 100% eaten?" She responded, "Happy," "Excited," "Nothing—everything would be gone!" I cannot credit this exchange for entirely convincing her to eat (many other factors played into this), but she now eats most of her lunch at school.

Use the *fantasy analogy* technique to think of fantastic, far-fetched, and ideal solutions. Out of these far-fetched fantasies, creative, yet often practical, ideas emerge. Using the fantasy analogy technique involves thinking of what you ideally want and then figuring out how to reach that goal. In the figuring out, you imagine anything is possible without censorship. For example, to improve class attendance, one day I asked my Cal Poly Pomona students "What in your wildest imagination would make you attend class?" Offering students $100 per class was a wild idea offered. Although I do not offer $100 to students to attend class, I do offer activity points (toward their final grade) for in-class participation.

To use a *symbolic analogy,* create two-word phrases that seem contradictory but could relate to a particular problem and stimulate ideas. In a creativity course I taught, we were discussing analogical thinking right before the long-awaited Spring Break vacation period. I asked the students to use the phrase "cheap luxury" to come up with ideas for vacation during their Spring Break. Many inexpensive but fun ways to pamper themselves emerged out of our discussion.

Suggestions for Using Analogical Thinking in Virtual Teams. Analogical thinking can be done individually or in a team session. In either case, it is sometimes helpful to construct questions that may stimulate team members to make an analogical connection. These questions may be created by the team and posted onto its Intranet Web page, or pre-packaged sets of stimulator questions may be found in idea generator software programs (to be described in the section on creativity software tools). Archiving the analogies created in shared files or in threaded discussion boards may be useful to stimulate analogical thinking in later sessions.

Drawing

Remember the old adage, "a picture is worth a 1000 words"? In the technique of drawing, the basic idea is to sketch your understanding of a particular problem and how it might be solved. The drawings may be symbolic, abstract, or realistic. Drawings help bring out your creativity and encourage you to develop new insights and dialogue about problems. Martha Graham, a creative genius in modern dance, used drawings to help her defy the conventions of traditional ballet. Her notebooks were full of drawings and sketches that she used to help conceptualize her dances (Michalko, 1998).

Because intuition emerges out of images and symbols better than it emerges out of words, drawing is an effective way to pull out intuitive creativity. Drawings can both evoke and record creative insight (Miller, 1987). One of the ways I begin creativity seminars is to ask participants at the beginning to create a drawing of what they think creativity means to them. At the close of the seminar, I ask participants to create another drawing of what creativity means to them. By viewing their drawings, participants witness the transition and growth they have made in their thoughts on the role of creativity in their lives. The second set of drawings typically illustrates a deeper personal view of how creativity impacts their lives on a daily basis.

You and your team members may want to try a drawing exercise to better understand the current reality of your virtual team or your own life situation.

Exercise

1. Draw a picture that represents your view of your team's current reality (or your current life situation). Use whatever images come to mind to describe the current situation.

2. Draw a picture that represents what you feel the future holds for your team or what you would ideally like to see for the team or for yourself. Use whatever images come to mind to describe your future or ideal situation.

3. Examine the two sets of drawings. What have you learned about your current and ideal team reality (or life situation)? Record the insights that emerge from your reflections.

4. Now consider what you might do to make that second drawing more of a reality in the future.

In a course I teach on *The Psychology of Creativity,* I have students do the previous drawing exercise. As most of the students in the class are graduating seniors, they are both apprehensive and excited about their upcoming transition into either full-time career work or graduate school. Many of the students gain insight into what they want their newfound reality to be. I also go through the exercise with the students. Figure 6.2 shows the set of drawings I created during one session. Even though the drawings are somewhat simplistic, they helped me to understand my current inability to gain work–life balance and my desire to do so.

Suggestions for Using Drawing in Virtual Teams. Teams may also participate in drawing activities. In teams, members are allowed a period of time to independently draw sketches of a problem and its solution. Then each team member passes his or her drawing to another team member, who reviews it, adds features, modifies it, or makes a new sketch on the same page. Finally team members collect and examine all the drawings and either select a final solution or construct a final solution from a composite of different sketches. Virtual teams may benefit from using the drawing technique. Members may use the graphics capabilities inherent in any word processing program to draw, or may use computer programs specifically designed for drawing. For an interactive session, in which team members construct drawings jointly, interactive whiteboards and drawing programs (such as SMART Board™, which was discussed in Chapter Five) are useful. All team members can see what is being drawn and can add to the drawing, as well. In addition, many EMS and groupware software packages have a whiteboard feature (such as the whiteboard feature in GroupSystems OnLine). During or after creating the drawings, team

Figure 6.2 Drawings Illustrating Current and Ideal Reality

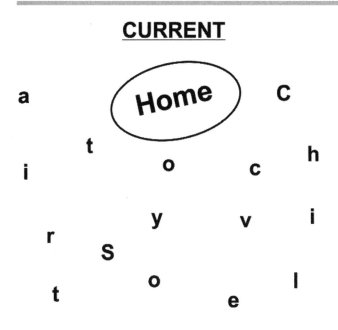

CURRENT

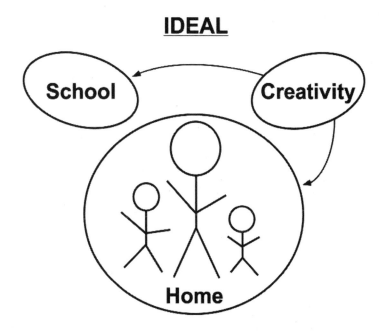

IDEAL

members discuss and record insights. Combining the use of interactive white-boards with video and audio links in synchronous computer meetings can assist in processing the drawings and sharing results.

Meditation (or Mind Clearing)

William Miller (1999) explains how Meditation, or Mind Clearing, works.

> Creative ideas happen when we open ourselves to something big-ger than our own mind, just as they are spurred by being com-mitted to a purpose larger than ourselves. Our most original ideas emerge from the space *between* our thoughts. Most of us, however, have such a constant stream of thoughts, there is very little space between them. Creating more stillness and serenity allows greater space between thoughts and thus greater opportunities for break-through ideas. (pp. 79–80)

Mediation allows one to access that space between thoughts. Unfortunately, meditation (and for that matter, many of the intuitive techniques that were pre-viously described) is regarded with suspicion in business settings. For that rea-son, Miller (1999) suggests mind clearing or concentration as more accepted terms for meditation in business. Many mistakenly believe that meditation is a losing of awareness, which is why they have misgivings about the technique. On the contrary, meditation involves a heightening (not a loss) of awareness, which is useful for tapping into one's inner source of creativity. From the inter-nal quietness achieved through meditation, one's mind becomes open to per-ceiving responses to questions that may otherwise continue to be puzzling. Meditation reduces anxiety and alleviates stress and tension; stress and tension inhibit one's ability to access intuitions. Scientific research has indicated that people who practice meditation are able to achieve a high degree of bodily relaxation and mental calmness. They also experience deeper levels of insight into themselves and their surrounding situations (Walker, 1975).

More than twenty years ago, I went through a training program in Tran-scendental Meditation (TM). At the time, I was involved in a summer acting program at the American Conservatory Theatre (ACT) in San Francisco. The hours were long and the work was emotionally intense. During this period, I regularly meditated twice daily. Even though it was a grueling (and invigorat-ing) schedule, I felt relaxed and energized. A year later, I began a career in film editing and let the practice of meditation go. During the nearly twenty years I spent as a film editor, where sixty- to eighty-hour work weeks were standard, I never felt as relaxed as I did that summer during my stay at ACT. I believe my meditation practice helped me maintain my high level of energy during that period.

Read the following exercise and then give the process of meditation a try.

Exercise

1. Sit on the floor and cross your legs, with your right foot resting on your left thigh, and your left foot resting on your right thigh (called the lotus position). Hold your back in a straight but comfortable position. Your neck and head should be held comfortably erect. Allow your hands to rest in your lap. You may choose whether to leave your eyes open and focused on a specific point a few feet in front of you or to keep them closed. If the lotus position is uncomfortable for you, then sit in a straight-backed chair with your feet on the floor, back and head comfortably erect, and hands placed in your lap. It is most important that you assume a comfortable position.

2. Once in position, take a few deep breaths. Then, imagine a warm drizzle of rain has just begun to fall. Feel the first few drops of the warm rain touch your forehead and scalp. As the raindrops touch you, release any tightness or tension you may feel. Next allow the warm rain drizzle to touch the other parts of your body—your face, neck, shoulders, chest, arms, waist, and thighs down to your knees, calves of your legs, ankles, feet, and toes. As the rain touches each part of your body, breathe deeply and let all tension, worry, anxiety, and tightness be washed away.

3. Breathe slowly and deeply. Establish a pattern of deep, slow breaths. On each inhalation, say the word "um," and on each exhalation say the word "ah." Continue to breathe in this fashion for a period of time (some indicate 20 minutes is an appropriate time to meditate).

   If you do not want to use the terms "ah" and "um," choose your own two neutral sounds to say on each inhalation and exhalation. Or try meditating to soothing music or sounds (such as bird chirps, wind, or ocean). Some people prefer to meditate by repeating a mantra over and over. A mantra in some forms of Buddhism is a sacred sound passed from the master to his disciple. In India, a common mantra is "Om." To use this mantra, separate the word "Om" into three syllables of equal length. Take a deep breath and as you exhale, make the sound of "oww" (as in cow), then "oou" (as in blue), then "mmm." Take another breath and continue repeating the mantra each time you exhale. You may also choose to develop your own mantra.

4. When you are ready to bring the meditation period to a close, allow yourself a few minutes to emerge. Do not come out too abruptly. You may wish to revisit each part of your body, reawakening (but not tensing) these parts. Once you reach your eyes, if they are closed, open them slowly. Then enjoy the rest of the day relaxed and refreshed.

Suggestions for Using Meditation in Virtual Teams. There are a variety of products to support virtual meditation. I was actually surprised to discover how much material is available over the Internet to support virtual meditation. Products range from simple tools such as books and audiotapes, to Internet Web sites offering soothing images and sounds to focus on while meditating, to discussion boards for meditators, to virtual meditation chambers. One meditation chamber, a virtual reality-based program, has been developed by researchers at the Georgia Institute of Technology (Larry Hodges, Diana Bromala, and Christopher Shaw). Meditators wear a head-mounted display with audio and video that guides them through a series of sunset and moonrise scenes and muscle-relaxation exercises. The headgear is connected by computer to three devices that monitor the meditator's breathing, heart rate, and galvanic skin response. As people relax, the images change. For example, as one relaxes, the sun begins to set or the moon begins to rise. The company under which this chamber is being produced (Virtually Better) is developing a PC-based desktop version of the meditation chamber for home and office use. This particular system may be useful for virtual team members wanting to use meditation techniques (Georgia Research Tech News, July, 2002).

Of course, virtual teams do not have to access chambers to practice meditation. One idea is for virtual teams to design their own "virtual meditation"

Web site, perhaps in a particular location on their team's Intranet. Team members may post their favorite soothing images or sounds and relaxation exercises for all members to share and be able to take a "mental vacation" when needed. On the team Web site, there might also be a discussion board where team members could post their reactions and share intuitive insights from meditation experiences. Although we often think of meditation as an individual activity, virtual teams may sponsor "team meditation sessions" with help from synchronous computer-meeting tools (discussed in Chapter Five). Virtual teams might even begin their meetings with a relaxing meditation before they dive into their work.

Creativity Software Tools

I am certain a few readers of this book may recall life before we began to use home computers and word processing software programs. I recall drafting papers in junior high and high school by hand and typing the final draft on a typewriter. Today, most students (even in elementary school) use computers with fairly sophisticated word processing programs to form and build their assignments. Word processing programs do not directly help students create better papers, but they do make steps in the process easier, such as moving text around and deleting and inserting text in the middle of sentences.

In the 20 years I spent as a film editor, I witnessed a similar influence of computers in facilitating and making creative tasks easier. Early in my career, I edited films using an upright moviola, an awkward machine that an editor hunched over to view the film on a little screen. I had to use a grease pencil to mark the frames where I wanted the scene to stop or start. Then I used a splicing block to cut out the portion of unwanted film and tape together the two adjoining pieces of film. With practice, you could get rather fast; nevertheless the process was manual and cumbersome. In the early 1990s, the concept of nonlinear editing emerged, which used film software in a fashion similar to word processors. Film was electronically digitized into a computer, and an editor could electronically select portions of scenes, put them together, add or delete as much as he or she liked, without the manual labor of a splicing block. I would not say that nonlinear editing systems made me a better editor. Those skills were inherent and developed through education and work experience. But the computer did make the process less tedious and more efficient. As an editor on a nonlinear system, I was more efficiently able to play around with different combinations of scenes.

So, computers are not the actual creators. But they can be helpful tools to use during the creative process. There are a series of computer software programs that have been developed to assist individuals and teams in generating, trying out, recording, and finally implementing ideas. Creativity software tools can be categorized into five distinct areas: idea generators, idea outliners, idea processors, idea implementers, and group decision-making tools (see Table 6.9). This section briefly describes the overall purpose of each category of creativity software and describes some useful programs within each category. In describing these programs, it is not my intent to endorse them. The descriptions are included to offer an example of what creativity software can do within each particular category. Certainly, many other useful creativity software programs exist that are not covered.

Table 6.9 Some Creativity Software Tools

Category	Overall Purpose	Sample Programs
Idea Generators (brainstorming, questioning, and prompting)	User provides input on problem or challenge, and then sets of questions, keywords, or exercises are presented to help provoke new ideas.	• Brainstorming Toolbox— NetStorm feature supports brainstorming in teams across a network. • IdeaFisher™ • ThoughtPath™ • Creative Whack Pack® Online
Idea Outliners (text-based and visual)	• *Text-based* outliners allow users to enter written text in a random or unstructured fashion and facilitate the reordering and restructuring of entries in a more meaningful way. • *Visual* outliners automate the process of drawing graphical outlines, mind maps, and concept maps.	*Text-based:* • Built in outline mode in word processors. • Specialized outliners like Acta or MORE. • Most visual outliners also have option of displaying what is generated in a text-based outline mode. *Visual:* • Inspiration® • MindManager®

Table 6.9 Some Creativity Software Tools, Cont'd

Category	Overall Purpose	Sample Programs
Idea Processors	Programs to assist with the processing of ideas. These programs offer a wide variety of options, including functions from other categories of creativity software programs as well.	• Axon Idea Processor • Idea Generator Plus
Idea Implementers	Programs to assist in the implementation of ideas, in turning ideas into action; may include project and task management programs, simple "to do" list manager programs, and Personal Information Managers (PIMs) to track tasks, contacts, and appointments.	• Microsoft Project • FastTrack Schedule • Milestones Professional • In Control • Project KickStart
Group Decision Making Tools: Electronic Meeting Systems (EMS)	Set of collaborative technologies designed to improve the productivity and quality of team meetings and other group activities.	• GroupSystems—Online version supports collaborative work across a network.

Idea Generators

How can you or your team break out of a rut, see things from a new perspective, climb over a creative block? Enter the Idea Generators (some call these questioning programs; see Proctor, 1999), a series of computer software packages designed to help you toss around ideas. These programs poke, prod, and question you to view things in a new light. The user provides a relatively small amount of input and then the program generates questions, keywords, or exercises to help provoke new ideas. Programs may also display random images or words, quotations, or affirmations useful for triggering ideas. Examples of idea generator programs are described as follows.

1. *The Brainstorming Toolbox* offers a series of interactive creative prompts that can be used by individuals or teams to assist in generating new ideas. The program provides thousands of original prompts to spark

ideas and specialized questions to help the problem solver explore alternative solutions. The Brainstorming Toolbox includes a series of tools such as Random Word, Random Picture, SCAMPER, FalseRules, What-Problem, FrameChange, and Challenge Facts. Each tool has its own screen designed specifically for software users to generate ideas with the aid of that particular tool. At any time, the list of ideas generated can be saved for later use. The NetStorm feature supports brainstorming in groups across a network.

2. *IdeaFisher*™ helps to stimulate mental associations starting from the input of a word or concept. IdeaFisher is built around a database called the IdeaBank, which contains more than 60,000 words organized by major categories (such as Animals, The Senses, and Emotions) and topical categories (groups of related concepts). Entries in the IdeaBank are cross-referenced by concept and association. An individual engages in free association, jumping from one related word or phrase to the next. Associations are recorded on the Idea Notepad and can be exported to a text file. IdeaFisher also includes a feature called QBank, a collection of more than 5000 questions that help an individual probe, evaluate, and flesh out ideas. It is also possible for users to construct and store their own list of questions for future use. IdeaFisher compiles a list of words users tend to use when answering QBank's questions. From this list, IdeaFisher extracts key ideas. Specialized QBank modules can also be purchased for helping to create a mission statement and produce long-range plans, for preparing grant proposals, or helping create speeches, lectures, and other presentations.

3. *ThoughtPath*™ (formerly MindLink Problem Solver) has been recommended for first-time users of idea-generation software because of its strong process orientation and simple interface. A problem or challenge is typed in and the program presents questions and exercises that allow a user to examine the problem from different angles. ThoughtPath is divided into components that work together to assist participants in generating creative ideas. These components include:

- The Gym—a series of self-paced exercises to improve creative thinking skills.

- Idea Generation—a tool for generating ideas about a problem.

- Triggers—exercises that allow participants to see fresh and new perspectives on problems, using prompts such as imagery, writing, word analogies, and role playing.

- Problem Solving—a complete tool for generating and organizing wishes, ideas, and potential solutions to problems.

- Thought Warehouse—the storage area for recording ideas and database for organizing, retrieving, and managing the knowledge base created while using ThoughtPath. Database queries can be performed on the warehouse with simple keyword assignments and text searches, giving users direct access to the accumulated bank of ideas, solutions, and thoughts from past ThoughtPath sessions.

Source: Copyright © 2003, thoughtpath.com. Used by permission of Inventive Logic, Inc.

Idea Outliners

Some individuals do not want a series of creative prompts, questions, or scenarios to solicit creative thinking. For those who simply need a way of recording, organizing, and arranging the ideas as they come, outliner programs are beneficial. Most programs offer support in both text-based and visual outlining.

Text-Based Outliners

Text-based outliner programs allow users to input written text in a random or unstructured fashion and then reorder and restructure the entries in a more meaningful way. Text-based outliners are useful for developing ideas from initial concept through to finished product. These programs allow individuals to start with an idea, add in main topics or categories, add sub-topics, and then flesh out text in each topic area. These systems are designed to help structure users' thoughts when they are preparing reports or designing processes. Although most word processors have a built-in outline mode (as does Microsoft Word), specialized textual outliners like Acta or MORE are also available. In addition, most visual outliners also have the option of displaying what is generated in a text-based outline mode.

Visual Outliners

Visual outliners attempt to automate the process of drawing graphical outlines, mind maps, and concept maps. There have been a number of visual outliner programs produced commercially. Two well-known visual outliner programs are described below.

1. *Inspiration®* is a tool for visual thinking and outlining to develop ideas into written documents and diagrams. Inspiration supports users in a variety of tasks—visual and textual outlining, idea or mind mapping, concept mapping, creating storyboards, and drawing diagrams such as organizational charts and flow charts. Inspiration helps individuals to create and organize ideas in both graphic and outline forms. In the diagram mode, one can create free-form visuals, diagrams, mind and concept maps, and presentation graphics. Using the integrated outline mode, ideas can be expanded into outlines and written documents. Although Inspiration has been classified as a visual outliner, it can also function as a textual outliner, as a brainstorming tool, and as a Web design tool.

2. *MindManager®* (developed by Mindjet LLC) is a visual tool for brainstorming and planning that helps users capture, organize, and communicate ideas, information, and data. MindManager uses both words and visual clues (such as proximity, color, graphics, and icons) to express ideas and relationships. From a graphic symbol in the center of the screen, users capture ideas and information with cascading layers of topics and sub-topics—each topic representing an idea or piece of information. Users can connect thoughts with relationship arrows, add graphic images and icons, emphasize key points with color highlighting, and hyperlink topics to Web sites, documents, files, applications, and email addresses. The result is a visual map of the thinking process and related information that can be shared via the Internet, used for interactive presentations, or exported via Microsoft Office® applications, XML, or as a Web page. A sample mind map generated through MindManager is seen in Figure 6.3.

Figure 6.3 Sample Mind Map from MindManager

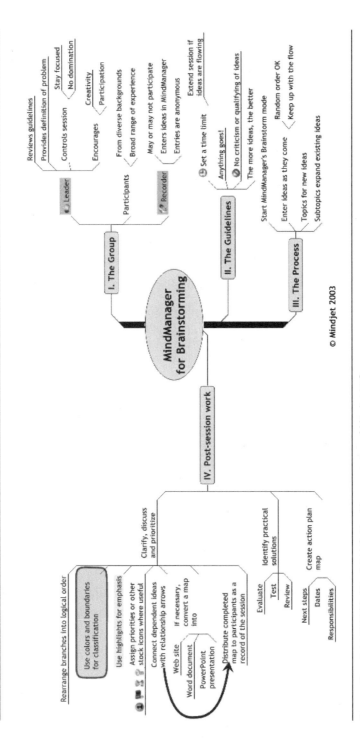

Source: Copyright © 2003. Mindjet LLC. Used by permission of Mindjet LLC.

There are a variety of functions that can be accomplished with Mind-Manager, including:

- Manage and track progress on projects visually, prepare and make presentations, and make budgets and "to-do" lists. (This feature can be used as an idea implementer.)

- Brainstorm individually or within a group. (This feature can be used as an idea generator.)

- Conduct strategic and project planning.

- Analyze data and model processes.

- Create reports, project plans, presentations, and Web sites.

- Export to PowerPoint, Word, Project, Outlook, HTML, and XML.

- Capture, store, and share project information with others.

MindManager provides users with an intuitive way to think quickly and broadly about a project or topic. Once thinking has been captured in the Mind-Manager interface, it can then be shared in whatever form is most appropriate to the team (i.e., a text report, slide presentation, Web site, or exported directly into an information system, application, or database). Virtual teams can also share MindManager maps in real time over the Internet, using any of the leading Web conferencing software to collaborate around the globe.

Idea Processors

Similar to what word processors have done for processing words, idea processor programs are available to assist with the processing of ideas. These programs actually offer a wide variety of idea processing options.

1. The *Axon Idea Processor*, invented by Chan Bok, offers a visual workbench with a range of tools to record, process, and manipulate ideas. The Axon Idea Processor functions as an idea processor, but also has features that allow it to be used as an idea generator, visual outliner, and idea implementer. The Axon Idea Processor is primarily a sketchpad for creating diagrams to relate ideas. Ideas and diagrams are the basic abstractions of the Axon Idea Processor. Ideas are shown as graphical objects and relationships among them shown as links. Diagrams may be multilevel and three-dimensional. Color, shape, size, scale,

position, depth, link, and icons may all be used in representing ideas. Visual cues facilitate recall, association, and discovery. Users can also get a sense of the bigger picture, with details which can be hidden from view, if needed. Diagrams help the thinker to model and subsequently solve complex problems. The Axon Idea Processor supports the user in creating both visual diagrams (concept maps, mind maps, clusters) and working with text (analyzing sentence structure). It also assists in idea generation, with a checklist of question prompts, and offers templates for assisting with project management. A simulation feature can also be used to map out and create animated movements to make concepts come alive. A brief description of the Axon Idea Processor's set of tools follows:

- Analyzer—analyze sentence structure, word frequency, and so on.

- Checklists—capture and store knowledge and wisdom.

- Clusters—organize ideas into trees and branches (mind mapping).

- FreeWriter – a pre-writing tool.

- Generator—generate sentences, poems, inventions, and the like.

- Questions—generate generic questions.

- Random Words—prompt with words or word pairs.

- Sequencer—assign sequence to your ideas.

- Simulator—make concepts come alive with animation.

- Templates—a resource containing pictorial templates (referred to as pictures of wisdom) to help in modeling and analyzing complex systems, and in project management.

- Ticker—a continuous/modeless prompting tool. Tickers are similar to the horizontal scrolling texts seen on television news channels. Text contents can be user specified or auto-generated.

Source: Copyright © 2003 Axon Research. Used by permission of Axon Research, Singapore.

Following is a sample screen from the *Axon Idea Processor* software program illustrating the checklist tool. (A mind map illustrating the cluster tool was included earlier in this chapter.)

Figure 6.4 Checklist Tool from Axon Idea Processor

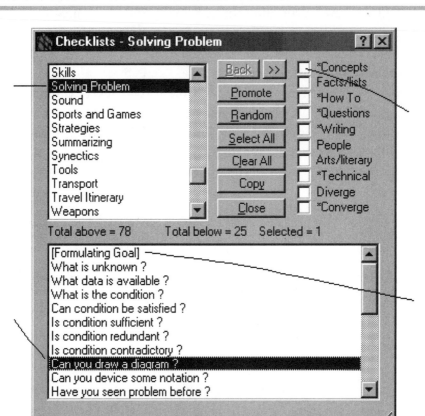

Source: Copyright © 2003 Axon Research. Used by permission of Axon Research, Singapore.

Some idea processor programs are grounded more firmly in theoretical conceptualizations of the creative problem-solving process and provide a series of creative thinking skills for each identified stage. An example is The Idea Generator Plus program.

2. The *Idea Generator Plus* takes users through a series of structured interactive exercises designed to help them look at problems or situations from new points of view and develop and evaluate ideas. Idea Generator Plus has a series of creative thinking and planning skills to support three logical parts of the problem-solving process.

- Problem statement—In this first section of the program, users succinctly define their problem, their goals, related objectives, and list all the people involved.

- Idea generator—Next, users choose from a series of seven thought-provoking techniques to create new ideas and solutions. These techniques are as follows:

  - *Similar Situations*: directs users to take lessons from similar situations they have encountered in the past.

  - *Metaphors for the Situation*: prompts users to search for parallels between familiar activities and the situation they face. For example, marketing campaigns may be described as military operations.

  - *Other Perspectives*: asks users to play the pessimist and optimist and see their situation through the eyes of others, real or imaginary. For example, users may ask themselves, "What would Lee Iacocca do in a situation like this?"

  - *Focus on Your Goals One by One*: lets users treat each objective as the only goal. This frees users from trying to solve too many problems at the same time.

  - *Reverse Your Goals*: prompts users to generate ideas from opposites of the goals they want to achieve.

  - *Focus on the People Involved*: asks users to analyze qualities in other people, helpful or hostile, as a source of new ideas.

  - *Make the Most of Your Ideas*: permits users to improve bad ideas, dump ideas that make no sense, and group ideas together in categories.

- Evaluation—The third section of the program is where users evaluate their ideas by ranking ideas against objectives and considering long- and short-term costs and benefits and determining potential effects on other people. Reports can be generated to list ideas numerically ranked for further consideration and analysis.

Source: Copyright © 2003, projectkickstart.com. Used by permission from Experience In Software, Inc.

An on-line note pad is available for users to capture thoughts as they occur. Reports can then be generated and viewed on the computer screen or printed out.

Idea Implementers

After an idea has been generated and further developed, it needs to be further improved and then implemented or turned into action. A series of programs may assist in the implementation of ideas. Depending on the size and the scope of the implementation, a project or task management program (for example, Microsoft Project, FastTrack Schedule, and Milestones Professional) can be used; or perhaps a to-do list manager, like In Control, will suffice. One unique brainstorming and project management tool is Project KickStart (developed by Experience In Software). This software tool has a dual emphasis on both planning a project strategy and building a project schedule. Eight planning icons guide individuals or teams through a process of defining project phases, clarifying goals, establishing tasks, anticipating obstacles and needed resources, delegating assignments, and consideration of other strategic project-related issues as well. There is a built-in Gantt chart for scheduling. Users can also send their project data to Microsoft Office Applications, such as Word, Excel, and Microsoft Project (Source: Copyright © 2003, projectkickstart.com. Used by permission of Experience In Software). Personal Information Managers (PIMs) electronically keep track of tasks, contacts, and appointments. They may also aid in organizing notes in a variety of ways for ongoing projects. Outliner programs (discussed earlier) also assist with idea implementation.

Group Decision-Making Tools: Electronic Meeting Systems

It's 5 p.m. and your team has been meeting for nearly four hours. At 2 p.m., you began to look at the clock every five minutes. The meeting has lasted way too long, the discussion has been dominated by two or three individuals, and the rest of you have said little. The meeting adjourns at 5:30 p.m., at which time you are left wondering, "What was accomplished?" On the drive home, you conclude pretty much nothing of any merit was accomplished.

Well, you get the picture and we have all been there. Organizations have been struggling with the problem of how to increase team meeting effectiveness for years. To meet this need, a particular subset of collaborative technologies called Electronic Meeting Systems (EMS) have been designed to improve the productivity and quality of team meetings and other group activities. The list of business activities being accomplished through EMS continues to grow, including activities such as negotiation, group decision support, proposal development, conflict resolution, strategic planning, business process re-engineering, policy development, product development, brainstorming, focus groups, and just plain team meetings.

What Is EMS?

The EMS software is a set of programs or tools that runs on networked computers. This software can support both same-time and same-place meetings (in what are termed meeting rooms) or Internet-enabled different-time and different-place meetings. Participants engage in synchronous or asynchronous electronic exchanges with each other, but with direction and purpose and under the guidance of a skilled facilitator who is not a member of the group and who doesn't necessarily know anything about the meeting topic, but does thoroughly understand the EMS software. Members contribute ideas anonymously without fear of criticism. Everyone has equal opportunity to participate. Ideas are evaluated on their merit rather than on the personal traits or political clout of the individual proposing the idea.

Hardware needed for EMS applications includes more than just computers and peripheral equipment. Same-time and same-place meetings also require conference facilities, audiovisual equipment, networking equipment that connects everyone, and meeting facilitators and staff to keep the hardware operating correctly. However, many companies are bypassing the specially-equipped meeting rooms in favor of having participants attend EMS meetings through their individual desktop computers. In addition, EMS's can be integrated with other conferencing systems such as desktop video or audio links, so that the interpersonal dynamics of a face-to-face meeting can be captured. In this case, team members can see one another on their desktop screens or hear them at the same time the information is generated.

What Is EMS Best Used For?

Common uses for EMS software are described in Table 6.10.

EMS software has been shown to enhance both productivity and efficiency in business meetings. These systems offer a series of advantages for teams, whether virtual or not. Some of the advantages and disadvantages of EMS (when compared to traditional, non-automated team meetings) are as follows.

Table 6.10 Common Uses for Electronic Meeting Systems (EMS)

Brainstorm and generate ideas: Team members enter ideas about a topic or potential problem from their computers simultaneously (and often anonymously) and are able to see the ideas from other team members immediately on their computer monitors. Team members can add comments or opinions to other members' ideas as well. Because brainstorming is free flowing and can be anonymous, this reduces the social pressure to conform. Results of these brainstorming sessions are also recorded electronically.

Group and categorize ideas: Team members can collectively take the initial list of ideas generated and move them into different categories, collapsing or subsuming them into a smaller list of categories.

Prioritize and evaluate ideas and potential solutions: Team members can vote to gauge the degree of consensus about ideas generated and potential solutions or decisions. Results can then be displayed for the team to view and discuss. If voting is done anonymously, this may free individual team members from feeling pressure to respond one way or another.

Organize ideas into preliminary outlines of products: Team members can jointly organize ideas into outlines that the entire team can then view and comment on. Individual team members can then take the outlines and associated comments away to work on them.

Advantages of EMS

1. *More participation*—Because EMS software offers anonymity, members may participate more fully and be more willing to ask "foolish" questions or make unpopular comments. Similarly, participants will not be as subject to Groupthink or conformance pressure (holding back due to politeness or fear of reprisals). Each participant actually has more "air time" to contribute ideas throughout the entire meeting. In a traditional group meeting, members may only have a few minutes to express their ideas; they have to listen to others speak, and certain individuals often dominate the discussion. EMS software allows every participant to speak in parallel (at the same time).

2. *More structure*—EMS software provides structure, making it more difficult to deviate from the problem-solving cycle and make incomplete or premature decisions. In addition, team members using the software stay focused more fully on the issues throughout the meeting. This is in part because they have fewer non-task interactions, like gossiping, when working on-line.

3. *Triggering*—EMS software allows each participant to add his or her thoughts in the discussion and to review others' ideas and comments. Because every member can see everyone else's work (without knowing their identity), new ideas and thoughts are triggered. People are more willing to share even budding or embryonic ideas. These budding ideas may in turn stimulate ideas that might not have surfaced in a more traditional face-to-face meeting.

4. *Automatic organizational memory*—EMS software is able to record all comments generated during the meeting, and consequently, participants need not take notes or minutes. This automated log of the discussion supports the development of an organizational memory from meeting to meeting.

5. *Benefits and savings*—Studies involving the use of EMS software show that time spent in meetings was reduced by seventy-one percent and calendar time required for projects relating to meetings was reduced ninety-one percent. Many organizations that have used EMS software (such as IBM, Boeing, US Army, BellCore, and Marriott) have reported significant reduction of labor costs, increased return on investment, and overall company savings (Marsh, Collins and Stohr, 1997).

Disadvantages of EMS

1. *Slow communication*—Most people speak much faster than they type and thus usually prefer a verbal environment. On the other hand, an EMS allows participants to review recorded comments and some people may read and scan faster than they are able to hear and process. In addition, anonymity and parallel communication are advantages that may compensate for slow typing speed. And if the group is made up of at least eight people, it may be more efficient to type in parallel rather than type and read in sequence.

2. *Not all tasks are amenable to EMS*—Group meetings that involve one-to-many communication (for example, a leader lecturing to the group) would not benefit from EMS software. Only those tasks that require team members to exchange ideas efficiently are appropriate for EMS.

While EMS software has many advantages, it is not always the best tool for the task. Table 6.11 outlines the usefulness of EMS for virtual teams (adapted from Duarte and Snyder, 1999).

Table 6.11 Electronic Meeting Systems' Usefulness

EMS are useful for	EMS may not be useful for
• Brainstorming, prioritizing, outlining, and voting on ideas	• Depicting complex concepts, process flows, scenarios, or sketches
• Defining problems with answers and reaching a consensus	• Displaying and diagramming data and performing in-depth and complex analysis
• Listing and prioritizing options and making decisions	• Debating options and making judgments about ambiguous topics
• In negotiating conflict, stating and discussing opinions, deciding among optional approaches, and reaching compromises	• Resolving interpersonal conflict

Source: Adapted from Duarte, D., & Snyder, N. (1999). *Mastering Virtual Teams: Strategies, Tools, and Techniques That Succeed.* San Francisco: Jossey-Bass Publishers. Used by permission of John Wiley and Sons, Inc.

GroupSystems: An EMS Software Program

A number of groupware options are available to support dispersed team creativity and decision-making efforts. *GroupSystems,* developed at the University of Arizona in cooperation with IBM and other manufacturers, and offered by GroupSystems.com (originally Ventana Corporation), is most commonly recognized as the pioneer and leader in the field of collaborative EMS technology. GroupSystems is built around idea generation, idea organization, alternative evaluation and consensus building, decision-making, and the immediate creation of an accurate group record and action plan. GroupSystems offers the following three major products.

1. GroupSystems MeetingRoom and Workgroup edition, for same time and same place network-based collaboration.

2. GroupIntelligence, a Web-reporting tool that makes it possible to combine, publish, and apply results from GroupSystems sessions.

3. GroupSystems OnLine, which is an Internet-enabled version of the MeetingRoom product. The GroupSystems OnLine version has particular applications for virtual teams.

GroupSystems OnLine offers a series of electronic interactive tools to allow virtual team members to work collaboratively and create together. The following three main features apply to the GroupSystems tools.

- Simultaneous contribution—Everyone speaks at once, which saves time and increases productivity.

- Anonymity—The identity of each contributor is unknown, so participants tend to feel freer to express opinions and to evaluate ideas based on merit.

- Complete records—At the end of a meeting, participants can easily produce a complete and accurate report of ideas and comments generated, and vote results.

The tools, each of which provides a unique way to guide interactions, are as follows.

Agenda—Provides the framework for team activities. It prompts the team leader to develop a plan for the business process that details the intended results, information needed, and participant list.

Categorizer—Used to collect a list of ideas, then categorize those ideas into logical groupings. The group can brainstorm on one single list or enter ideas directly into categories.

Vote—A series of eight voting methods (rank order, ten-point scale, true and false, yes or no, four- and five-point agree or disagree scales, multiple selection, and a customized point scale). This feature is commonly used to evaluate, make decisions, and build consensus on appropriate ideas and solutions.

Group outliner—Used to generate and organize ideas into a hierarchical structure. Outlines can be displayed in bulleted or numbered format. Meeting facilitators can distribute the entire outline to all participants or allow them to work in subgroups. This feature is commonly used to support action planning, group writing, and process design.

Topic commenter—The meeting facilitator enters a list of topics and asks meeting participants to comment on those topics. This feature is commonly used for discussing strengths and weaknesses and in focus group research.

Alternative analysis—Used to evaluate a list of alternatives based on multiple criteria (for example, easy to use, saves time, saves money, and so on). Some common uses include assessing risks and evaluating options.

Electronic brainstorming—Used for simultaneous and anonymous idea sharing on a specific question or issue. This feature is used for broad or more focused brainstorming and visioning or strategic planning sessions.

Survey—Used to build, distribute, and collect survey forms. In business, common uses are employee feedback surveys, three hundred sixty-degree performance reviews, and customer surveys.

Source: Copyright © 2003, GroupSystems.com. Used by permission of GroupSystems.

A sample screen illustrating the Electronic Brainstorming tool can be found in Figure 6.5.

Figure 6.5 Electronic Brainstorming Tool from GroupSystems

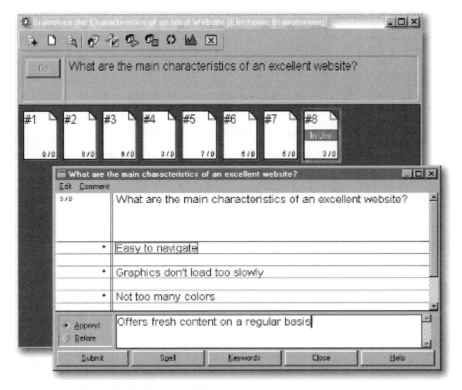

Source: Copyright © 2003, GroupSystems.com. Used by permission of GroupSystems.

In addition to the interactive tools, GroupSystems includes several resources for the leader or facilitator of a GroupSystems meeting. A few examples include a whiteboard that allows team members to draw on separate pages or on the same page; an opinion meter that allows the leader to take a quick read on group opinion on a particular issue; and a personal log, where the meeting leader can take notes that are not shared with the rest of the team.

It is a fact that in contemporary business more and more decisions are being made by groups. Sadly enough, it is also a fact that a large number of team meetings in which these decisions are being made are inefficient. Especially with larger teams, EMS software helps remove many of the process obstacles and interpersonal barriers that develop and exist in face-to-face decision making sessions. With EMS software, team meetings are more efficient, communication is more directed, and the subsequent decisions are made more efficiently.

Tool: Pulling Together Your Team's Creative Toolbox

Your team's preference for creativity techniques and software programs will depend on team goals and philosophies and individual creative styles. Linear techniques help teams find new areas to look for new innovations. Intuitive techniques complement linear thinking by allowing individuals to tap into inner sources of creative insight. It is important that your team be fluent in both intuitive and linear techniques, mixing them together and crafting your own team creative toolbox. You may find it beneficial to use Table 6.12 while selecting the appropriate creativity techniques and software tools for your team. The table includes the following information:

- a summary of each linear and intuitive technique
- a brief description of suggestions on how to do each technique in a virtual team
- suggestions for creativity software that may assist in using each technique
- an analysis of whether the technique is best accomplished by individual team members (who then later share their results with the entire team) or best accomplished by the entire team working together (whether synchronously or asynchronously)

Table 6.12 Appropriate Creativity Techniques and Software Tools

Technique	Description and Purpose	Suggestions for Virtual Teams and Relevant Software Tools	Supports Use by Individuals or Entire Team?
Linear			
Attribute listing	Useful for improving tangible objects. Properties or attributes of a product are listed and then reviewed one at a time with a view toward improving each attribute.	If feasible, face-to-face meetings with few resources (i.e., flipchart, whiteboard) can be used. Can also be done via synchronous computer meetings with interactive whiteboards and audio-conferencing or through asynchronous threaded discussions. Idea generator programs (for example IdeaFisher™) offer questions or idea triggers that may be beneficial. Outliner programs assist in organizing and structuring ideas generated.	Can be done individually with results shared to the entire team, but probably more fun and enjoyable when done by entire team or subset of the team.
Morphological synthesis	Extension of the attribute-listing procedure. Involves listing specific ideas for one dimension of a problem along one axis of a matrix and ideas for a second attribute along the other axis. Within each cell of the matrix lies a new idea or potential solution to a problem.	To create the matrix, use drawing programs, electronic or interactive whiteboards, or visual outliners. Even simple word processing programs (creating a table) will work for two-dimensional matrices.	Individual or team.
Force-Field Analysis	Identify forces contributing to or hindering a solution to a problem; specify actions to strengthen or add a new positive force and weaken a negative force.	Have team members post individual statements to shared database systems, shared files, or to a private section of team's Intranet Web page. Then schedule a face-to-face, audio-conference, or synchronous computer meeting	Begin with individuals constructing their own personal catastrophe and ideal statements. Then bring team together for rest of the process.

Table 6.12 Appropriate Creativity Techniques and Software Tools, Cont'd

Technique	Description and Purpose	Suggestions for Virtual Teams and Relevant Software Tools	Supports Use by Individuals or Entire Team?
		(with access to interactive whiteboards, word processing, outliner programs, audio link) to form joint catastrophe and ideal statement, list negative and positive forces, and generate actions moving the team closer to the ideal.	
Mind Mapping	Start with central theme and then depict thoughts and associations as branches growing in all directions from the central theme.	Mind maps can be created with a variety of tools: • visual outliners (for example Inspiration®, MindManager®) • interactive whiteboards (for example SMART Board™)	Individual or team.
Idea Checklists	Series of structured questions or exercises that prod one into seeing a problem from a new perspective (for example, SCAMPER).	Several idea generator (questioning) programs have built-in lists to prod team members into new insights (for example, Brainstorming Toolbox; IdeaFisher™; Thought-Path's™ Idea Triggers; Creative Whack Pack® Online). EMS software also has this feature.	Individual or team.
Brainstorming	Problem is stated. Participants give ideas for solving the problem off-the-top-of-the head, under the conditions of deferred judgment and quantity breeding quality.	Most widely-developed electronic creativity technique. Many idea generator programs (for example, Brainstorming Toolbox) are available. EMS software (Group-Systems' Electronic Brainstorming option) is also set up to support electronic brainstorming.	Individual or team.

Table 6.12 Appropriate Creativity Techniques and Software Tools, Cont'd

Technique	Description and Purpose	Suggestions for Virtual Teams and Relevant Software Tools	Supports Use by Individuals or Entire Team?
Intuitive			
Imagery	Use of symbols, scenes, or images as windows to creative thought and insight.	Creativity software programs that display random images or words, quotations, or affirmations (for example, Axon Idea Processor) are useful for triggering images and resulting ideas. Virtual meditation tapes and on-line resources may also be helpful in practicing imagery.	Mostly individual generation of images. Then a sharing of results with the entire team can occur through various synchronous or asynchronous communication tools.
Analogical thinking	Involves taking ideas from one context and applying them in a new context. Four major types—direct, personal, fantasy, symbolic.	Use either pre-packaged sets of stimulator questions found in the idea generator software programs or custom-tailored questions (perhaps made available on team Intranet Web page) to prod individuals into making analogical connections. Archive analogies created in shared files, databases, or in threaded discussion boards.	Individual or team.
Drawing	Draw a picture or sketch of one's understanding of a particular problem and how it might be solved. Drawings may be symbolic, abstract, or realistic.	Teams can perform joint drawings, supported by interactive whiteboards or drawing programs (e.g., SMART Board™, GroupSketch). Many EMS and groupware software packages also have a whiteboard feature (such as whiteboard feature in GroupSystems Online; whiteboard function in NetMeeting).	Individual or team.

Table 6.12 Appropriate Creativity Techniques and Software Tools, Cont'd

Technique	Description and Purpose	Suggestions for Virtual Teams and Relevant Software Tools	Supports Use by Individuals or Entire Team?
Meditation	Also known as mind-clearing or concentration; consciously directing one's attention to heighten awareness and achieve inner calmness; useful for tapping into one's inner source of creativity.	Tools to support individual virtual meditation range from books and audiotapes to Internet Web sites offering soothing images and sounds to focus on during meditation, to discussion boards where meditators exchange ideas and seek support, to a PC-based desktop version of a meditation chamber.	Mostly individual meditation sessions, from which insights that emerge can later be shared and processed with team members, using one of the many groupware options. One idea is for team members to create a "virtual meditation" room in their team Intranet Web page. Joint team meditation sessions may also be useful as lead-ins to synchronous computer meetings.

Now it is your turn to formulate your creative toolbox. As a team, decide which creativity techniques you find most useful in your work. Also discuss (and perhaps demonstrate) various software tools. Then decide on your team's creative toolbox and enter your decisions in Table 6.13.

Table 6.13 Your Team's Creative Toolbox

Linear techniques our team prefers:
Intuitive techniques our team prefers:
Creativity software tools our team would like to utilize (or already has):

Final Thoughts

Some have suggested that computers are necessary to assist with creativity. Gerhard Fischer argues that "the power of the unaided, individual mind is highly overrated—much of our human intelligence and creativity results from the collective memory of humankind and of the artifacts and technology surrounding us" (in Edmonds, Fischer, Mountford, Nake, Riecken, and Spence, 1995). Others assert the opposite, that computers are basically useless in creative domains. According to Joy Mountford, "The tools of creative businesses are typically paper and pencil, whiteboards and physical objects" (in Edmonds et al., 1995). Remember, none of the creativity techniques and software programs discussed in this chapter can replace your team. Techniques and software cannot come up with an idea or make a decision for you. However, the most appropriate creativity techniques and the most suitable creativity software programs can function as tools to make it easier for your team to sort through a jumble of ideas and transform them into a highly creative outcome—maybe even a great one. But a team will be hard-pressed to effectively sort through any jumble of ideas without establishing agreed-upon norms and protocols to guide and monitor its creative activities. Part IV outlines a series of norms for communication behavior and project and task management that are essential for virtual teams doing creative work.

Points to Remember

- Approaches to stimulating creativity fall into two major categories, linear and intuitive. Linear techniques provide a structure within which we can seek and find alternative solutions. We use a logical pattern or sequence of steps to arrive at solutions. Intuitive techniques assist individuals or teams in achieving an inner state of calmness, out of which unpredictable inspirations or insights may appear.

- In the pursuit of optimal creativity, both linear and intuitive approaches are necessary. A typical pattern is linear thinking or logic preceding and following intuitive insight.

- Software programs have been developed to help individuals and teams in generating, trying out, recording, and finally implementing ideas. However, it is important to remember that while computers can be helpful tools to use during the creative process, they are not the actual creators.

- Which creativity techniques and software programs your team will find most useful depends largely on the philosophy of the team and style of the individual members in approaching creative work. Linear techniques are beneficial for helping teams to find new areas to look for new innovations. Intuitive techniques complement linear thinking by allowing individuals to tap their inner source of creative insight. It is important for the team to be fluent in both intuitive and linear techniques, mixing them together in a well-rounded creative toolbox.

- Techniques and software cannot come up with an idea or make a decision for you. But they may make it easier for the team to sort through a jumble of ideas and transform them into a creative outcome.

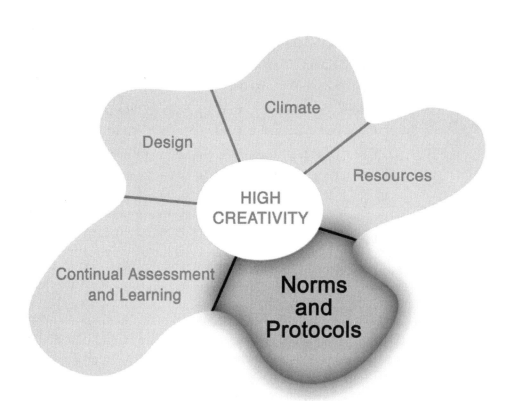

PART IV

Norms and Protocols

NORMS ARE CRITICAL FOR SPECIFYING what the acceptable standards of behavior are within a team. Norms tell individual team members what is expected of them and what they can expect of their colleagues as well. Working virtually through collaborative technology gives individual members new levels of autonomy and freedom that may not be possible on a traditional team. However, this does not mean virtual team members can use this new freedom to escape the pull of their team. Armstrong and Cole (1996) suggest that a shared agreement across distance concerning how to use technology is just as important as the technology itself. Such a sense of shared agreement can be developed by having your team take the time to seriously address, define, and agree on what is acceptable (and unacceptable) behavior. Two key categories of *norms and protocols* needed for virtual teams doing creative work are communication behavior and project and task management norms and protocols. Chapter Seven describes a series of communication behavior and project and task management norms and protocols. A step-by-step process is also offered to help virtual teams develop norms that govern their communication patterns and approaches to accomplishing shared creative work.

CHAPTER 7

Establishing Appropriate Norms and Protocols

I don't think we can usually get through a week without phone contact with each of our partners. That's just one of those expected norms. An example is that if one of my partners calls me, for whatever reason, I am expected to, as soon as possible, get back to him or her. If I have a problem at 11:00 at night on how to do something the next day, I know that it's okay for me to call these people, and they have to respond. If I have that need, and call, generally within 24 hours, more often within a few hours, I'm going to get a return call. People check in.

Matt, ACI

ALL TEAMS HAVE NORMS. Norms establish what the acceptable standards of behavior are that are shared among the members of any team, whether virtual or not. Norms tell team members what they ought and ought not do under certain circumstances. They tell each individual team member what is expected of him or her in certain situations. Norms guide

233

participation, communication, conflict management, project and task management, problem solving and decision-making, and how to pursue creative efforts. Virtual teams require unique and more detailed norms than co-located teams do. When all team members agree on norms, they act to influence the behavior of team members with a minimum of external controls. In this chapter, two critical types of norms needed by virtual teams doing creative work are reviewed: communication behavior and project and task management norms. *Communication behavior* norms guide the team's communication patterns and exchange of information to accomplish and perform their knowledge work. *Project and task management* norms assist the team in organizing and managing their work. The specific norms that will be reviewed in this chapter are listed in Table 7.1.

Table 7.1 Two Critical Types of Norms

Communication Behavior Norms	Project and Task Management Norms
Availability and acknowledgment	Developing a creative process project lifecycle map
Appropriateness of specific communication tools	Distinguishing between routine and creative tasks
Protocols for usage of specific communication tools	Assigning roles and responsibilities
Rules governing subgroup information exchange	Timeframes and accountability measures
The balance of structured and unstructured communication	Protocols for shared workspaces and files
	Norms for project review, revision, and final approval

Communication Behavior Norms
Availability and Acknowledgment Norms

Developing standards for availability and acknowledgment means creating agreements between team members about when and how they will be available for collaboration and how quickly they will respond to requests (Haywood, 1998). These types of norms are needed to: (1) establish acceptable timeframes and frequency for individuals to check in various communication tools, (2) confirm that individual team members received messages, and (3) respect an individual team member's personal time.

Availability and acknowledgment norms need to be defined and agreed on by all members of the team and then respected and practiced. The frequency of checking in must be fair to all members and may also need to be adjusted depending on project demands. Unless clear protocols are set for how often to check in each type of communication tool, team members may disagree about what is considered up-to-date project-related information.

Individual team members, in consultation with the entire team, need to establish and communicate what their working hours are and how often they will check and respond to specific types of communication. (For example, when do they check voice mail, e-mail, interoffice mail, and so on.) The team also needs to specify standards of acknowledgment for various communication tools. Different communication tools may require different forms of acknowledgment. For example, sending a Fax may not always guarantee that a particular individual received it. (Faxes may be received in central mailrooms.) Team members may require additional confirmation (perhaps by e-mail) that a Fax was received.

Availability and acknowledgment norms work best when clearly spelled out in written form, especially with larger multi-organizational or globally-dispersed teams. Teams may want to post agreed-upon availability and acknowledgment norms on their Intranet pages, in essence displaying a "virtual availability board."

Availability standards may vary for each team member based on that individual's task and role in the team. For example, in the ACI team, consultants did not need to check in daily, but the current rotating team leader (RIOU) needed to telephone the support staff daily to discuss business-management issues. If availability standards vary depending on a particular team member's role, then these differences need to be clearly defined in the team's availability and acknowledgment norms.

Examples of Availability Norms

The ACI Team

E-mail: A guiding norm is for team members to commit to responding to e-mail at least three to four times a week. Consultants on the road must travel with computers.

Telephone: A norm is for team members to return phone calls as soon as possible, generally within twenty-four hours, even when traveling and working out of client sites. Another norm for telephone contact is that the designated team leader (RIOU) is required to telephone the support office daily.

The Jacobs/Taylor Team

Telephone: A norm agreed to by all senior members of the team is daily phone contact, even on weekends. Chad, a member of the Jacobs/Taylor team, elaborates on this norm: "Senior members of the team have agreed on daily contact times. We talk to each other every day, including weekends. I know every night at 5:30 Pacific time, my partner is going to call me from wherever he is at, or I will call him. Another rule is that the person out of town calls home base. And so I can save up all of the things during the day, and I don't even have to think about that 'cause I know when that communication is going to take place."

The VTG Team

Shared database system (Lotus Notes®): Team members agreed to replicate (post information in shared databases) daily (except weekends), even when traveling and working at client sites. Cristina, a member of the VTG team, explains that daily replication is required on weekdays: "Even if you're out there delivering work, you replicate when you come back. So the different consultants who will be on the road are all replicating in their hotel rooms."

The ELC Team

E-mail: Team members are expected to work on-line daily, actively using the main avenues of communication available to the team: synchronous conversations through the team's computer conferencing system and asynchronous communication through the team's Intranet and Internet e-mail.

The WN–Current Events Team

E-mail: E-mail exchanges occur as needed. Team members are in contact daily through either e-mail or the telephone.

Availability and acknowledgment norms are critical to give team members the connection and assurance they need to perform shared work. However, it is important not to overdo availability. Think about what is appropriate, respect what has been agreed on, and allow team members their personal time.

Appropriateness of Specific Communication Tools

In Chapter Five, a series of communication tools available to virtual teams and the purposes for which each are appropriate were offered. Members of virtual teams need to think clearly about what types of communication tools they will use and for what specific purposes or circumstances and put this forward in an agreed-upon norm statement. These norms should be incorporated into the team's communication plan (also discussed in Chapter Five).

Protocols for Usage of Specific Communication Tools

Much has already been written about certain forms of etiquette for different types of communication tools, such as face-to-face meetings, e-mail, and video-conferencing. It is important for teams to consider what their specific forms of etiquette or guidelines are for using each type of communication tool. These guidelines are more specific than for what purpose each tool is used (as touched on in the previous section, and in detail in Chapter Five). They offer protocols for how the team should use a particular communication tool. Below are suggestions of protocols for some of the more frequently-used communication tools. However, each virtual team will need to customize and construct a set of protocols that meets its own needs.

Face-to-Face or Synchronous Computer Meetings

Face-to-face meetings that require travel are costly for virtual teams, so preparation is key. When meetings cannot be held face-to-face, synchronous computer meetings are a feasible alternative. However, meetings held through team members' networked computers require even more planning and facilitation than face-to-face meetings. Consider the following protocols when holding either a face-to-face or synchronous computer meeting:

- Identify who has the authority to call a meeting.
- Determine who needs to attend the meeting.
- Assign someone to coordinate, plan, and facilitate the meeting.
- Determine a protocol for scheduling and responding to a meeting request and define the appropriate timeframe for notification. (For example, attendees must have at least two weeks' notice.)
- Carefully plan the agenda with team input and send it out prior to the meeting.

- Identify what prework or preparation needs to be done ahead of the meeting and who should do what. Establish ways to ensure that team members complete assignments prior to meeting, and also establish adequate timeframes to review prepared material before the meeting.

- Select appropriate technology given the purpose of the meeting; have a backup plan if technology fails.

- If the team works in multiple time zones, rotate synchronous computer meetings based on time zones.

- Make sure all attendees have access to all materials that will be used in the meeting.

- Allow time at the beginning of meetings to break the ice and make sure team members are introduced. Also allow time at the close of the meeting to debrief and summarize decisions and action items.

- Assign someone to synthesize meeting notes or resulting products immediately after the meeting. Consider documenting and recording the meeting for playing back later for absent members.

- Create a way to ensure that all participants have an opportunity to participate, including soliciting input from silent members. Actively search for ways to create involvement.

Videoconferencing and Audioconferencing

Each team needs to define what its own set of "manners" are for video and audioconferences. If you have ever attended one of these types of meetings, you know that you have to work harder to concentrate and participate than in a face-to-face meeting. The tendency may be to drift off or to multi-task (especially in audioconferences, when no one is looking). Preparation is key for these types of meetings. Planning an agenda, sending out relevant information prior to the session, and making sure all team members complete what they need to prior to the meeting is important. You may want to consider assigning meeting roles (someone to ensure full participation, someone to keep track of and distribute meeting notes, and the like). Some general protocol guidelines for video and audioconferences are discussed next.

Protocols for Videoconferences

- If possible, limit the time of the conference to no more than two hours. Since these meetings require more effort to concentrate, they can be tiring.

- Make sure to explicitly thank those who are attending at inconvenient times.

- Think about the room setup and make sure everyone is visible to those at other locations. (Focus the camera so members may see one another's facial expressions.)

- Test equipment prior to the meeting to make sure it is working properly, and have a backup plan in case of technical difficulties.

- Make sure microphones are placed so that all speakers may be heard. Use the mute function when you are not talking.

- Make use of the visual element in a videoconference by using visual or graphical materials.

- Encourage interaction with team members in other locations rather than focusing only on those in the room with you.

- Proceed to closure more slowly. Consider polling each location to ensure all opinions have been heard and considered.

- Raise your hand to be recognized.

Protocols for Audioconferences

- If possible, limit the conference time to no more than two hours. Since these meetings require more effort to concentrate, they can be tiring.

- Announce your name when you are joining a call, and, if needed, identify yourself each time you speak. If a team member leaves the session, make sure he or she notifies members beforehand.

- Make sure to explicitly thank those who have phoned in at inconvenient times.

- Close your office door or use a headset.

- Keep the phone on mute when you are not talking.

- Because of the lack of visual cues, be more conscious about soliciting input and reactions from others, especially when there is unexpected silence.

- Circulate any relevant visual materials to team members prior to the audioconference for review.

Telephones, Cell Phones, and Voice Mail

Today, technology has given us the ability to have instant access to other team members any time of day. But when that instant access is synchronous (such as in a telephone call) rather than asynchronous (such as in e-mail or voice mail), the need to set up boundaries is crucial. I remember going through similar issues when I began teaching graduate students. After a series of late-night phone calls from frantic dissertation students trying to complete their research projects, I realized the importance of setting protocols and specifying boundaries. I designed my own availability statement, which included what my working hours were, my scheduled office hours, my off-hours availability, any extended periods for which I would not be available, preferred media to get in touch with me, and best ways to send in working drafts for review and feedback. From then on, I distributed this availability statement to the students I worked with. The result—life was a lot quieter around the house after 9 p.m. I reiterate an earlier point—team members need to be allowed their own personal time. With respect to telephones and cell phones, norms need to be in place to set boundaries for their usage. Consider the following protocols for telephones and cell phones:

- Determine appropriate times to call (for example, after 9 a.m. and before 9 p.m.).

- Be sensitive to and respect the time zones of other team members when you call.

- Determine when it is necessary to contact someone on his or her cell phone. (Also consider who needs a cell phone; all team members may not need one.)

- Establish times when cell phones must be turned off (such as during important meetings).

- When calling unannounced, ask initially if it is a good time to talk.

- Establish a timeframe for when members can expect return phone calls.

- Minimize interruptions and distractions during a telephone exchange.

Voice mail and answering machines have allowed individuals to set boundaries for receiving calls, while still getting the message of who it was that called and the purpose of the call. However, protocols must be in place for their use as well. I have, at times, fallen into the trap of getting so busy at the office that

I have left after an entire day of working, realizing I did not check my voice mail. I now realize the importance of establishing protocols for checking and using voice mail. Suggestions for voice mail usage are as follows:

- Establish how often you will check your voice mail.
- Keep voice mail messages short and to the point. Make sure to leave your name and telephone number.
- Determine when are the appropriate times for using codes to voice stamp messages as urgent.
- Make sure that when you send a broadcast message, you only send it to those who need it.
- Leave out emotionally-charged information or dialogue from voicemail messages.
- Send critical messages through multiple forms of communication to ensure on-time delivery.

E-mail

A variety of sources today outline proper e-mail etiquette. Your team will need to establish its own rules of e-mail etiquette, which may include some of the following:

- Create norms for the frequency with which individuals should check their e-mail (availability) and then respond.
- Establish proper lengths for an e-mail message. For example, Fisher and Fisher (2001) suggest the *no-scroll* rule, which means an e-mail message should be no longer than one page and should not require the receiver to scroll down.
- Spell out protocols for when to send or reply to messages to the entire group.
- Construct guidelines for who should get copied or blind copied, if needed.
- Establish rules for whether or not e-mail can be forwarded to others outside of the team (and agree on who those individuals are).
- Consider and agree to the style or tone of e-mails (for example, formal or informal). This may vary depending on who is communicating with whom and what the purpose of the e-mail is.

- If a distribution list is used, decide whether the list should be blind (addresses not revealed for privacy) or open (posted so anyone can access any e-mail address from the distribution list).

- Use subject lines appropriately as a flag, sorter, or indicator of key information. Decide on what topics are urgent and how this will be indicated in the subject line.

- Consider what may not be appropriate to send via e-mail (for example, no conflicts held via e-mail, no forwarding of Internet stories or jokes).

- Agree on what files can be included as attachments and what cannot. Some team members may not want to receive large documents through e-mail.

- Determine what information is confidential and should not be discussed via e-mail.

- Agree as to whether team members need to leave an extended absence greeting on their e-mails if they are on vacation or away from the office for an extended period of time.

One of the recurring complaints among individuals working in the virtual world is information overload, getting more information than you can realistically process and take in. This is especially true with e-mail. One helpful way to deal with information overload is to create protocols for prioritizing and filtering information. For example, many e-mail systems allow users to filter or delete messages based on a sender's name or words in the subject line, to create different folders to store e-mails in similar categories, to forward e-mails to an assistant, or see whether a message was specifically for them or copied to them. Another simple yet helpful technique to prioritize e-mail messages is to add to the subject line a number that indicates to the receiver the priority of the e-mail sent (1 = read now, 2 = read today, 3 = read this week, 4 = read at your leisure).

Chat Rooms, Bulletin Boards, and Calendaring and Scheduling

Here are some additional protocols to consider with regard to chat rooms, bulletin boards, and the use of calendaring and scheduling software. For *chat rooms,* consider the following:

- Determine the appropriate size. Synchronous, linear chat rooms tend to work better with smaller numbers of participants. Threaded chats are useful for larger group discussions on a variety of topics.

- Spell out the specific purpose of the chat room and limit the number of topics to be discussed in one session. (Unless you have a threaded discussion with specific topics set up.)

- Decide who will have access to the chat room exchange and establish ways to deal with lurkers (individuals who are watching the chat without participating).

- Agree on a way for participants to indicate when someone has completed a statement. For example, when posting more than a few words, post in phrases followed by an ellipsis (. . .). That way all individuals know not to post anything until that person has indicated with periods that he or she is finished.

- In linear chat rooms, try to post messages that flow logically from the previous posting. If the logic between messages is not apparent, refer to the message you are responding to in your post.

- If necessary, establish ways to create virtual body language indicating when one has something to interject, wants to clarify something, ask a question, or has something to add before the topic of discussion is changed. For example, when you want to ask someone to clarify something, type a question mark and an ellipsis (?. . .) and post. Then ask your question.

- Consider using some relevant and commonly-used chat acronyms. Acronyms can save time, but do not get carried away using too many of them. A list of useful acronyms is as follows:

BTW: by the way	HTH: hope this helps
FAQ: frequently asked questions	IAC: in any case
FYI: for your information	IMO: in my opinion
FWIW: for what it's worth	IOW: in other words
GA: go ahead	OTOH: on the other hand

Your team may choose to design its own set of acronyms. The point is, the team should decide whether to use acronyms or not, and if so, which to use.

- Of course, never use emotionally charged or offensive language in chat room discussions. (This applies to all other forms of communication tools as well.)

- If you are participating in a public Internet chat room, never give out any personal information or arrange to meet someone. Remember, people on-line may not be who they say they are. Anyone with access to the Internet can enter public chat rooms, regardless of the subject matter of each room. If you feel threatened or uncomfortable, exit the chat room. You may also report problems to the moderator or forum leader.

Virtual teams will need to decide how to manage a shared discussion forum such as a *bulletin board* or asynchronous computer meeting. These forums also need to define protocols, including the following:

- Determine which topics are appropriate to discuss in a shared forum and which are not. Some teams may be more open to allowing for controversial debates than others, but all teams benefit from discouraging the use of shared forums for voicing personal differences and attacks.

- To light the initial spark to an on-line discussion forum, it may be necessary to assign specific individuals to post the first messages in bulletin boards or to post weekly messages to keep the discussion active. For example, in a virtual discussion board I lead with Executive Management students from Taiwan and Thailand, I posted weekly discussion topics for the students to respond to.

- Use other techniques to maintain participation. For example, update team members on what is happening in the on-line forum. Without these reminders, members may drift away from these discussion forums as other needs take precedent.

- Consider assigning someone the task of pruning the shared forum by eliminating old, outdated, or irrelevant information as time goes on. This individual also needs to devise ways to ensure the team members are posting all relevant information to the forum rather than simply e-mailing it to one another.

In using *calendaring and scheduling* programs, it will be important for teams to specify how often team members need to check their calendars and schedules (availability). Teams will also need to decide who has access to each team member's calendar and schedule and who has the authority to schedule appointments on another team member's calendar or schedule.

Rules Governing Subgroup Information Exchange

When virtual teams are small in size, norms for governing subgroup communication may not be important. However, as teams increase in size, so too may the need to establish norms to guide the information exchange between subsets of individuals within the team. Larger teams need to ask themselves— should all members on the team receive every communication? If not, when is it appropriate for subgroups to communicate and exchange information between only themselves? Teams can avoid potential misunderstandings, conflict, and wasted duplication of efforts by establishing subgroup communication norms. For example, the JSC team initially had some problems with team members "holding onto information" due to some self-serving interests. This team was the largest team I interviewed, with twelve members in all. Team members eventually created a guiding norm that determined how e-mail (the most common way this team communicated) would be sent to members. A distribution list including the twelve team members' e-mail addresses was created. Individual team members agreed to send all e-mail correspondence using this distribution list. So whenever an individual team member sent or replied to an e-mail, it was sent to the entire team. Even when the team was broken down into subsets to work on particular projects, the e-mail exchanges between those subsets of members were copied to the rest of the team as well. Other teams I spoke with, like the ACI team, were more comfortable with allowing communication to occur only between team members working on a similar project. The ACI team, an organizational consulting team, realized the need for subsets of members to be assigned to different projects. Those sub-teams made use of face-to-face meetings (when possible), telephone conversations, and exchanges of information and files via e-mail. The entire team was only consulted when team input was needed. The team was also updated at appropriate times during a project's development and implementation.

The Balance of Structured and Unstructured Communication

Common sense may suggest that when individuals are geographically-dispersed, it takes a lot of structure to create communication exchanges between these individuals. Unstructured, spontaneous "water cooler" types of discussions are not easily accomplished in virtual teams. One key communication norm that virtual teams need to discuss, specify, and agree on is the degree of structure or lack of structure that will be incorporated into their communication behavior patterns. In my own investigation of virtual teams, I found there was no magical mixture or balance. Of the nine teams I spoke with, varying levels of structure were incorporated into each team's communication behavior. Some teams had a high level of structure, while for others communication was merely a random exchange of information.

Structured Communication

Teams with a relatively high level of structure established formal rules to guide their communication behavior. Structure was also integrated into a team's communication behavior through formally-scheduled face-to-face meetings and teleconference calls. Two examples of teams with high levels of structure in their communication behavior are described in the following section.

Case Examples of Structured Communication

The ACI Team

The ACI organizational consulting team formally schedules face-to-face meetings three times a year. Each one of these meetings lasts from two to three days. Team members dub the meetings the "gathering of the clan." As Matt from ACI explains, team members come together at these meetings, to *"look at the work and to pay attention to something that we need to do to run our business."* An interesting characteristic, one that helps solidify the personal bond between team members, is that the meetings are held in the team members' homes. Cheryl, a team member, elaborates about these meetings. *"We have breakfast, lunch, and dinner together. We stay at each other's houses. And when we have meetings where we are staying in each other's homes, I mean you really get to know somebody when you spend the night with them [laughs]."* The ACI team also holds a teleconference call every four weeks. Matt explains the purpose of these calls is to *"keep an eye on the marketing business development involved, kind of have a walk through of where we are with prospects and with ongoing clients. And it's also a personal check-up."* Conference calls are scheduled in advance and last from one to two hours. Prior to each conference call, Cheryl, one of the support staff, tracks the marketing efforts and prepares a report to go out to all consultants. The report details the status of each client project. Consultants elaborate on this information during the conference calls. Conference calls are not held during the same months that face-to-face meetings are scheduled. There are nine scheduled conference calls a year (and three face-to-face meetings). Conference calls may also be scheduled when an emergency arises.

Other rules that ACI team members established and followed with respect to communication behavior include: (1) return phone calls from other team members in 24 hours, (2) all consultant members are required to notify the support staff of their whereabouts, and (3) the rotating team leader is required to check in daily with the support staff.

The JSC Team

For the JSC team in the field of education, face-to-face meetings are formally held twice a year. A one-day meeting, located at one of the twelve schools, is held in the spring for members to plan for the career recruiting event. The other face-to-face meeting is held just prior to the recruiting event. Team members actually spend a week together, meeting a couple of days prior to the recruiting event, and then for the event itself, which lasts two and a half days.

The JSC team also has a yearly teleconference call, usually scheduled in the fall that follows the team's summer marketing efforts. Members assess where they are in terms of recruiting employers for the job search event and motivate and encourage one another to recruit even more employers to participate.

The JSC team also requires all team members to be on-line at least twice a week and to send e-mail correspondence regarding team issues to all members of the team. Even if subsets of individuals are working together, they still copy their correspondences to the rest of the team.

Unstructured Communication

Two of the teams (OfficeTech and WN–Religion Forum) lacked structure in their communication behavior. Even in looking at ACI, which had nine conference calls and three face-to-face meetings, the majority of contact came through unstructured e-mail and phone exchanges. On a day-to-day basis, the majority of communication between team members in all nine teams was unstructured, occurring electronically as needed.

Although much of the unstructured forms of communication occurred through e-mail, some teams supported unstructured (unplanned) face-to-face encounters as the need developed. For example, in addition to the gatherings of the clan, the ACI team allows for face-to-face contact between consultants when a particular client request or product development issue requires input. For the JSC team, face-to-face contact also occurs throughout the year when two or three members may meet to hold luncheons with prospective employers. The VTG team allocates financial resources for unexpected face-to-face meetings, which, although they are rare, are held when essential. The VTG team leader considers each team member's differing needs for face-to-face contact. Nicole, one of the team members, needs more human contact, and the VTG team leader arranges for her to visit the corporate office about every six weeks. Susan, the VTG team leader, explains that her team "had to come up with a mix of how much contact people want. Because we are extraordinarily virtual, she [Nicole] would ring up and say, 'I need warm contact' [laughs]. And then we'd call a meeting so that we could be together."

Three case examples of teams with less structure in their communication behavior are described in the next section.

Case Examples of Unstructured Communication
The ELC Team
For the ELC team who designs and manages an educational virtual community, members are in contact with each other daily through e-mail and computer conferencing. There are no formal, written rules on how the team should communicate. The only norm that guides its communication behavior is an unwritten expectation to communicate anything that is unusual or different (for example, to offer suggestions to the learning community or to share information about a technical problem).

The OfficeTech Team
The OfficeTech team, whose task is to develop and sustain a company virtual community, has no formal rules for communicating, most likely because it only has two core members and one peripheral member. Communication occurs as needed. However, when a

junior person joined the team, senior members began to realize the need to structure their communication exchanges. Richard, the team leader, shares the following: *"We communicate informally. We have talked about formalizing it a bit. For a period of time up until about two weeks ago, we had a young man work with us. He was a junior member of the team and less self-directed, and we came to the conclusion a bit belatedly that it would have been advisable to have made an effort to have a regular morning meeting where we talk about what was done yesterday, and what needs to be done today. Since Keith and I are a little more self-directed senior practitioners, we tend to only touch base when we need to."*

The WN–Religion Forum Team

The team with perhaps the least amount of structure interwoven into its communication behavior is the WN–Religion Forum team, which manages an on-line forum on religion. Communication in this team is more of a random exchange and occurs only when needed. One team member said staff meetings were held occasionally in chat rooms, while another member recalled only having one chat room staff meeting. Clearly, no regularly-scheduled meetings are in place. Interestingly, team members did see the need to add structure to their random exchanges. Scott explains that adding structure to communications is *"something we're going to put in place. I think it's very important and we have been neglectful of it."*

Eryn, the leader of the WN–Religion Forum team, sees the need for a system to organize the massive number of random daily e-mail exchanges. *"What we need now is not this random exchange, I mean a sort of moment-by-moment exchange of notes. We write each other literally 50 times a day. We exchange that many conversations, okay? We need a system where we flag things by color or code and where we more actively utilize shared files. That way we will all know what other team members have done and what has not yet been done. We are now trying to develop and tailor a system for our particular needs."*

One may wonder how these virtual teams who work across physical distance and different time zones can survive when the majority of their communication behavior is unstructured. The answer may lie in the type of individual who seems most appropriate to work in these teams—someone who is *self-disciplined, self-motivated*, and *self-directed*.

Creating an Appropriate Balance

Even if virtual teams are composed of self-motivated individuals, protocols must be defined to create a balance of structured and unstructured communication. In the teams studied, structured exchanges were used, for the most part, to review and assess work and the overall business, and to keep personal bonds alive. Unstructured exchanges were used to exchange information, ask for advice, and keep one another informed. It is interesting to note that in the two teams that lacked structure in their communication behavior (OfficeTech and WN–Religion Forum), the team leaders were planning to add structure to their communication exchanges.

Tool: Developing an Agreed-Upon Set of Communication Behavior Norms

Communication behavior norms in virtual teams may be less obvious than in more traditional, co-located teams. Thus, it becomes critical to highlight communication norms in a more explicit and forthright way. Once norms are defined, the team needs to make a commitment to honor what has been agreed to and to jointly modify the norms if needed. Table 7.2 can be used to assist virtual teams in developing an agreed-upon set of communication behavior norms.

Table 7.2 Communication Behavior Norms Tool

For Availability and Acknowledgment Norms, consider:

Team's overall availability norms:

Individual team members' norms (list for each team member):
- contact information
- time zone
- available working hours, off-hour availability
- preferred media contact (for example, e-mail first, voicemail second, cell last)
- typical check-in frequency and response time for each media (if not set by overall team norms)

For Appropriateness and Guiding Protocols of Specific Communication Tools, consider:

Communication Tool	When to Use	When Not to Use	Guiding Protocols

Table 7.2 Communication Behavior Norms Tool, Cont'd

For Subgroup Communication Norms, consider:

1. In what situations should all members on the team receive every communication? What types of communication tools should be used?

2. When would it be accepted for subgroups within the team to communicate and exchange information between only themselves? What types of communication tools should be used?

For Creating a Balance Between Structured and Unstructured Communication, consider:

1. What is the team's overall philosophy in terms of formality and rules guiding communication behavior? Does your team prefer random, less structured or more formally, rule-driven exchanges of information?

2. What types of communication exchanges (either synchronous or asynchronous) should be formally scheduled? How often should they occur? What will be the overriding purpose(s) of these scheduled communication exchanges? A simple chart can help your team to clearly map this:

Communication Tool	How Often	For What

3. In what situations should unplanned, informal (not formally scheduled) synchronous communication exchanges be supported? Who has the authority to call these meetings? What communication tools will the team use to fill this need?

4. Re-visit availability standards to clarify and guide random, unstructured communication exchanges (both asynchronous and synchronous). How formalized and detailed are the norms of availability and acknowledgment that guide the team's communication behavior? Especially in teams where random, unstructured communication exchanges are the norm, it becomes even more crucial to clearly specify availability and acknowledgment norms. (For example, if you get the creative urge at 2 a.m. it is most likely more appropriate to send the idea to your colleague through e-mail, rather than placing a telephone call to his or her home.)

Project and Task Management Norms
Developing a Creative Process Project Lifecycle Map

Virtual teams must create a set of shared expectations about communication behavior. They must also create norms about how to accomplish their creative work. A virtual team needs to develop an agreed-upon set of project and task management norms, which should ultimately be published internally (perhaps on a team Web page).

To begin, a team needs to create a shared process for working on joint projects such as documents or products. In order to do this, the team needs to define what the lifecycle of the project will be (or has been in the past) and record that process. This allows the team to develop a shared working picture of the creative process and to determine the boundaries and scope of the work so that it has a clear beginning, transition points, and ending. In creating this process map, team members jointly determine what tasks need to be accomplished and who will be assigned to which tasks on a project. Then people who are working on similar tasks coordinate their work with each other. (See Mohrman, Cohen, and Mohrman, 1995, for more information on process analysis.)

To start outlining a project's lifecycle map, list the inputs needed to begin the process. Inputs may include relevant suppliers and vendors; needed resources, materials and supplies; additional staff; and necessary knowledge, expertise, or information. Next, examine and outline the series of tasks that support each stage in the creative process. What actions need to be taken in each stage? What is the actual work that the team needs to perform during each stage of the creative process? A key ingredient in outlining these tasks is to indicate which tasks can be routinely done (as they have been in the past, using previously developed forms or templates) and which tasks will need to be developed from scratch, requiring creativity. This allows a team to decipher where in the project's lifecycle creativity is necessary and where it is not. (See the next section for more information on norms for distinguishing between routine and creative tasks.)

Once projects are finalized, brought to closure, and subsequently evaluated, the last major step is to specify any changes that need to be implemented in the next lifecycle. So the process continues in a circular fashion. A template for constructing a creative process project lifecycle map is shown in Table 7.3.

Table 7.3 Template for Constructing a Creative Process Project Lifecycle Map

	Creative Process—Tasks to Perform				
Suppliers/ Resources/ Inputs Needed to Begin	Idea Generation	Development	Finalization/ Closure	Evaluation	Changes to Implement/ Next Cycle Action Steps
Resource 1:	Task A-1:	Task B-1:	Task C-1:	Task D-1:	Task E-1:

Distinguishing Between Routine and Creative Tasks

Many virtual team members told me that their work does not always require creativity. Project by project, task by task, virtual teams need to address and draw the line between what is routine and what requires creativity. Norms need to be established so that throughout a project's lifecycle, it is evident to the team what will be done routinely and what will be done with creativity. These norms are necessary to allow for both efficient and creative outcomes. Without norms, tasks that can be effectively accomplished using routine work may use up the resources needed for tasks that require creativity. A simple example from my own job demonstrates this.

Case Example: College of Letters, Arts and Social Science, Cal Poly Pomona

Every ten weeks, all of the faculty members within the College of Letters, Arts and Social Science at Cal Poly Pomona, where I teach, are required to fill out a report documenting their scholarly and academic activities for that period. All the individual faculty reports are integrated by College of Letters, Arts and Social Science staff into a written report that is delivered to the Dean of the College for review. For many years, each faculty member took it upon himself or herself to create a format in which to report this information. What resulted was a massive number of reports in all different shapes and sizes. In addition, new faculty who were required to fill out these forms had little guidance in creating these reports. So the problem continued, as each new faculty member also created his or her own way of constructing the report. Now you probably can guess that the poor staff members who had the task of integrating these different reports into one report to be seen by the Dean had quite a lot of work.

Enter one staff member, Diane, in the Psychology and Sociology Department. Diane is responsible for collecting and integrating reports from the Psychology and Sociology Department and then forwarding them to another staff member in the Dean's Office. The staff member in the Dean's office integrates all reports within the College of Letters, Arts, and Social Science for the Dean's perusal. Diane saw the need to standardize a process that people were accustomed to doing creatively. So she created a standard template on which all faculty could list their accomplishments. All faculty members now use this template to complete their scholarly and academic activity reports.

The end result was a happier faculty and staff. Faculty members now spend less time filling out bureaucratic reports and more time writing books like this one. And staff finds it easier and more efficient to integrate all the reports into one. The entire process is more efficient and no longer wastes valuable human resources that should be used creatively elsewhere.

The question "Is creativity always necessary?" has haunted me since the early days of my research. I believe creativity is essential for an organization to survive. However, virtual team members helped me to see that creativity is *not* always necessary. There were periods in which these virtual team members needed to be creative, and there were other periods in which team members simply carried out routine work. In fact, some team members had difficulty remembering high and low team creativity stories; they did not consider what they did on a daily basis to be creative. Other team members suggested that creativity was necessary, but not all the time. For example, Elaine, a JSC team member, shares that throughout the year her team follows a set system (which they do not consider to be creative), but that when the team comes together for face-to-face planning sessions, a creative environment is established.

Throughout the year we have our system and it functions very well. It's evolved to the point where every person who performs a specific duty knows it, does it, and communicates it. So we don't really have to talk about it too much. When we do get together, we have reports about the different areas [and] what's new. And that usually lasts half an hour, where every person provides information about the area of their responsibility. And then we move on to the creative part, what are we going to do now? We have all these different ideas that we're pursuing as to how we can work more collaboratively to provide services to employers and attract them to our Consortium. So when we do get together, it's usually a planning meeting or a marketing meeting, and it's really a very creative environment.

So virtual teams vary in their needs for creativity. And in order for these teams to not waste valuable resources and time, members need to actively develop norms for distinguishing between which types of tasks or phases of project development require creativity and which do not. For which tasks have prior work already been completed and can prior templates be used? For which tasks does the process need to be reinvented? After answering these questions, protocols for routine work or work that is based on prior work need to be established.

Virtual teams need to clearly assess for what purposes such standard forms, predefined templates, or standard ways of working can be used. Common uses include scheduling, cost estimates, requirements from customers, assigning tasks, reporting work status, and action plans. In the early stages of the team's development, members may need to capture templates from their current and previous project lifecycle maps. As often occurs, what may begin as a creative task evolves into a routine task in later project lifecycles. In Grenier and Metes' (1995) book, *Going Virtual: Moving Your Organization Into the 21st Century*, they advise "Design everything, then do it again when things change" (p. 137). As team members become more accustomed to using appropriate templates, templates become more efficient to work with. For example, most companies that have document management capabilities on their Intranet routinely publish corporate documents and routine forms on-line and also reuse simple company graphics, charts, and logos in multiple documents. One of the teams I interviewed, the WN–Current Events team, provides a good case example for how to distinguish between routine and creative tasks.

Case Example: The WN–Current Events Team

The WN–Current Events team members, whose major responsibility was to create an on-line publication, had clearly taken the time to distinguish between when they could use more standard ways to work and when they needed to have creativity integrated into their product development process. The team looked at the project's lifecycle for publishing materials on the on-line current events pages. Certain promotional tasks were designated as routine (with help from standard forms and use of shared databases). Other more design-related tasks were designated as creative, so the team needed networked tools to help team members work together on the design. Managing promotional information (such as people sending information about current events to publish on-line) became the routine portion of their work. A standard form (called an e-form) was created for clients to fill out their promotional requests. These e-forms were assembled into a shared database system. The creative portion of the project's lifecycle was to develop the content and design the on-line publication. For these activities, the team used networked design tools and other synchronous forms of communication (such as face-to-face meetings and audioconferencing).

The WN–Current Events team (from prior experience) had also developed an awareness of when using templates was not creative enough. Lianna, the WN–Current Events team leader, said the team went through a time where they relied too heavily on old ways of doing business. When they assessed the situation they realized they needed to generate new action steps to revitalize creativity during the design phase. One major action step was to hold regular meetings to assign work and brainstorm ideas. Team members that worked offsite attended the meetings through teleconferencing. Lianna describes these meetings: *"Every Monday morning we actually have a team meeting. Well the meeting is scheduled for every Monday, it's sort of a standing meeting, but we cancel it sometimes because we don't need to meet all the time. We meet for probably a half an hour or so, and we usually begin by going through all of the e-forms. It's [e-form] like an e-mail, but it's automated in a standard-format electronic form for content partners to tell us what events they would like to have promoted in our on-line publication. So, we usually go through all the e-forms that have come in and decide which events we're going to promote and put them on the schedule together. We then assign who will design promotion materials for which events. Then, as a team, we begin to brainstorm ideas for those promotions."*

Assigning Roles and Responsibilities

It is not enough to just map out what tasks will make up the creative process. A key element of what makes up a creative and high-performing team is clearly assigning roles and responsibilities to individual team members with respect to the tasks that need to be completed. Responsibility for obtaining the overall creative goal is shared by the entire team, but responsibility for individual tasks rests with team members. As we saw in the modular approach (discussed in Chapter One), members are accountable for their "piece of the creative pie." So teams need to be clear about who does what and who is responsible for what. If individual roles and responsibilities are not clearly specified and understood by all the members of the team, confusion and redundancy result. Some team members may take on more than their share of responsibility and become stressed and frustrated. Other team members may take on less than their share of responsibility and become disenchanted and bored. The result in both these situations may be poor and shoddy performance. For virtual teams, these problems can intensify greatly.

How can a virtual team gain agreement on what roles individual team members will play and the responsibilities each team member will be accountable for? After a team has carefully laid out its creative process project lifecycle map, it next clarifies which individual team member(s) will be responsible for each of the tasks listed in the project lifecycle map. I call this section of the lifecycle map, the *Task Accountability Chart* (Mohrman, Cohen, and Mohrman [1995] refer to this as a responsibility chart). The chart identifies which individual(s) are to be involved in the project's lifecycle and what their type of involvement will be (see Table 7.4). For each task, the team defines who is *responsible* for completing the task, who may offer *support and consultation*, who needs to be kept *informed* about the task, and who is to *review and approve* the output of each task. Following is a list of suggested codes that may be used to designate an individual's role with respect to a particular task:

P = Primary person responsible for completion of this task; has ultimate accountability for accomplishing this task.

C = Person who can be consulted, if needed, to provide project-related support, advice, or expertise.

R = Person who is responsible for reviewing and approving the task-related output.

N = Person who needs to be notified about the status of the task and needs this information to perform his or her own task.

Table 7.4 Template for Constructing a Creative Process Project Lifecycle Map with Embedded Task Accountability Chart

Creative Process—Tasks to Perform

Suppliers/ Resources/ Inputs Needed to Begin	Idea Generation	Development	Finalization/ Closure	Evaluation	Changes to Implement/ Next Cycle Action Steps
Resource 1:	Task A-1:	Task B-1:	Task C-1:	Task D-1:	Task E-1:
	*TM #1—P	TM #1—P	TM #1—P	TM #1—P	TM #1—P
	TM #2—C	TM #2—C	TM #2—C	TM #2—C	TM #2—C
	TM #3—R	TM #3—R	TM #3—R	TM #3—R	TM #3—R
	TM #4—N	TM #4—N	TM #4—N	TM #4—N	TM #4—N

*TM = team member, indicates where names of team members are to be listed.

In addition, each team may want to modify the chart with respect to its individual team needs. Other issues that may be added include specific target dates for delivery or completion of each task, who should task-related outputs be sent to (and in what format), and what accountability measures may be taken to ensure delivery. Norms for establishing timeframes and accountability measures are discussed in the next section.

Timeframes and Accountability Measures

Timeframes clarify when certain actions must be completed. Accountability norms spell out what actions will be taken to ensure on-time delivery of task-related output and what will occur if members do not meet their deadlines. When developing appropriate timeframes for task completion, it is crucial that, as much as possible, individual team members are asked for input on what they see as feasible and reasonable. When individuals are subjected to unrealistic timeframes in which they had no input, anxiety, stress, and lower levels of creativity result. Virtual teams need to have honest discussions about these issues and develop jointly agreed-upon norms to ensure accountability and on-time completion of their work.

Agreement on timeframes and accountability norms is essential to avoid the "out of sight, out of mind" mentality that may occur with dispersed virtual team members. Jeff, a JSC team member, shares how a goal, communicated clearly and agreed to by members of his team in a face-to-face brainstorming meeting, was later forgotten and finally dropped as team members dispersed.

> At our meeting in May, I said, "I know we're all doing some kind of information packet for our students about this event as far as how it works and how much it costs and what the agenda is and how to prepare for it." And I said, "Wouldn't it be great if we all could put together a single student packet from the Consortium that everybody can use?" Everybody's like, "Oh, it's a great idea." I thought it was too because I wanted to see what other people did. And so I said well, have your stuff to me by June. Well, I got one [packet]. And then I'm sitting there thinking about it, and I was into a million other things and I'm like, well, I can send an e-mail to everybody and say, "Hey, send me your stuff," and I just decided to let it go. That year we ended up just doing our same old thing.

As discussed in Chapter Three, accountability and trust go hand in hand. If team members know they can rely on others to deliver what they said by when they said, trust is built. If not, trust either does not get built or disintegrates rapidly. Following are some questions your virtual team may find helpful when drafting realistic project timeframes and accountability norms:

- How will realistic timeframes for delivery be set? Who will have input in establishing timeframes? Who will ultimately be responsible for setting the timeframes? What circumstances may be justifiable reasons for altering established timeframes?

- How will the team ensure that shared work (for example joint-authored document or designed product) be moved through the project lifecycle in a timely manner?

- How will appropriate timeframes in the project's lifecycle vary with respect to tasks in each stage of the creative process? Will even amounts of time be allotted for idea generation, for development work, modifications, and revisions, for finalization and closure, and for evaluation efforts? Or will timeframes be tailored to each individual stage? In what stages does the team want to expend most of their time and resources?

- How will the team assess whether team members are accountable and following established timeframe protocols? What should the team do if problems arise in terms of accountability?

- How will the team ensure that next-cycle action steps are actually implemented? (That the team will not just go back to the way it was previously done, as the JSC team member shared above.)

Protocols for Shared Workspaces and Files

With the myriad of collaborative technologies now available, virtual teams may effectively author documents or design products collaboratively. The most qualified individuals can now be brought together to jointly develop a creative outcome, no matter where these individuals reside. However, even when the best and the brightest team members work together virtually in shared workspaces or with shared files, problems can still arise. One of the most common pitfalls is when each team member is not working from the same updated information, document, or product design prototype. As a result, misunderstandings, confusion, wasted time, and even the total or partial loss of creative efforts (such as when one team member overwrites the most current version with a previous version) can result. And as the number of individuals working with a particular shared file increases, so does the risk of loss of creative output. Thus, the need to establish norms for working on shared files is quite real. When virtual team members work in a shared workspace and exchange files back and forth, established norms ensure that all team members have current project-related information and that the shared workspace is organized and not confusing. Following are some issues your virtual team will want to discuss before you share tools or files:

1. Decide on how the shared work will be stored (for example, in a document database). Then team members need to agree to use the system the team has set up for a particular project. If team members exchange information and add to joint products via other electronic or non-electronic communication tools, this may be troublesome.

2. Agree on what types of information or documents need to be updated regularly and how often they should be updated. Determine who should be responsible for making updates. AutoMax team members suffered because information in their shared workspace was not always updated accordingly. Dana, an AutoMax team member, points out that computer

problems can cause communication problems. When the computer is slow or down, she says, "we can't access some information resources we need. The schematics, the wiring diagrams are not always updated. In fact, on this job, I put in a request to get it [wiring diagrams] updated about three days ago and I'm still waiting for that information."

3. Agree on the particular software applications members will use to create and exchange their shared work.

4. Establish mechanisms for tracking the work. Similar to how one can track a letter or an Express mail document once it has been sent, virtual team members must also be able to track where the shared work is at any given time. Virtual team members function much like volleyball players, passing their work back and forth in iterative cycles. Kimball and Mareen Fisher (2001) in their book, *The Distance Manager: A Hands-On Guide to Managing Off-Site Employees and Virtual Teams,* share a technique to use when multiple individuals are working on the same project. The technique is called "Who's got the football today?" Team members are aware of who is currently working on the project. When the individual leaves the project, he or she passes the football to someone else. Other techniques that help track shared work include the following:

- Attach dates or version numbers to files when saving so that team members know which file is most current.

- Make sure input into the shared workspace is searchable by time or date, subject, and person responsible.

- Structure the work so that team members never work on the same files at the exact same time.

- Organize the workspace to avoid confusion and decide in what folders the files will be located; set up separate areas for different project pieces, individuals, or subgroups—whatever makes sense to the team.

- Create a team space (perhaps on the team's Intranet Web page) where team members may check the schedule, review past work, follow the project's progress, or check on other projects' status.

5. Develop norms to ensure security and confidentiality of the work. The team will need to agree on who has access to which documents and decide who has the authority to release documents to outsiders.

Norms for Project Review, Revision, and Final Approval

In addition to norms ensuring that team members are accountable for their parts of the shared work, norms also need to be established for how the work, once completed, will be reviewed, revised, and approved. Questions virtual teams need to discuss and answer when developing norms and protocols for project review, revision, and final approval are next. (Note: revisiting the team's task accountability chart will assist members in answering several of these questions.)

- At what increments in the project's lifecycle should review of work take place? How often should resulting feedback be given?

- How will the team ensure that proper reviews are completed and feedback is given as promised? For example, some virtual teams schedule and require all team members to attend weekly review sessions (held through some form of electronic, synchronous communication). At these review sessions, current work is reviewed, revisions are discussed, and next action steps are outlined. It is important that teams state how often they will meet to discuss and review the status of their shared work.

- Who has the authority to add, change, or delete portions of a shared work product?

- Who has the authority to make recommendations or offer input for revision?

- Who has the authority to give final approval of the shared work?

- Who needs to be kept informed of project revisions or final approval of the project (because their own work is affected by or dependent on the outcomes of this effort)?

Tool: Developing an Agreed-Upon Set of Project and Task Management Norms

As stated earlier, once norms are specified, the team needs to make a commitment to honor the agreements laid out, but be open to modifying them as needed. Use the steps listed in Table 7.5 to develop an agreed-upon set of project and task management norms and protocols for working and creating together virtually.

Table 7.5 Project and Task Management Norms Tool

Step 1—Develop a creative process project lifecycle map: Use the template in Table 7.3 to construct a *Creative Process Project Lifecycle Map,* outlining the creative process for each project to be completed by your team.

Step 2—Distinguish between routine and creative tasks: As a team, ask and answer:

- For what tasks has prior work been completed and can predefined templates be used?
- For what tasks does the process need to be re-invented?
- For what tasks is creativity vital?

Step 3—Assign roles and responsibilities: Use the *Task Accountability Chart* template in Table 7.4 to delineate the roles and responsibilities of each team member that will be involved in the project's lifecycle, and what their involvement will be for each task. Specify those individuals who are responsible for completing each task, who may offer support and/or consultation, who need to be informed because their work is interdependent, or who will review and have the authority for approval of the task-related output.

Step 4—Establish Timeframes and Accountability Norms: As a team, clarify the following:

- The procedure the team will use to set realistic timeframes for delivery.
- The individuals who will have input in establishing timeframes and specific delivery target dates, and those who will be ultimately responsible for setting the timeframes and dates.
- The circumstances in which established timeframes may be justifiably altered.
- The procedure for assessing whether team members are accountable for their assignments.
- The actions to be taken if problems do arise in terms of accountability.
- How the team will ensure next cycle action steps are actually implemented.

Step 5—Develop Protocols for Shared Work: First, come to an initial agreement that all team members involved in the shared work will use the document storage system created for the project. Then, gain agreement on the following:

- The types of information or documents that need to be updated regularly and how often and by whom they should be updated.
- The particular software applications team members will use to create and exchange their shared work.
- The established mechanisms for tracking the work.
- What documents are confidential, with access given only to internal team members.
- Who has the authority to release documents to outsiders.

Step 6—Agree on Project Review, Revision, and Final Approval Norms: First, decide how often the team will meet to discuss and review the status of their shared work. Then, gain agreement on the following:

- How the team will ensure that proper reviews are completed and feedback is given as promised
- Who has the authority to add, change, or delete portions of a shared work product
- Who has the authority to make recommendations or offer input for revision
- Who has the authority for final approval of the shared work
- Who will need to be kept informed of project revisions or final approval of the project

Final Thoughts

Just as there are seasons in life, so are there seasons in the development of norms. Team norms emerge over time. Virtual teams using new collaborative technologies need to allow themselves the flexibility to evolve and develop their own norms for working together. The process of developing mutual expectations is not always clear until team members have had some experience working with one another and on their team tasks. Thus, frequent checkpoints, lessons learned sessions, and group reflections on the process should be one of the most stable norms of a virtual team. Norms typically develop gradually as team members learn what behaviors are necessary for them to function effectively. Those norms that are most often enforced are, of course, those considered important to the team—norms that facilitate the team's survival, increase the predictability of behavior, reduce interpersonal problems, and allow members to express the core values of the team and clarify their team's identity. A core value that needs to be seeded in creative teamwork is to continually emphasize and appreciate assessment and learning. In Part V, you will have the opportunity to learn from other virtual team members and to assess and learn from your own team's creative experiences.

Points to Remember

- All teams have norms. Norms establish acceptable standards of behavior that are shared among team members, whether virtual or not. Virtual teams require unique and more detailed norms than co-located teams. Two critical types of norms needed for virtual teams doing creative work are communication behavior norms and project and task management norms.

- Availability and acknowledgment norms are critical to ensure the connection members need to perform shared work. However, it is important not to overdo availability. Members need to think about what is appropriate, respect what has been agreed on, and allow team members personal time.

- Both structured and unstructured interactions need to be incorporated into a team's communication plan. Structured exchanges are typically used for reviewing and assessing work and the overall business and for keeping personal bonds alive. Unstructured exchanges are frequently used to exchange information, ask for advice, and keep one another informed.

- It is important to realize that creativity is *not* always necessary. There are periods in which virtual teams need to be creative, and there are other periods in which teams simply carry out their work by following an existing system. In order for virtual teams to use resources and time efficiently, members need to develop norms to identify which tasks require creativity and which do not.

- When developing timeframes for task completion, it is crucial that, as much as possible, individual team members are respected and asked for input on what they see as feasible. Asking individuals to adhere to timeframes they had no input in setting and ones they feel are unrealistic results in high levels of anxiety and stress and lower levels of creativity for those involved.

- To ensure accountability, virtual teams need to have honest discussions and to jointly develop and agree on actions that will guarantee accountability and success at meeting deadlines.

- As the number of individuals creating in shared workspaces increases, so does the risk of loss of creative output. Thus, virtual teams need to establish norms to ensure that all team members have current project-related information and that the shared workspace is organized and not confusing.

- Once the team has finalized its set of agreed-upon communication behavior norms and project and task management norms, it needs to document and internally publish these norms (perhaps on a team Intranet Web page) for the entire team to refer to as needed.

- Team norms emerge over time. Virtual teams need to remain flexible enough to evolve and develop their own norms for working together.

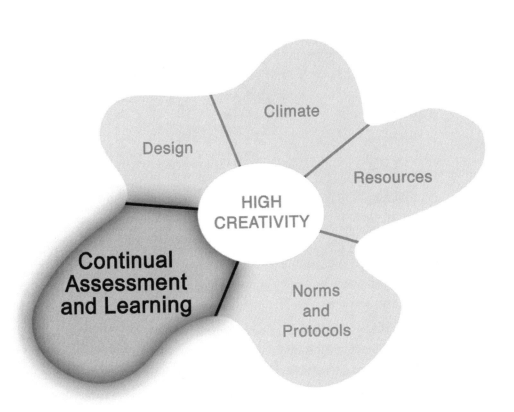

PART V

Continual Assessment and Learning

AS A VIRTUAL TEAM NEARS THE END of its creative process on a particular project, finalizes it, and brings closure to that specific creative effort, there is a tendency for the momentum to slow down. Team members may decrease their energy and concentration as they begin to focus on other future projects. But as you read in Chapter One, the final stage in the creative process is not finalization and closure but rather evaluation. At the close of each creative outcome, virtual teams (and any team for that matter) need to take the time to evaluate and assess their efforts. What worked? What could be improved on? Out of evaluation and assessment come seeds for growth and improvement leading to potentially even more creative and successful future projects and ways of working together. The fifth and final component to creativity in virtual teams is *Continual Assessment and Learning.* In every ending is another beginning and another opportunity for growth and improvement. Chapter Eight brings this book to a close by offering a series of key lessons learned from the virtual teams I interviewed. These lessons may suggest ways for future growth and improvement in your virtual team. In addition, this concluding chapter offers an opportunity for your virtual team to take one last look at its functioning with respect to the five key components for creativity in virtual teams. But remember this is NOT the last time your team will assess itself on these issues. Assessment and learning is continuous. You may use the tools in the next chapter, or any of the tools throughout this book, or any other tools available to you to continue to learn how to increase your virtual team's creativity.

CHAPTER 8

Lessons Learned and Final Assessment

THE THIRTY-SIX VIRTUAL TEAM MEMBERS (representing nine different teams) interviewed provided a wealth of insight, expertise, and knowledge on what it takes to be creative in this new form of working together virtually. You have witnessed their accounts of how they developed and maintained each of the four previously discussed key components—Design, Climate, Resources, and Norms and Protocols. The fifth component, Continual Assessment and Learning, has actually been discussed in each chapter in this book. This final chapter offers even more food for thought in striving for continual assessment and learning. From the stories the teams members shared spring forth a series of important lessons and strategies for encouraging creativity in virtual teams. This chapter describes these key learnings. It also offers additional suggestions for continual assessment and learning to develop and maintain high levels of creativity in your virtual team.

Lessons Learned

Component One – Design

Creative Process and Work Design Approaches

Lesson 1 *It is imperative that none of the four stages of the creative process be short-changed. Doing any one stage inadequately will impact the results of all the rest.* As virtual teams are typically formed to meet or solve a pressing customer need or market demand, the time allotted for development and finalization and closure is often more lengthy than the time given to generating or evaluating ideas. Less emphasis is placed on sorting through a variety of problem definitions, and more emphasis is placed on assessing whether presented problems are worthy to pursue. In addition, in virtual teams, problems and challenges are often presented by clients or managers, thus eliminating the need for extended work on finding and defining problems. However, while it does appear that in the creative process of virtual teams there is more of a push to get to development quickly, that should not imply that it is any less important to generate appropriate ideas or take the time to adequately evaluate creative outcomes. In reality, the boundaries between the four stages of a virtual team's creative process can often become blurred.

Lesson 2 *Assess whether the type of creative project is really best accomplished in a virtual team design.* Virtual teams are task-focused teams. It is common for virtual teams, in pursuing creative work (and probably any type of work for that matter), to break a task down into components, assign those components to individual team members who work alone on their assigned pieces, and then come back together for feedback, revisions, and finalization of the entire project. However, not all creative efforts may be so easily divided into sections. Managers or team leaders need to consider whether the creative task at hand can be effectively accomplished with a virtual team design.

Lesson 3 *Although a common work design approach for virtual teams is the modular approach, each team needs to integrate in its work pattern an appropriate portion of iterative togetherness on the path of the creative process.* Many of the teams used a modular approach to accomplish their creative work. Work was divided and parceled out to team members based on their individual knowledge, expertise, and interest. A modular approach gives geographically dispersed team members, with little or no face-to-face contact, "walking papers" (as one participant shared) or "clear actions" (as another participant shared) from which to work. However, to avoid the loss of feedback from fellow members and others on the work, it is crucial that the team has periods of iterative feedback and review. How much time team members spend apart or together varies, depending on the individual needs of each team and the tasks or projects they are presented with.

Leadership Structures

Lesson 1 *Virtual teams need to choose the type of leadership structure that is appropriate for the values and skills of team members and the vision, objectives, and tasks that guide the team's work.* There are many ways to lead a virtual team. My interviews with virtual team members revealed different leadership structures that all proved to be productive. But appropriate leadership does not emerge by chance. Taking the time prior to setting up a virtual team to assess what leadership structure will most benefit the team is key. Continual assessment as the team develops is also necessary. Every parent knows that as a child grows from infancy to adulthood, the strategies and techniques to guide that child into being a successful individual may need to change. The same may be said for virtual teams. What works to guide and manage a virtual team in one phase of team development may not necessarily work in later stages of the team's life.

Lesson 2 *A critical shift for members in virtual teams is realizing that they will most likely be required to, at some point in the team's lifecycle, fill the dual roles of team member and team leader.* As more and more virtual teams begin to use shared-leadership structures (self-managed teams, rotated project team leaders), members in these types of teams will need to develop a tolerance for performing dual roles of team member and team leader, and will also need to be able to shift back and forth between these roles as the need arises. But we cannot ask individuals to play the role of team member and leader without offering them the appropriate training. If virtual team members are to take on the roles of team member and team leader interchangeably, then, in addition to their individual areas of expertise, they will need to develop skills and competencies in project and task management, communication, conflict resolution, strategic planning, and the like.

Component Two—Climate

Task and Interpersonal Connection

Lesson 1 Managers and team leaders of virtual teams may build task connection by establishing procedures and forums for team members to clarify team goals, to give and get feedback from one another, and to ensure accountability from all team members. A manager or leader of a virtual team cannot merely assume the members of the team will check in with one another when necessary. Formal systems must be developed and put in place for members to periodically clarify team goals and give and receive feedback on their work. However, there is no magic formula for how often and at what points of a project's cycle these forums should be integrated into the creative process. Each team will need to design a framework to meet its own needs. A key thing to remember is that virtual teams may need to over-communicate about the work they are performing. They will need to have more structured communication systems in place than their co-located counterparts. Using multiple methods to communicate may also assist in ensuring task connection. In addition, team managers and leaders will need to carefully and clearly communicate team goals and tasks. Managers and leaders need to continue to develop their writing skills to ensure clear communication of the goals and tasks.

Lesson 2 Managers and team leaders of virtual teams can build interpersonal connection among team members by providing funds and opportunities that will allow virtual team members to bond personally. Allowing time to play games, share humor, or respond to one another's personal issues and crises, perhaps thought of as inappropriate behavior in conventional teams, may not be inappropriate at all in the virtual world of work. These simple sharing activities help develop a strong personal bond between virtual team members, a bond that transcends geographic and time boundaries. Some team members may feel that work is work, and that developing such a personal bond is a waste of time. On the contrary, establishing this type of personal bond can actually save time, as virtual teams that are personally bonded are less likely to suffer from wasted time and indecision as a result of misunderstandings, confusion, and incorrect assumptions. Funds should be provided for team members to get together initially to discuss common goals and shared values and to build trust. Furthermore, once the team is up and running, having periodic face-to-face, social get-togethers or celebrations after completing a project also helps encourage and maintain team identity. Organizations, managers, and team leaders can also use strategies besides face-to-face meetings to encourage interpersonal connection and, as a result, creativity in virtual teams. Companies or teams may sponsor team games. Or one team member may function as a team historian, documenting team stories and sending them out electronically to members. For teams that do not meet face-to-face, even strategies such as sending all team members pictures of one another can be beneficial. Any number of techniques may be used to help establish an interpersonal connection among team members.

Team Member and Management Conditions and Competencies

Lesson 1 *Virtual team managers and leaders need to encourage and support the creative endeavors of the teams they supervise.* A key starting point is to make sure managers and team leaders understand the importance of establishing a climate that fosters creativity. Without such a climate, even the most creative individual team members will quickly lose their desire to shine creatively.

Lesson 2 *When appropriate, virtual team managers and leaders need to search for ways to allow individual team members freedom in accomplishing their work assignments.* Individuals who are attracted to working virtually tend to be self-disciplined and self-motivated. These individuals value freedom in how to do their work. Freedom may be integrated in virtual work by offering team members a flexible pace and schedule, and autonomy when accomplishing work assignments. Additionally, virtual team leaders may work actively to identify and eliminate unnecessary forms of constraint, such as unnecessary criticism, restrictive evaluation, or over-controlling and inflexible managers and team members.

Lesson 3 *Virtual team managers and leaders need to construct work assignments that are individually challenging for each team member.* A first step is to develop a clear understanding of what motivates each individual team member and then to make work assignments based on this level of understanding. Team leaders need to make sure that all team members have an even balance of tasks they find enjoyable and tasks they do not find enjoyable.

Lesson 4 *Virtual teams need to develop a climate that supports a high level of acceptance of ideas generated.* Team members need to respect one another's offered ideas, input, and contributions. They also need to be able to openly and honestly give and receive feedback. This is not to say that all ideas and input generated need to be actually implemented. But all ideas shared need to be heard, valued, and evaluated fairly.

Lesson 5 *Managers, leaders, and team members involved in virtual work will need to master a wide range of interpersonal competencies in addition to maintaining a high level of expertise in their specific domain.* Virtual team members need to be trained in how to use a range of collaborative software and information technology to enhance the team's work. Training, however, needs to go beyond how to use the technology to incorporate how to communicate effectively and supportively through these kinds of technologies. Virtual team members need training also in conflict resolution, problem-solving, and cross-cultural communication. In addition, managers and team leaders need to be coached on how to modify managerial tasks in a virtual work environment. For example, techniques used in conventional teams to motivate and reward members and to make consensus decisions may not work the same way in a virtual team. And as the pace of virtual work continues to intensify, and as the boundaries between work and home continue to blur, virtual team members need to add stress and time management to their skill set to achieve a comfortable work and personal life balance. Furthermore, taking the time to know and appreciate yourself and the others in your virtual world will help you be able to work with diverse colleagues. Through self- and interpersonal exploration, virtual team members develop an appreciation for team members' different working styles. Team members who understand and appreciate themselves and their teammates and who trust one another are less likely to attach negative interpretations to incomplete or unclear communications. This type of exploration, if conducted early in the team's development, will help eliminate misunderstandings that may disrupt the creative process.

Component Three – Resources

Communication Tools

Lesson 1 *There is no ideal set of technologies for all teams. The communication tools needed may vary depending on the particular task or project presented to the team.* A virtual team needs to have a clear strategy for selecting appropriate communication tools. In doing so, the team will need to first consider what the needs of the task are. How can the task be accomplished effectively? What levels of social presence and information richness are needed to facilitate work on a particular task or project? Answering these questions will give the team the needed information to select the appropriate communication tools for each situation and create a *personalized communication plan* for the team. One key section in a team's communication plan is a description of how often they will use particular communication tools and for what purposes.

Lesson 2 *Establish guidelines for appropriate matching of the message with the communication tool to be used to communicate that message.* It is crucial that all team members discuss and agree on what purposes and in what situations specific communication tools are appropriate and not appropriate. In general, communication tools high in social presence and information richness are used to transmit complex, non-routine, and ambiguous messages. More straightforward, routine, and simple messages may be transmitted with tools lower in social presence and information richness.

Lesson 3 *Face-to-face communication, often expensive, is best reserved for idea generation and evaluation.* It was evident in this investigation that virtual team members did use different forms of communication behavior in the four stages of the creative process. Face-to-face contact was reserved for idea generation and, in some cases, evaluation. Development work was almost entirely accomplished through electronic means. For most of the teams, finalization and closure took place electronically. A knowledge of the communication tools that tend to be used in the various stages of the creative process is valuable information for those who manage or lead virtual teams doing creative work. In particular, if travel funds are limited, it would be most effective to bring team members together for initial idea generation sessions and then again for evaluation sessions once the particular effort is completed.

Lesson 4 *Development work requires technology that allows for interactive sharing of creative efforts. E-mail, while useful, is usually not sufficient.* Although development work can be reserved for electronic forms of communication, the type of information technology used can influence how smoothly development work evolves. Shared databases or networked computer systems, where team members can share one another's work and simultaneously review designs, can assist in making the development stage more efficient.

Lesson 5 *Tailor the integration of information technology and face-to-face communication to the individual needs of a specific virtual team and to a particular creative effort as well.* At the outset make sure all team members are comfortable with and can easily use available information technology to generate creative results. Then, assess and align the importance of face-to-face communication and different methods of information technology with each stage of the creative process. Make sure that each stage of the creative process is properly supported by sufficient information technology and face-to-face contact. The specific type of creative effort may also guide the integration of communication methods. For example, complex projects that potentially have many solutions may need more face-to-face time upfront. Brainstorming ideas in less complex projects may best be done electronically, with face-to-face contact reserved for closure and evaluation, if needed.

Lesson 6 *Don't underestimate the importance of synchronous exchanges in the creative process. When face-to-face contact is not feasible, integrate into the team's communication repertoire tools that can electronically simulate face-to-face contact.* Virtual teams that utilize either periodic face-to-face encounters or information technologies that simulate face-to-face contact, or both, are more likely to be able to create *as a team.* Furthermore, they are more likely to achieve joint creative insight. If teams build into the repertoire of communication tools more frequent use of tools that allow for real time, synchronous communication, the misunderstandings and miscommunications that often occur in virtual teams may be lessened.

Lesson 7 *Use a variety of communication tools, and integrate into the communication repertoire tools that allow for video and audio links to augment text-only communication when possible.* Text only communication is good for basic communication, but it is not a replacement for graphics and images. Remember, a picture is worth a thousand words. In addition, if you include audio links, team members may hear and respond to the words of their fellow team members, which creates an experience of "being there."

Creativity Techniques and Software Tools

Lesson 1 *Although intuitive techniques for creativity may be viewed with suspicion in business settings, virtual team members need to be fluent in and utilize both linear and intuitive techniques for high levels of creativity.* In reality, intuitive techniques may be even more essential for virtual teams. The rapid pace with which business moves in the virtual world may leave little time for the series of steps outlined in some of the linear techniques. Intuition and insight can be used to assist team members in reaching initial agreement on what intriguing ideas should be further developed. And remember, intuition does not emerge out of nowhere. Intuition is grounded in logical thought based on prior experience and learning.

Lesson 2 Creativity software tools should not be over-used. These programs are helpful in facilitating creative tasks, but they do not replace the minds and exper-tise of team members. These software tools also do not replace the synergy and excitement that emerges when a team creates in a face-to-face session. Put the use of these software tools into perspective, use them when needed, and remember that it is team members who do the actual creative work.

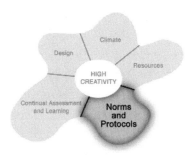

Component Four— Norms and Protocols

Communication Behavior

Lesson 1 Establish agreed-upon norms for regu-lar communication early on. These norms can and should be tailored to the individual needs of a par-ticular team. The important point is that what-ever the established communication behavior norms are, team members need to commit to them and follow through. So if the team has a norm that all mem-bers will call one another back within twenty-four hours, team members need to follow through with the appropriate calls. Virtual teams need to realize that regular and consistent communication is an absolute must. Without informa-tion exchange and communication, there simply is no team, virtual or not.

Lesson 2 Make sure to discuss how the team will handle communication within subgroups of the team. Open discussion about this issue and subsequent agreement as to how the team will handle this will lead to more positive working experiences. With-out this discussion, members may not disclose information to all members of the team and may withhold information to fulfill their own self-interests. Hav-ing a plan to guide subgroup exchanges may eliminate misunderstandings and miscommunications, which lead to wasted efforts (such as two team members doing the same task) or to interpersonal conflicts (such as individual team members wondering, "Why was I not included in the loop?").

Lesson 3 *Although much communication between virtual team members may appear random and occur as needed, there needs to be a balance of structured and unstructured communication.* And as the size of the virtual team increases, so may the need for more structure in the communication behavior between members.

Lesson 4 *Teams need to create a personalized communication plan for the team.* Earlier it was mentioned that a key element of this plan is to describe how often particular communication tools will be used and under what circumstances. A team's communication plan must also include norms for guiding communication behavior. The team's communication plan needs to be captured, documented, and posted so that all members can revisit it when needed for clarification.

Project and Task Management

Lesson 1 *Keep team members and their efforts visible.* Established availability norms allow team members to know when and how they may get in touch with one another. But beyond availability, virtual teams need to work on keeping individual team members' actions visible to the team. Achieving a high level of visibility serves many purposes. Accountability can be observed as team members post their work on-time to shared workspaces. In addition, members may see who is working on what portion of the project, which eliminates duplication of efforts and the loss of creative work resulting from costly misunderstandings (such as saving over the wrong file). Another benefit of visibility is that the efforts of the team and individual team members can be seen by members of other teams or the entire organization, and by members external to the organization as well.

Lesson 2 *Keep the team's overall creative project visible.* To avoid an out of sight, out of mind mentality, progress on the project needs to be visible. This visibility includes, but is not limited to, the project's lifecycle, where team members are with respect to that lifecycle, the overall schedule, any necessary revisions to that schedule, progress toward goals and tasks, and an explicit description of how individual team members fit in and what they are responsible for with regards to those goal and tasks. In addition, there needs to be clearly defined roles for team members and for those who have the authority to review and approve various stages of the creative work. With the use of a team Intranet Web site, relevant project elements can be easily accessed electronically. Keeping the project visible once again assists with accountability and eliminates duplication of efforts. It also helps in keeping all team members informed in a timely fashion of any changes in the project's requirements.

Lesson 3 *Within a project's lifecycle, virtual teams need to realistically assess where creative resources should be allocated and where tasks can be more routinely handled.* The practical side of most creative work is that there are deadlines to meet and clients to please. And recall that one defining characteristic of creativity is the appropriateness of an idea or response. Simply stated, there are times when creativity is necessary and other times when following the status quo will better accomplish what is needed.

Lesson 4 *Team member input needs to be solicited on what types of procedures should be used to ensure individual team member and overall team accountability.* If individuals have helped set up the measures for ensuring accountability, they are a lot more likely to follow through. The same holds for setting appropriate timeframes and delivery dates of individual tasks and the entire project. As much as possible, individual members of the team should have a voice in setting up a realistic schedule.

Component Five—Continual Assessment and Learning

Lesson 1 *Virtual teams need to have explicit procedures and forums in place for evaluating and assessing the creative work and process.* Only two of the teams interviewed mentioned they went through a formal period of evaluation and assessment after a project was completed. However, most teams probably performed some type of informal evaluation and assessment. It is generally best to build in a balance of formal and informal ways to evaluate and assess the team's work and functioning.

    Lesson 2 *Virtual teams benefit from taking the time to archive and document their creative efforts and then reviewing those archived documents for continual evaluation, assessment, and learning.* The ability of virtual teams to archive and document their creative process through various communication and creativity software opens up a wealth of exciting and practical implications for continual growth, assessment, and evaluation of creative work. Organizations and the teams within them will be able to either reuse or modify previous work and apply this to current organizational needs. Further, being able to follow and track activities in each stage of the creative process deepens the team's understanding of how it actually creates. This newfound understanding can be used to assess and further refine the team's unique creative process. The archive capability of virtual teams allows team members to read and witness the creative process after the fact. Creative insights often use prior knowledge that an individual or team had but whose relevance may not previously have been obvious. Making sure this prior knowledge is archived for team members to be able to review at a later time may add to the development of creative insights in solving newly-generated problems, unmet needs, challenges, or opportunities. Documenting and archiving knowledge generated allows teams to *learn from their own experiences.* Data collected over time may be organized into knowledge bases, FAQs, and other useful forms of information.

Final Assessment and Team Action Plan

This book has offered a variety of opportunities for your virtual team to assess its current functioning with respect to the key components that lead to high levels of creativity in virtual teams. As our discussion comes to a close, make sure you have captured what you have learned. *Take the time once again to assess your virtual team's creative functioning with respect to each of the five key components and, as a result of this assessment, capture actions for growth and improvement.* The final assessment activity in Table 8.1 synthesizes the work you have previously generated while reading through this book.

Table 8.1 Actions for Growth and Improvement

Directions: For each of the questions in the left-hand column, if the answer is yes, consider actions that would lead to further growth. If the answer is no, consider actions that would lead to improvement. List appropriate actions for growth and improvement for the component in the right-hand column.

Component	Actions for Growth and Improvement
Design: • Are there adequate opportunities for idea generation, development, finalization and closure, and evaluation? • Is there an appropriate balance of periods for the team to work together, work apart, and then work together again? • Is the chosen leadership structure optimal for guiding the team in its path toward creative results?	
Climate: • Does the team have adequate procedures and forums for establishing task connection? • Does the team have ways to build and maintain interpersonal connection? • Are appropriate team member and management conditions for creativity established and maintained? • Do team managers and leaders have appropriate competencies to support the team's creativity? • Do team members have appropriate competencies to support the team's creativity? • Are there adequate opportunities for training and development of needed competencies?	
Resources: • Does the team have an agreed-upon personalized communication plan in place to specify the communication tools used, the frequency of use of those tools, and the purposes for which they are used? • Does the team use a balance of intuitive and linear techniques to stimulate and enhance creative thought?	

Table 8.1 Actions for Growth and Improvement, Cont'd

Component	Actions for Growth and Improvement
• Does the team make use of relevant creativity software tools?	
Norms and Protocols: • Does the team have an agreed-upon personalized communication plan in place to specify the norms and protocols that guide its communication behavior? • Does the team have an agreed-upon set of norms to assist in the management and accomplishment of team projects and tasks?	
Continual Assessment and Learning: • Does the team have procedures in place for capturing knowledge for later assessment and learning? • Does the team set aside adequate time to actively review and assess its work and subsequently learn from this assessment?	

Revisiting Your Team's Values for Supporting Creativity

You will recall that in Chapter Six I asked you and your team members to try out an imagery exercise to find out what key values could guide your virtual team to high levels of creativity. Now that you have completed the components in this book (in whatever order you chose to do so), it is time to revisit those values. Consider the following questions:

- How well is your team achieving each of the values it feels are important to support high levels of creativity within the team?

- What actions might be needed to ensure further growth and improvement in achieving those values?

- And finally, what values did you not consider earlier that have subsequently occurred to you and your team members as essential for helping your team achieve high levels of creativity while working virtually? (You may want to revisit the imagery exercise in Chapter Six.) Capture additional values that have now emerged.

Why You Need Creativity

To close our journey together, I would like to share my thoughts on why you and your virtual team need to be creative. You and your virtual team need creativity for the following reasons:

1. *It helps your organization survive.* Organizations need the creative efforts of their teams and individual employees to survive in the global economy, to keep up with competitive market demands and pressures, to create new types of technology, to effectively adapt to changes due to new knowledge work, and to adapt to the changing demographic makeup and values of the contemporary workforce.

2. *It can contribute to a healthier and happier you.* Creativity can contribute to achieving job satisfaction and personal health (Puccio, 1989; Runco, 1995). In addition, creativity is an important element of self-actualization, defined as using all of one's potential talents to become what one is capable of becoming (Davis, 1999; Maslow, 1954; Rogers, 1962).

3. *It can contribute to broader necessary social change.* As the world and our society evolve, so do the problems and issues of contemporary life. How can we solve broader societal problems? One way is to look at these problems and issues with a new perspective. Creative thought offers individuals, teams, organizations, and the broader society the ability to see things in new ways.

In closing, I ask you to *make room for creativity in your life and in your team's lifecycle.* Believe in creativity and believe in the process you use to achieve creative outcomes. The real value of this book is not in its content, but in the ways you and your teams use the content to build and maintain each of the five key components within your virtual teams to ensure high levels of creativity and success.

How Trustworthiness Was Established

THIS APPENDIX GIVES FURTHER DETAILS on the methodology that provided the data for the content of this book. Specifically, this appendix looks at the issue of trustworthiness. For qualitative researchers, issues of reliability and validity are recast into the broader concept of trustworthiness (Lincoln and Guba, 1985). Trustworthiness of a particular investigation considers the following:

- Confidence in the truth of the findings (validity and credibility)
- Extent to which the findings of a particular inquiry have applicability in other contexts or with other respondents (transferability)
- Extent to which the findings of an inquiry could be repeated if the inquiry were replicated with the same or similar subjects under the same conditions (reliability)
- Degree to which the findings of an inquiry are determined by the subjects and conditions of the inquiry and not the biases of the researcher (neutrality)

A variety of techniques were used to enhance this study's trustworthiness.

To establish *internal validity and credibility,* during data analysis I searched for contradictory evidence and negative cases, with the intent of constantly revising developing categories (Glaser and Strauss, 1967). To increase *external validity and transferability,* I used maximum variation sampling. Maximum variation sampling is a form of purposive sampling in which the researcher deliberately selects a heterogeneous sample (in terms of people and sites) and observes the commonalities of their experiences. Furthermore, I gathered evidence to produce thick descriptions, in-depth descriptions of the context or setting within which the investigation took place. Thick descriptions are necessary to determine whether the theory that emerged from one context can be transferred to another (Lincoln and Guba, 1985). Information on the experiences of the virtual team members was collected through interviews, background surveys, and, in a few cases, company documentation to help create thick descriptions.

Several steps were taken to ensure the *reliability and dependability* of the inquiry. First, both the interview protocol and background survey were piloted and pre-tested. Second, triangulation, or the use of multiple methods, was incorporated by collecting information through interviews, background surveys, and, in a few cases, company documentation. Third, a thorough audit trail was maintained so that other researchers would be able to witness how the data collection and analysis processes evolved. The audit trail was composed of the following (all recommended by Halpern, 1983):

1. *The raw data*—original tapes of interviews and backup copies of each; transcribed interviews in both hard copy and on disk; original background surveys and photocopies of each.

2. *A participant recruiting content notebook*—contact summary sheets that included contact information, logs of each exchange, and all written correspondences (letters and e-mail messages).

3. *A data collection chart*—chart that tracked the dates that interviews were scheduled, completed, transcribed, and first-level coded. The chart also tracked dates when the background surveys were sent to each participant, when reminders were sent out, when surveys were returned, and when the data was entered into the Statistical Package for the Social Sciences (SPSS) for Windows.

4. *A methodological journal and memos*—a diary of what was done in the data collection process; memos that followed each interview to outline reactions and problems; memos written to comment on methodological issues and problems.

5. *An analysis journal and memos*—a diary outlining the data analysis procedure and theoretical development; more than one hundred memos on codes and their relationships, emerging theory, and on personal biases, feelings, and frustrations during the data analysis process.

Colleague reviews and check coding were also used to establish reliability. Meetings with colleagues were used to discuss the utility of the categories and codes generated and to further brainstorm conceptual connections. The reliability of codes within categories was tested with two independent raters coding selected portions of the interview transcripts.

Neutrality was established by reflecting on potential sources of bias and error in methodological memos, using effective listening skills during the interview process, and being respectful and nonjudgmental of what participants said during their interviews.

REFERENCES

Adams, J. L. (1986). *The Care and Feeding of Ideas: A Guide to Encouraging Creativity.* Reading, Mass.: Addison-Wesley.

Aiken, M., and Riggs, M. (1993). Using a group decision support system for creativity. *Journal of Creative Behavior, 27,* 28–35.

Amabile, T. M. (1983). *The Social Psychology of Creativity.* New York: Springer.

Amabile, T. M. (1988). A model of creativity and innovation in organizations. In B. M. Staw and L. L. Cummings (Eds.), *Research in Organizational Behavior* (Vol. 10, pp. 123–167). Greenwich, Conn.: JAI Press.

Amabile, T. M. (1996). *Creativity in Context.* Boulder, Colo.: Westview Press.

Amabile, T. M., Conti, R., Coon, H., Lazenby, J., & Herron, M. (1996). Assessing the work environment for creativity. *Academy of Management Journal, 39* (5), 1154–1184.

Amabile, T. M., and Gryskiewicz, S. S. (1987). *Creativity in the R&D Laboratory.* Technical Report 30. Greensboro, N.C.: Center for Creative Leadership.

Amabile, T. M., & Gryskiewicz, N. D. (1989). The creative environment scales: Work Environment Inventory. *Creativity Research Journal, 2,* 231–253.

Andrews, F. (1975). Social and psychological factors which influence the creative process. In I. Taylor and J. W. Getzels (Eds.), *Perspectives in Creativity* (pp. 117–145). Chicago: Aldine.

Armstrong, D., and Cole, P. (1996). Managing distances and differences in geographically distributed work groups. In S. Jackson and M. Ruderman (Eds.), *Diversity in Work Teams*. Washington, DC: American Psychological Association.

Baran, S., Zandan, P., and Vanston, J. H. How effectively are we managing innovation? *Research Management,* 1986, January–February, 23–25.

Basadur, M. (1994). Managing the creative process in organizations. In M. A. Runco (Ed.), *Problem Finding, Problem Solving and Creativity* (pp. 237–268). Norwood, N.J.: Ablex.

Crawford, C. B., Brungardt, C. L., and Maughan, M. (2000). *Understanding Leadership: Theories and Concepts.* Longmont, Colo.: Rocky Mountain Press.

Daft, R. L., and Becker, S. W. (1978). *Innovation in Organizations.* New York: Elsevier North-Holland.

Daft, R. L., and Lengel, R. H. (1984). Information richness: A new approach to managerial behavior and organization design. In B. M. Staw and L. L. Cummings (Eds.), *Research in Organizational Behavior* (Vol. 6, pp. 191–233). Greenwich, Conn.: JAI Press.

Daniels-McGhee, S., and Davis, G. A. (1994). The imagery-creativity connection. *Journal of Creative Behavior,* 28, 151–176.

Davidow, W., and Malone, M. (1992). *The Virtual Corporation.* New York: HarperCollins.

Davis, G. A. (1999). *Creativity is Forever.* 4th edition. Dubuque, Iowa: Kendall/Hunt Publishing.

Digman, J. W. (1990). Personality structure: Emergence of the five-factor model. In M. R. Rosenzweig and L. W. Porter (Eds.), *Annual Review of Psychology,* Vol. 41, (417–440). Palo Alto, Calif.: Annual Reviews.

Drucker, P. F. (1985). *Innovation and Entrepreneurship: Practice and Principles.* New York: Harper & Row.

Duarte, D. L., and Snyder, N. T. (1999). *Mastering Virtual Teams: Strategies, Tools, and Techniques That Succeed.* San Francisco Jossey-Bass.

DuBrin, A. (2004). *Human Relations: Interpersonal, Job-Oriented Skills.* 8th ed. Upper Saddle River, N.J.: Pearson Educational/Prentice Hall.

Edmonds, E., Fischer, G., Mountford, S. J., Nake, F., Riecken, D., and Spence, R. (1995). Creativity interacting with computers (panel presentation). In *Proceedings of the Human Factors in Computing, Computer Human Interaction (CHI) Conference* (Denver, Colo., May 7–11, 1995). New York: ACM Press.

Ekvall, G. (1983). *Climate, structure, and innovativeness of organizations* (Report 1). Stockholm: Swedish Council for Management and Organizational Behavior.

Ekvall, G., Arvonen, J., and Waldenstrom-Lindblad, I. (1983). *Creative organizational climate: Construction and validation of a measuring instrument* (Report 2). Stockholm: Swedish Council for Management and Organizational Behavior.

Eveland, J. D. (1990). Technological innovation as a process. In L. Tornatzky and M. Fleischer (Eds.), *The Processes of Technological Innovation* (pp. 27–50). Lexington, Mass.: Lexington Books.

Feldman, D. H., Csikszentmihalyi, M., Gardner, H. (1994). *Changing the World: A Framework for the Study of Creativity*. Westport, Conn.: Praeger.

Finke, R. A., Ward, T. B., and Smith, S. S. (1992). *Creative Cognition: Theory, Research, and Applications*. Cambridge, Mass.: MIT Press.

Fisher, K., and Fisher, M. D. (2001). *THE DISTANCE MANAGER: A Hands-On Guide to Managing Off-Site Employees and Virtual Teams*. New York: McGraw-Hill.

Fritz, S., Brown, W., Lunde, J. P., and Banset, E. (1999). *Interpersonal Skills for Leadership*. Upper Saddle River, N.J.: Prentice Hall.

Gardner, J. W. (1990). *On Leadership*. New York: Free Press.

George, J. (1996, November). Virtual best practice: How to successfully introduce virtual team-working. *Teams, 38–45.*

Georgia Research Tech News. (July 2002). Modernizing Meditation: Researchers Create Virtual Environment to Teach and Enhance Meditation. http://gtresearchnews.gatech.edu/newsrelease/MEDITATION.htm

Gibb, J. R. (1995). Defensive communication. *The Journal of Communication,* 1961, 11 (3), 141–148.

Glaser, B., and Strauss, A. (1967). *The Discovery of Grounded Theory*. Chicago: Aldine.

Gordon, W.J.J. (1961). *Synetics*. New York: Harper & Row.

Gordon, W.J.J., and Poze, T. (1972). *Strange and Familiar*. Cambridge, Mass.: SES Associates.

Gordon, W.J.J., and Poze, T. (1980). *The New Art of the Possible*. Cambridge, Mass.: Porpoise Books.

Grenier, R., and Metes, G. (1995). *Going Virtual: Moving Your Organization Into the 21st Century*. Upper Saddle River, N.J.: Prentice Hall.

Gruber, H. E. (1989). The evolving systems approach to creative work. In D. B. Wallace and H. E. Gruber (Eds.), *Creative People at Work: Twelve Cognitive Case Studies* (pp. 3–24). New York: Oxford University Press.

Halpern, E. S. (1983). *Auditing naturalistic inquiries: The development and application of a model.* Unpublished doctoral dissertation, Indiana University.

Handy, C. (1995, May–June). Trust and the virtual organization. *Harvard Business Review,* 2–8.

Havelock, R. G. (1970). *Planning for Innovation.* Ann Arbor: Center for Research on Utilization of Scientific Knowledge, University of Michigan.

Haywood, M. (1998). *Managing Virtual Teams: Practical Techniques for High-Technology Project Managers.* Boston: Artech House.

Holt, R. R. (1964). Imagery: The return of the ostracized. *American Psychologist,* 19, 254–264.

Holton, J. (2001). Building trust and collaboration in a virtual team. *Team Performance Management,* 7(3/4), 36–47.

Houtz, J. C., and Patricola, C. (1999). Imagery. In M. A. Runco and S. R. Pritzker (Eds.), *Encyclopedia of Creativity* (Vol. 2, pp. 1–11). San Diego: Academic Press.

Isaksen, S. (1985). Facilitating small group creativity. In S. S. Gryskiewicz and R. M. Burnside (Eds.), *Blueprint for Innovation: Creativity Week VIII* (pp. 71–84). Greensboro, N.C.: Center for Creative Leadership.

Isaksen, S. (1988). Innovative problem solving in groups: New methods and research opportunities. In Y. Ijiri and R. L. Kuhn (Eds.), *New Directions in Creative and Innovative Management* (pp. 145–167). Cambridge, Mass.: Ballinger.

Johnson, D. W., and Johnson, F. P. (1997). *Joining Together: Group Theory and Group Skills.* 6th edition. Boston: Allyn and Bacon.

Jung, C. (1923). *Psychological Types.* London: Routledge and Kegan Paul.

Kanter, R. M. (1983). *The Change Masters.* New York: Simon and Schuster.

Katz, D., & Kahn, R. (1978). *The Social Psychology of Organizations* (2nd ed.). New York: John Wiley & Sons.

Kayworth, T., and Leidner, D. (2000). The global virtual manager: A prescription for success. *European Management Journal,* 18 (2), 183–193.

Kiesler, S., Siegel, J., and McGuire, T. (1991). Social aspects of computer-mediated communication. In C. Dunlop and R. Kling (Eds.), *Computerization and Controversy: Value Conflicts and Social Choices* (pp. 330–349). Boston: Harcourt Brace.

Koestler, A. (1964). *The Act of Creation.* New York: Dell.

Lincoln, Y. S., and Guba, E. G. (1985). *Naturalistic Inquiry.* Newbury Park, Calif.: Sage.

Lipnack, J., and Stamps, J. (1997). *Virtual Teams: Reaching Across Space, Time and Organizations With Technology.* New York: Wiley.

Lubart, T. (1999). Componential models. In M. A. Runco and S. R. Pritzker's (Eds.), *Encyclopedia of Creativity* (Vol. 1, pp. 295–300). San Diego, Calif.: Academic Press.

Lubart, T. (1990). Creativity and cross-cultural variation. *International Journal of Psychology,* 25, 39–59.

Majchrzak, A., Rice, R., Malhotra, A., King, N., and Ba, S. (2000). Technology adaptation: The case of a computer-supported inter-organizational virtual team. *MIS Quarterly,* 24 (4), 569–600.

Marsh, B., Collins, C., and Stohr, R. (1997). *Tools and technologies—Electronic Meeting Systems: Computer-assisted collaboration in a distributed environment* (Report 47350). National Aeronautics and Space Administration (NASA) [http://www.nasa.gov/doc/47350main_tools-6.doc].

Maslow, A. H. (1954). *Motivation and Personality.* New York: Harper.

Mayer, R. (1999). Problem solving. In M. A. Runco and S. R. Pritzker's (Eds.), *Encyclopedia of Creativity* (Volume 2, pp. 437–447). San Diego, Calif.: Academic Press.

Michalko, M. (1998). *Cracking Creativity: The Secrets of Creative Genius.* Berkeley, Calif.: Ten Speed Press.

Mill, C. R. (1976). Feedback: The art of giving and receiving help. In L. Porter and C. R. Mill (Eds.), *The Reading Book for Human Relations Training* (pp. 18–19). Bethel, ME: NTL Institute for Applied Behavioral Science.

Miller, W. C. (1987). *The Creative Edge: Fostering Innovation Where You Work.* Reading, Mass.: Addison-Wesley.

Miller, W. C. (1999). *Flash of Brilliance: Inspiring Creativity Where You Work.* Reading, Mass.: Perseus Books.

Mohrman, S. A., Cohen, S. G., and Mohrman, A. M. (1995). *Designing Team-Based Organizations: New Forms for Knowledge Work.* San Francisco: Jossey-Bass.

Mumford, M. D., Mobley, M. I., Uhlman, C. E., Reiter-Palmon, R., and Doares, L. M. (1991). Process analytic models of creative capacities. *Creativity Research Journal,* 4 (2), 91–122.

Nemiro, J. (1997). Intepretive artists: A qualitative exploration of the creative process of actors. *Creativity Research Journal,* 10, 229–239.

Nemiro, J., & Runco, M. A. (1995). Creativity and innovation in small groups. Unpublished paper. Claremont Graduate University, Claremont, CA.

O'Hara-Devereaux, M., and Johansen, R. (1994). *Global Work: Bridging Distance, Culture, and Time.* San Francisco: Jossey-Bass.

Osborn, A. (1963). *Applied Imagination: Principles and Procedures of Creative Problem-Solving.* New York: Charles Scribner's Sons.

Parnes, S. J. (1981). *Magic of Your Mind.* Buffalo, N.Y.: Bearly Limited.

Pelz, D. C., and Andrews, F. M. (1966). *Scientists in Organizations.* New York: Wiley.

Peters, T. J., & Waterman, R. H. (1982). *In Search of Excellence: Lessons from America's Best-Run Companies.* New York: Harper & Row.

Policastro, E. (1999). Intuition. In M. A. Runco and S. R. Pritzker (Eds.), *Encyclopedia of Creativity* (Volume 2, pp. 89–93). San Diego: Academic Press.

Poltrock, S. E., and Sharma, K. (1995). Some groupware challenges at Boeing. In D. D. Coleman (Ed.), *Groupware 95.* San Mateo: Morgan Kaufmann.

Proctor, T. (1999). Computer programs. In M. A. Runco and S. R. Pritzker (Eds.), *Encyclopedia of Creativity* (Vol. 1, pp. 301–307). San Diego: Academic Press.

Puccio, G. J. (1989). Rationale for the study of creativity: A review and a summary. In T. Rickards and S. Moger (Eds.), *Creativity and Innovation Yearbook* (pp. 13–26). Manchester, UK: Manchester Business School.

Rogers, C. R. (1954). Toward a theory of creativity. *ETC: A Review of General Semantics, 11,* 249–260.

Rogers, C. R. (1962). Toward a theory of creativity. In S. J. Parnes and H. F. Harding (Eds.), *A Source Book for Creative Thinking* (pp. 63–72). New York: Scribner's.

Rogers, C. R., and Farson, R. E. (1976). *Active Listening.* Chicago: Industrial Relations Center of the University of Chicago.

Runco, M. A. (1994). Creativity and its discontents. In M. P. Shaw and M. A. Runco (Eds.), *Creativity and Affect.* Norwood, N.J.: Ablex.

Runco, M. A. (1995). The creativity and job satisfaction of artists in organizations. *Empirical Studies of the Arts, 13,* 39–45.

Runco, M. A., and Chand, I. (1995). Cognition and creativity. *Educational Psychology Review, 7* (3), 243–267.

Schutz, W. C. (1958). *FIRO: A Three-Dimensional Theory of Interpersonal Behavior.* New York: Holt, Rinehart & Winston.

Stein, M. I. (1975). *Stimulating Creativity* (Vol. 2). New York: Academic Press.

Steiner, G. (1965). *The Creative Organization.* Chicago: University of Chicago Press.

Steinfield, C. W. (1986). Computer-mediated communication in an organizational set-ting: Explaining task-related and socioemotional uses. In M. L. McLaughlin (Ed.), *Communication Yearbook, 9,* 777–804. Newbury Park, Calif.: Sage.

Sternberg, R. J., and Lubart, T. I. (1991). An investment theory of creativity and its development. *Human Development,* 34, 1–32.

Thomas, K. (1976). Conflict and conflict management. In M. D. Dunnette (Ed.), *Hand-book of Industrial and Organizational Psychology* (pp. 900–902). Chicago: Rand McNally.

Toynbee, A. (1962). Is America neglecting her creative minority? In C. W. Taylor (Ed.), *Widening Horizons in Creativity* (pp. 3–9). New York: Wiley.

Treffinger, D. J., Isaksen, S. G., and Dorval, K. B. (1994). *Creative Problem Solving: An Introduction* (revised edition). Sarasota, Fla.: Center for Creative Learning.

Tuckman, B. (1965). Developmental sequence in small groups. *Psychological Bulletin,* 63, 384–399.

Tuckman, B., and Jensen, M. (1977). Stages of small group development revisited. *Group and Organizational Studies,* 2, 419–427.

VanGundy, A. (1987). Organizational creativity and innovation. In S. G. Isaksen (Ed.), *Frontiers of Creativity Research: Beyond the Basics.* Buffalo, N.Y.: Bearly Limited.

von Oech, R. (1992). *Creative Whack Pack.* Menlo Park, Calif.

Walker, C. E. (1975). *Learn to Relax: 13 Ways to Reduce Tension.* Englewood, Cliffs, N.J.: Prentice Hall.

Wallas, G. (1926). *The Art of Thought.* New York: Harcourt Brace.

West, M. A. (1990). The social psychology of innovation in groups. In M. A. West and J. L. Farr (Eds.), *Innovation and Creativity at Work* (pp. 309–322). New York: Wiley.

Whetten, D. A., and Cameron, K. S. (1998). *Developing Management Skills.* 4th ed. Read-ing, Mass.: Addison-Wesley.

Wilson, J., George, J., and Wellins, R. (1994). *Leadership Trapeze: Strategies for Leadership in Team-based Organizations.* San Francisco: Jossey-Bass.

Woodman, R. W., Sawyer, J. E., and Griffin, R. W. (1993). Toward a theory of organiza-tional creativity. *Academy of Management Review,* 18, 293–321.

Woodman, R. W., and Schoenfeldt, L. F. (1990). An interactionist model of creative behavior. *Journal of Creative Behavior,* 24 (4), 279–291.

Yukl, G. (2002). *Leadership in Organizations.* 5th ed. Upper Saddle River, N.J.: Prentice Hall.

MICHAEL M. BEYERLEIN, PH.D., is director of the Center for the Study of Work Teams (www.workteams.unt.edu) and professor of industrial/organizational psychology at the University of North Texas. His research interests include all aspects of collaborative work systems, organization transformation, work stress, creativity/innovation, knowledge management and the learning organization, and complex adaptive systems. He has published in a number of research journals and has been a member of the editorial boards for *TEAM Magazine, Team Performance Management Journal,* and *Quality Management Journal.* Currently, he is senior editor of the JAI Press/Elsevier annual series of books, *Advances in Interdisciplinary Studies of Work Teams,* as well as this new series of books on collaborative work systems. In addition, he has been co-editor with Steve Jones on two ASTD case books about teams and edited a book on the global history of teams, *Work Teams: Past, Present and Future.* He has been involved in change projects at the Center for the Study of Work Teams with such companies as Boeing, Shell, NCH, Advanced Micro Devices, Westinghouse, and Xerox and with government agencies such as the Bureau of Veterans' Affairs, Defense

Contract Management Agency, the Environmental Protection Agency, and the City of Denton, Texas.

JAMES R. BARKER, PH.D., is director of research and professor of organizational theory and strategy in the Department of Management at the U.S. Air Force Academy. His research interests focus on the development and analysis of collaborative control practices in technological and knowledge-based organizations. His research projects include collaborations with scientists at the Los Alamos and Sandia National Laboratories and with scholars at the University of Melbourne and the University of Western Australia. Dr. Barker's work has appeared in a number of professional journals, including *Administrative Science Quarterly, Journal of Organizational and Occupational Psychology,* and *Communication Monographs.* His new book, *The Discipline of Teamwork,* is now available from Sage Publications. He won the 1993 Outstanding Publication in Organizational Behavior award from the Academy of Management and the 1999 *Administrative Science Quarterly* Scholarly Contribution Award for his research on self-managing teams. He has lectured on teamwork in organizations at many universities and organizations, including the Sloan School of Management at the Massachusetts Institute of Technology and the University of Western Australia. He served as associate editor of the *Western Journal of Communication* and on the editorial boards of *Administrative Science Quarterly, Journal of Organizational Change Management,* and *Management Communication Quarterly.*

SUSAN TULL BEYERLEIN, PH.D., holds a B.A. in English from the University of Oregon, an M.S. in general psychology from Fort Hays State University, and a Ph.D. in organization theory and policy with a minor in education research from the University of North Texas, Denton. Since 1988, she has taught a variety of management courses as an adjunct faculty member at several universities in the Dallas metroplex, with a particular focus on strategic management at both the undergraduate and MBA levels. Dr. Beyerlein has served as a research scientist/project manager with the Center for the Study of Work Teams at the University of North Texas and has been a recipient of research grant awards from the Association for Quality and Participation, the National Science Foundation, and corporate donors. Since 1995, she has co-edited the Elsevier/JAI Imprint annual book series, entitled *Advances in Interdisciplinary Studies of Work Teams,* and during the same period has served as an *ad hoc* reviewer for *The Academy of Management Review.* She has published book reviews on contemporary business offerings in *Business and the Contemporary World,* and her work has also appeared in *Structural Equation Modeling: A Multidisciplinary Journal, Teams: The Magazine for High Performance Organizations* (UK), *Journal of Management Education, Empirical Studies of the Arts,* and *Multiple Linear Regression Viewpoints.* She is a member of the Academy of Management, Beta Gamma Sigma—the honor society for collegiate schools of business—and Phi Kappa Phi National Honor Society.

JILL E. NEMIRO, PH.D., is an assistant professor in the Psychology and Sociology Department at California State Polytechnic University, Pomona, and an adjunct professor in the Human Resources Design Masters' Program at Claremont Graduate University. Her research interests are in the area of organizational and team creativity and the virtual workplace. She has published numerous articles on the topics of creativity and virtual teams. She recently co-edited *The Collaborative Work Systems Fieldbook: Strategies, Tools, and Techniques*. Her recent articles can be found in *Creativity Research Journal* and the *Journal of Creative Behavior*. Her recent book chapters can be found in *The Collaborative Work Systems Fieldbook: Strategies, Tools, and Techniques; Advances in the Interdisciplinary Study of Work Teams; The Encyclopedia of Creativity*; and *Knowledge Management and Virtual Organizations*. She has also presented papers and workshops at numerous professional conferences.

Professionally, Dr. Nemiro has worked for many years in the entertainment industry as a film and videotape editor, specializing in management training and corporate videos, children's television programs, and documentaries. She has worked as a consultant in creativity training and instructional design. She has also worked as a research associate for the Institute for the Academic Advancement of Youth with Johns Hopkins University, for the Milken Foundation, and for WestEd.

Dr. Nemiro received her Ph.D. in organizational psychology from Claremont Graduate University. She received her master's degree from California State University, Los Angeles, and a bachelor's degree from the University of California, Los Angeles. Dr. Nemiro may be contacted at jenemiro@csupomona.edu.

Pfeiffer Publications Guide

This guide is designed to familiarize you with the various types of Pfeiffer publications. The formats section describes the various types of products that we publish; the methodologies section describes the many different ways that content might be provided within a product. We also provide a list of the topic areas in which we publish.

FORMATS

In addition to its extensive book-publishing program, Pfeiffer offers content in an array of formats, from fieldbooks for the practitioner to complete, ready-to-use training packages that support group learning.

FIELDBOOK Designed to provide information and guidance to practitioners in the midst of action. Most fieldbooks are companions to another, sometimes earlier, work, from which its ideas are derived; the fieldbook makes practical what was theoretical in the original text. Fieldbooks can certainly be read from cover to cover. More likely, though, you'll find yourself bouncing around following a particular theme, or dipping in as the mood, and the situation, dictate.

HANDBOOK A contributed volume of work on a single topic, comprising an eclectic mix of ideas, case studies, and best practices sourced by practitioners and experts in the field.

An editor or team of editors usually is appointed to seek out contributors and to evaluate content for relevance to the topic. Think of a handbook not as a ready-to-eat meal, but as a cookbook of ingredients that enables you to create the most fitting experience for the occasion.

RESOURCE Materials designed to support group learning. They come in many forms: a complete, ready-to-use exercise (such as a game); a comprehensive resource on one topic (such as conflict management) containing a variety of methods and approaches; or a collection of like-minded activities (such as icebreakers) on multiple subjects and situations.

TRAINING PACKAGE An entire, ready-to-use learning program that focuses on a particular topic or skill. All packages comprise a guide for the facilitator/trainer and a workbook for the participants. Some packages are supported with additional media—such as video—or learning aids, instruments, or other devices to help participants understand concepts or practice and develop skills.

- *Facilitator/trainer's guide* Contains an introduction to the program, advice on how to organize and facilitate the learning event, and step-by-step instructor notes. The guide also contains copies of presentation materials—handouts, presentations, and overhead designs, for example—used in the program.

- *Participant's workbook* Contains exercises and reading materials that support the learning goal and serves as a valuable reference and support guide for participants in the weeks and months that follow the learning event. Typically, each participant will require his or her own workbook.

ELECTRONIC CD-ROMs and web-based products transform static Pfeiffer content into dynamic, interactive experiences. Designed to take advantage of the searchability, automation, and ease-of-use that technology provides, our e-products bring convenience and immediate accessibility to your workspace.

METHODOLOGIES

CASE STUDY A presentation, in narrative form, of an actual event that has occurred inside an organization. Case studies are not prescriptive, nor are they used to prove a point; they are designed to develop critical analysis and decision-making skills. A case study has a specific time frame, specifies a sequence of events, is narrative in structure, and contains a plot structure—an issue (what should be/have been done?). Use case studies when the goal is to enable participants to apply previously learned theories to the circumstances in the case, decide what is pertinent, identify the real issues, decide what should have been done, and develop a plan of action.

ENERGIZER A short activity that develops readiness for the next session or learning event. Energizers are most commonly used after a break or lunch to stimulate or refocus the group. Many involve some form of physical activity, so they are a useful way to counter post-lunch lethargy. Other uses include transitioning from one topic to another, where "mental" distancing is important.

EXPERIENTIAL LEARNING ACTIVITY (ELA) A facilitator-led intervention that moves participants through the learning cycle from experience to application (also known as a Structured Experience). ELAs are carefully thought-out designs in which there is a definite learning purpose and intended outcome. Each step—everything that participants do during the activity—facilitates the accomplishment of the stated goal. Each ELA includes complete instructions for facilitating the intervention and a clear statement of goals, suggested group size and timing, materials required, an explanation of the process, and, where appropriate, possible variations to the activity. (For more detail on Experiential Learning Activities, see the Introduction to the *Reference Guide to Handbooks and Annuals*, 1999 edition, Pfeiffer, San Francisco.)

GAME A group activity that has the purpose of fostering team spirit and togetherness in addition to the achievement of a pre-stated goal. Usually contrived—undertaking a desert expedition, for example—this type of learning method offers an engaging means for participants to demonstrate and practice business and interpersonal skills. Games are effective for team building and personal development mainly because the goal is subordinate to the process—the means through which participants reach decisions, collaborate, communicate, and generate trust and understanding. Games often engage teams in "friendly" competition.

ICEBREAKER A (usually) short activity designed to help participants overcome initial anxiety in a training session and/or to acquaint the participants with one another. An icebreaker can be a fun activity or can be tied to specific topics or training goals. While a useful tool in itself, the icebreaker comes into its own in situations where tension or resistance exists within a group.

INSTRUMENT A device used to assess, appraise, evaluate, describe, classify, and summarize various aspects of human behavior. The term used to describe an instrument depends primarily on its format and purpose. These terms include survey, questionnaire, inventory, diagnostic, survey, and poll. Some uses of instruments include providing instrumental feedback to group members, studying here-and-now processes or functioning within a group, manipulating group composition, and evaluating outcomes of training and other interventions.

Instruments are popular in the training and HR field because, in general, more growth can occur if an individual is provided with a method for focusing specifically on his or her own behavior. Instruments also are used to obtain information that will serve as a basis for change and to assist in workforce planning efforts.

Paper-and-pencil tests still dominate the instrument landscape with a typical package comprising a facilitator's guide, which offers advice on administering the instrument and interpreting the collected data, and an initial set of instruments. Additional instruments are available separately. Pfeiffer, though, is investing heavily in e-instruments. Electronic instrumentation provides effortless distribution and, for larger groups particularly, offers advantages over paper-and-pencil tests in the time it takes to analyze data and provide feedback.

LECTURETTE A short talk that provides an explanation of a principle, model, or process that is pertinent to the participants' current learning needs. A lecturette is intended to establish a common language bond between the trainer and the participants by providing a mutual frame of reference. Use a lecturette as an introduction to a group activity or event, as an interjection during an event, or as a handout.

MODEL A graphic depiction of a system or process and the relationship among its elements. Models provide a frame of reference and something more tangible, and more easily remembered, than a verbal explanation. They also give participants something to "go on," enabling them to track their own progress as they experience the dynamics, processes, and relationships being depicted in the model.

ROLE PLAY A technique in which people assume a role in a situation/scenario: a customer service rep in an angry-customer exchange, for example. The way in which the role is approached is then discussed and feedback is offered. The role play is often repeated using a different approach and/or incorporating changes made based on feedback received. In other words, role playing is a spontaneous interaction involving realistic behavior under artificial (and safe) conditions.

SIMULATION A methodology for understanding the interrelationships among components of a system or process. Simulations differ from games in that they test or use a model that depicts or mirrors some aspect of reality in form, if not necessarily in content. Learning occurs by studying the effects of change on one or more factors of the model. Simulations are commonly used to test hypotheses about what happens in a system—often referred to as "what if?" analysis—or to examine best-case/worst-case scenarios.

THEORY A presentation of an idea from a conjectural perspective. Theories are useful because they encourage us to examine behavior and phenomena through a different lens.

TOPICS

The twin goals of providing effective and practical solutions for workforce training and organization development and meeting the educational needs of training and human resource professionals shape Pfeiffer's publishing program. Core topics include the following:

Leadership & Management

Communication & Presentation

Coaching & Mentoring

Training & Development

E-Learning

Teams & Collaboration

OD & Strategic Planning

Human Resources

Consulting

What will you find on pfeiffer.com?

- The best in workplace performance solutions for training and HR professionals

- Downloadable training tools, exercises, and content

- Web-exclusive offers

- Training tips, articles, and news

- Seamless on-line ordering

- Author guidelines, information on becoming a Pfeiffer Affiliate, and much more

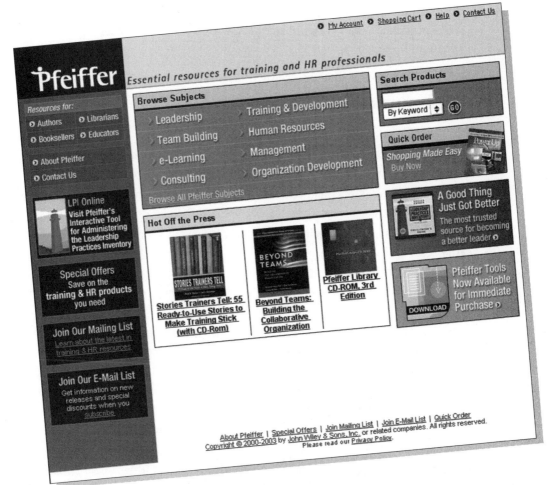

Discover more at www.pfeiffer.com

Customer Care

Have a question, comment, or suggestion? Contact us! We value your feedback and we want to hear from you.

For questions about this or other Pfeiffer products, you may contact us by:

E-mail: **customer@wiley.com**

Mail: **Customer Care Wiley/Pfeiffer**
10475 Crosspoint Blvd.
Indianapolis, IN 46256

Phone: **(US) 800-274-4434** (Outside the US: 317-572-3985)

Fax: **(US) 800-569-0443** (Outside the US: 317-572-4002)

To order additional copies of this title or to browse other Pfeiffer products, visit us online at **www.pfeiffer.com**.

For **Technical Support** questions, call **(800) 274-4434.**

For authors guidelines, log on to www.pfeiffer.com and click on "Resources for Authors."

If you are . . .

A **college bookstore, a professor, an instructor, or work in higher education** and you'd like to place an order or request an exam copy, please contact jbreview@wiley.com.

A **general retail bookseller** and you'd like to establish an account or speak to a local sales representative, contact Melissa Grecco at 201-748-6267 or mgrecco@wiley.com.

An **exclusively on-line bookseller**, contact Amy Blanchard at 530-756-9456 or ablanchard @wiley.com or Jennifer Johnson at 206-568-3883 or jjohnson@wiley.com, both of our Online Sales department.

A **librarian or library representative**, contact John Chambers in our Library Sales department at 201-748-6291 or jchamber@wiley.com.

A **reseller, training company/consultant, or corporate trainer**, contact Charles Regan in our Special Sales department at 201-748-6553 or cregan@wiley.com.

A **specialty retail distributor** (includes specialty gift stores, museum shops, and corporate bulk sales), contact Kim Hendrickson in our Special Sales department at 201-748-6037 or khendric@wiley.com.

Purchasing for the **Federal government**, contact Ron Cunningham in our Special Sales department at 317-572-3053 or rcunning@wiley.com.

Purchasing for a **State or Local government**, contact Charles Regan in our Special Sales department at 201-748-6553 or cregan@wiley.com.